Slaughter at the Chapel

Slaughter at the Chapel

The Battle of Ezra Church, 1864

Gary Ecelbarger

University of Oklahoma Press : Norman

Publication of this book is made possible through the generosity of Edith Kinney Gaylord.

Library of Congress Cataloging-in-Publication Data

Names: Ecelbarger, Gary L., 1962–
Title: Slaughter at the Chapel : the Battle of Ezra Church, 1864 / Gary Ecelbarger.
Description: Norman : University of Oklahoma Press, 2016. | Includes bibliographical references and index.
Identifiers: LCCN 2016002209 | ISBN 978-0-8061-5499-2 (cloth) ISBN 978-0-8061-6607-0 (paper)
Subjects: LCSH: Ezra Church, Battle of, Ga., 1864. | Gibson, Randall Lee, 1832–1892—Military leadership. | Walthall, Edward C. (Edward Cary), 1831–1898—Military leadership. | Sherman, William T. (William Tecumseh), 1820–1891—Military leadership. | Atlanta Campaign, 1864.
Classification: LCC E476.7 .E26 2016 | DDC 973.7/37—dc23
LC record available at http://lccn.loc.gov/2016002209

The paper in this book meets the guidelines for permanence and durability of the Committee on Production Guidelines for Book Longevity of the Council on Library Resources, Inc. ∞

Copyright © 2016 by the University of Oklahoma Press, Norman, Publishing Division of the University. Paperback published 2020. Manufactured in the U.S.A.

All rights reserved. No part of this publication may be reproduced, stored in a retrieval system, or transmitted, in any form or by any means, electronic, mechanical, photocopying, recording, or otherwise—except as permitted under Section 107 or 108 of the United States Copyright Act—without the prior written permission of the University of Oklahoma Press. To request permission to reproduce selections from this book, write to Permissions, University of Oklahoma Press, 2800 Venture Drive, Norman, OK 73069, or email rights.oupress@ou.edu.

Contents

List of Illustrations	vii
Acknowledgments	ix
Introduction	3
1. Sherman and His Army	9
2. Hood and His Army	31
3. Prelude to Battle	46
4. Vicious Volleys	69
5. Battle Hill	89
6. Gibson's Attack	118
7. Change of Plans	134
8. Walthall's Assault	148
9. Final Scene	168
10. Aftermath and Analysis	182
Appendixes	
A. Order of Battle	209
B. Interpreting the Battle of Ezra Church through the Words of Its Chief Confederate Commanders	217
C. The Ezra Church Battlefield after the Battle	229
Notes	235
Bibliography	257
Index	267

Illustrations

Figures

1. Major General William Tecumseh Sherman	110
2. Major General John A. Logan	111
3. Major General Oliver Otis Howard	112
4. General John Bell Hood	113
5. Lieutenant General Alexander P. Stewart	114
6. Lieutenant General Stephen D. Lee	115
7. Woods's Division, *Harper's Weekly,* August 27, 1864	116
8. Dead Brook and Ezra Church, *Harper's Weekly,* August 27, 1864	117

Maps

Opposing Armies at Atlanta, July 23–26, 1864	13
Hood's Lick Skillet Road Battle Plan, July 28–29, 1864	52
Opening Deployment, 10:30–11:45 A.M.	67
Brown Attacks Harrow and Morgan Smith, 11:45 A.M.	84
Brantly Seizes Battle Hill, 12:00 P.M.	93
Logan Rallies to Reclaim Lost Ground, 12:15 P.M.	99
Gibson's Attack, 12:45 P.M.	127
Battlefield Maneuvers, 1:15–2:00 P.M.	144
Walthall's Attack, 2:00–3:00 P.M.	162
Final Confederate Deployment, 3:00–6:00 P.M.	172
Ezra Church Battlefield, July 30, 1864	190

Acknowledgments

This book could not have been produced without the help of talented and dedicated friends and associates.

Chief among them is Hal Jespersen, the mapmaker for this work. Mr. Jespersen is the first professional cartographer to create a detailed series of troop movement maps depicting the Battle of Ezra Church. His dedication to the project and his patience—tested at times by the 3,000 miles separating him from the author—has gone neither unnoticed nor unappreciated.

I acknowledge the efforts of the editors at the University of Oklahoma Press, particularly Charles E. Rankin (editor-in-chief), Sarah C. Smith (manuscript editor), and Bob Fullilove (copy editor). Not only did they give this battle history a fine home, they collaborated to improve the project as it transitioned through publication.

I am also thankful for the staff at the numerous archival depositories, research libraries, and historical centers for their valuable aid provided to me in my quest to cull primary source material for this book. Particularly helpful were the historians and archivists at Kennesaw Mountain National Military Park and the Atlanta Historical Center. Both went out of their way to make my seven-hundred-mile research trips fruitful and rewarding.

Unlike the well-known big battles of the Civil War, Ezra Church has relatively few adherents who understand the battle and its participants. I am grateful for finding, meeting, and sharing information with this valuable group. This includes a decades-long friend, Scott Patchan, and a much newer associate, Bob Jenkins, who both made trips to the battlefield with me and lent their expertise in interpreting this battle. Thanks also to my friends David Powell, Keith Bohannon, and Dr. Stewart Bennett, who—along with Messrs. Jenkins and Patchan—generously provided me with important source material about this battle. I also wish to extend a special thank you to Bill Blackman for allowing me to view the captured flag he now owns of the 46th/55th Tennessee and inscribed by the 26th Illinois, a most important Ezra Church relic that rendered certain opposing regiment and brigade positions that heretofore were merely speculative.

I also wish to recognize all who have written and published works within the past forty years that included Ezra Church in detail. This includes (in ascending chronological order): Bill Erquitt, Stephen Davis, Albert Castel, Steven E. Woodworth, Russell S. Bonds, Bruce S. Allardice, and most recently, Earl J. Hess. Although my interpretation of this battle is often at variance with their analyses and conclusions, I appreciate all of them, individually and collectively, for their enlightening efforts to pull this important and fascinating battle out of obscurity.

Carolyn Ecelbarger deserves recognition for her role in this work. Our twenty-seven years of marriage includes nearly twenty years in which she has supported a book-writing spouse. I am forever grateful for her patience, her sacrifices, and her love.

Slaughter at the Chapel

Introduction

One of every three soldiers who attacked the defensive line at Ezra Church on July 28, 1864, was struck by a bullet.

This incredible testament of small-arms fire cannot help but force one to appreciate the experience the foot soldier endured. Add stifling hundred-degree heat, throat-choking smoke, ear-piercing screams, and head-swimming confusion; run the battle for six hours; strike down four generals—including a corps and a division commander; magnify by 3,000 both sides of the ratio written within the first four words of the above first sentence; place another 3,000 supporting men behind the attackers and 12,000 defenders on the heights in front of them; and sluggishly run the largest battlefield stream in crimson for the rest of the night. When that day's first light dawned upon the area, this contested field of gripping drama, horror, and chaos was simply a serene country church neighborhood. The battle's name alone evokes a mix of awe and sadness—and that feeling is not diminished one iota by the fact that this happened more than 150 years ago.

From an interpretive standpoint, the Battle of Ezra Church, perhaps more than any other battle of the Atlanta Campaign, has been a surprisingly tough nut to crack—surprising because the battle consisted of a series of repulsed headlong assaults with minimal counterstrikes, very few flank-turning efforts, and opposing battle lines that remained as close to the same position at the end as at the beginning of the contest. The lack of precipitous tactical challenges for historians to overcome should make for stability in its interpretation; remarkably, however, no two written histories of this battle, whether in chapter, essay, or book, produced in the past twenty-five years indicate any significant agreement on where troops were deployed on the battlefield, the relative shape and length of opposing lines of battle, the chronology of the attacks, or even the regiments of attackers and defenders. The score of troop movement maps published on this battle reveals the lack of agreement—from the location of brigades on the battlefield to their direction of advance and retreat; from the identity of commanders to even whether Ezra Church sat inside the defensive line or outside it.

What makes this variety of interpretations of troop positions and movements even more astounding is that all the battle histories produced within the past quarter century have, by and large, relied on the same primary source material from brigade, division, corps, and army commanders from both sides. Only one of the ten Union and Confederate division and corps commanders who stepped onto the Ezra Church battlefield on July 28, 1864, wrote an account of this battle after the war, and that account reveals almost nothing. Letters, diaries, and reminiscences during and after the war from the twenty-five brigade commanders (including replacements for wounded officers) are only slightly more numerous, just a handful of documents overall. Thus the battle reports of the higher commanders at Ezra Church are the chief sources to represent the thirty-five total officers; most of them were published in volume 38, part 3, of the 128-volume *Official Records of the Union and Confederate Armies*.

How has the heavy reliance on a single volume of the *Official Records* produced such a variety of interpretations of troop positions within a battle arena of less than two square miles? Ezra Church was the first battle of the Union campaign that was not reported in detail as a separate encounter, but rather as a small part of the entire May-to-September campaign document of all lines of commanders, from regiment to corps and army leaders. The truncated version of battle in the *Official Records* reads more as a summary than a report, providing few clues to battlefield tactics and maneuvers. The Confederate commanders continued to document Ezra Church independently as they had for previous battles of the campaign; however, reports from one of four division commanders, four of thirteen brigade commanders, and all but a quarter of the engaged regimental commanders have been lost, thus limiting comprehension of the battlefield. This combination of brevity from the Federals and sparsity from the Confederates regarding the Battle of Ezra Church in the *Official Records* leaves much open to interpretation.

The second problem in forming an accurate interpretation is the state of the battlefield today. What remains of the Ezra Church battlefield must be visually extracted from a western Atlanta neighborhood of houses, small businesses, a school, and a psychiatric facility that adorn the hills and lowlands, all tied together by a network of roads that did not exist in 1864. In addition, features such as a railroad and its requisite station, a community park with an inground public pool, and an interstate highway alter the terrain. Several points in this battlefield neighborhood are interpreted by informational markers created and placed in the mid-twentieth century, nearly all the result of the work of a dedicated Atlanta historian who clearly had a special interest in this battle. Unfortunately, the recent discovery that one of his markers misidentifies the site of the defensive flank during the battle now brings into question the validity of the locations selected for other battlefield signs.

The challenge of studying the modern battlefield is slightly ameliorated by contemporary visual documentation tools. Overlaying two decent maps of the Ezra Church battlefield, both created by army engineers within weeks of the battle, helps to convert the houses back to trees and the concrete and asphalt into fields. Unfortunately, both maps include postbattle earthworks, and both include hills, swales, and minor creekbeds that cannot be found today. Troop positions for the battle do not exist on these maps, but on one of them three faint arrows pinpoint where most of the 3,000 attacking soldiers were struck by bullets. Only a few nondescript turn-of-the-century photographs have come to light; the best visual documentation of the battle exists in two issues of an illustrated newspaper published within seven weeks of the bloodstained contest.

Fortunately, these challenges have not dissuaded documentarians from occasionally poking this sleeping bear of a battle from the 1940s through the 1970s, then effectively arousing it from hibernation late in the 1980s and into the second decade of the twenty-first century. Various narrations and analyses over the past thirty years have included newly discovered accounts from foot soldiers as well as company and regimental officers. The present narrative attempts to build on the recent documentation with additional primary source material, but also with a set of fresh and campaign-experienced eyes, to create a comprehensive narrative history of the Battle of Ezra Church. An updated tactical account of the movements and actions on the Ezra Church battlefield builds on previous work with additional source material and a reevaluation of maneuvers based on the distances measured on the modern battlefield.

Although the *what* of Ezra Church will be more thoroughly explicated, the other chief objectives of this battle study are to answer the *how* and *why* of Ezra Church, two questions that have remained unsatisfactorily answered for over a century and a half. Whereas the tactical story of the battle relies on a wide variety of source material, the reasons for the battle and the heretofore poorly comprehended decisions surrounding it have been obtained from a reevaluation of the *Official Records,* which has been nearly universally misread and misinterpreted regarding Ezra Church. With a careful study of officers' reports, dispatches, and orders, this account revises the understanding of the battle and the decisions and movements leading up to it with a new and more strongly supported battle history, which answers questions left open since the summer of 1864.

This study presents and supports the following: an entirely new reason for why one army commander fought at the Battle of Ezra Church (vanquishing the traditionally accepted reason); a detailed explanation of the only extant battle plans with a focus on the expected timetable; and a first-time case for why the plan changed so drastically. It offers conclusively a single reason for this battle's dramatic one-sided failure by arguing for a completely different scapegoat for that loss. Finally, this investigation unexpectedly but not completely exonerates the battle's traditionally accepted culprit, who has been blamed time and time again over the past quarter century. The fresh reinterpretation of the same sources used to convict him in recent literature cannot help but objectively recast him as a commander who performed soundly under the most trying circumstances and in complete compliance with the expectations of his commanding officer. An additional finding gleaned from this reinterpretation offers the strongest explanation available why one army commander curiously never attempted to visit the site of this seven-hour contest, fought within three miles of his headquarters.

Some decisions regarding style require justification. First, rather than explain controversy or conflicts between primary and secondary sources in the narrative, I have relegated important points of disagreement to the notes, in order to best capture the drama and intrigue of an intense day of battle. Second, since the two opposing armies confusingly carried nearly identical names, the Army of the Tennessee (Union) is preferentially identified as such, as it is often necessary to distinguish it from two other Northern armies attempting to capture Atlanta. The Confederate Army of Tennessee is frequently identified as "Hood's army," the "Southern army," or the "Confederate army," as it was the only army from that side in the region. All regiments, North and South, are identified by arabic numerals and complete state name; if no identifier is placed after the state name, it can be assumed that the force is infantry. Except in the order of battle (appendix A), no arabic numbers are used for brigades or divisions; instead, these units on both sides carry the names of the commanders who led them in *this* battle. The same applies to Confederate corps, while Union corps are identified traditionally by roman numeral or the name of the commander. Except in quoted material, all unit designations carry a lowercase first letter (e.g., *b*rigade, *c*orps), even though many such Confederate units are routinely styled in uppercase. On either side, a unit name changes at the point in the battle when a new commander takes over that unit. (First names are included with the surname "Smith" to prevent confusion.)

The time (e.g., 10:30 A.M.) is important throughout the battle narrative, and wherever possible, the sources for references to time, whether in a dispatch, report, diary, or letter, are cited in the corresponding note. However, other mentions of the time, particularly in descriptions of the course of the battle, are speculative best estimates based on preceding and subsequent events, since primary sources are not in agreement. Given that there was no time synchronization between commanders, tremendous variability exists regarding when a body of troops marched, entered, or ended a fight.

Any book devoted to a battle carries with it the assumption that the participants and the region were influenced by preceding events in the war, particularly those of the campaign in which the battle was waged. To pinpoint the focus on the battle presented herein, the context has been deliberately limited to a few days rather than a few months of the campaign or a few years of the war, with only a few exceptions.

The narrative introduces each opposing army in separate chapters beginning four days prior to the battle; the first chapter exclusively describes the Union armies around Atlanta, and the second focuses entirely on the Confederates defending the city. Chapter 3 combines the activities of the opposing armies from the day preceding the battle to the moment when the action commences on the disputed field. The following six chapters provide a detailed tactical history of the battle, occasionally panning out to opposing headquarters to appreciate what the army and army group commanders were doing while their respective troops were engaged in a life-and-death struggle. The final chapter explores the immediate aftermath of the battle with a look at the battlefield over the following few days, continuing a month later to analyze the immediate impact of the battle. Appendix B uniquely carries the documentation of the battle into the winter of 1865 and beyond, when posterity receives the first official and nonofficial documentation of these experiences on this particular field.

This book serves as a tribute to the Civil War soldiers who fought at Ezra Church regardless of the side for which they fought. The three-year veterans who served there were as skilled and experienced as any soldiers in the Civil War, more experienced in battle than any soldiers in American history before this battle, and more experienced in war than American professionals or volunteers for eighty years after this battle. At Ezra Church the American soldier fought for his cause; he fought for his country; he fought for his comrades; he fought for his president. In so doing, he also fought for an emblem that embodied all—his flag.

1

Sherman and His Army

Major General William Tecumseh Sherman awoke on Sunday morning, July 24, 1864, in command of a camp of 94,000 troops—a population greater than the tenth-largest city in America at that time. The red-headed, chain-smoking, forty-four-year-old mayor of this mobile metropolis had successfully led his infantry, artillery, and cavalry a hundred miles through northern Georgia, contested for more than half that mileage by an opponent that had stripped more than 20,000 residents from Sherman's city of blue. For Sherman the campaign had been hard fought, particularly during the past seven days, his first complete week on the southern side of the Chattahoochee River. But he could take solace in the fact that as he labored to choke off Atlanta from its supply lines, his command—the Military Division of the Mississippi—was assured a flowing lifeline of resources from Tennessee and the northern Georgia countryside.[1]

Sherman's push was the only aspect of Lieutenant General Ulysses S. Grant's four-pronged plan for simultaneous movements across all major arenas east of Tennessee that might achieve its objective before summer's end. The behemoth Army of the Potomac—accompanied by Grant himself—was locked in a siege against General Robert E. Lee's Army of Northern Virginia south of Richmond at Petersburg, Virginia. Grant held a numerical advantage over Lee, but their isolated contest was destined to drag into 1865. The Army of the Potomac naturally gained the attention of Lincoln's war machine in Washington, feeding it timely reports throughout the brutal Overland Campaign, which preceded the siege of Petersburg.

Two other Union offensives had met with disappointing and disastrous results. Major General Benjamin Butler had won early success moving up the James River toward Richmond, but he and his Army of the James entered the final week of July in the same aggravating position Major General George B. McClellan had found himself exactly two years earlier—neutralized on the James River with virtually no chance to capture the Confederate capital from the east. Butler's disappointment was a success compared to Union fortunes in the Shenandoah Valley, however, which realized their nadir on July 24. There—more specifically at Kernstown, Virginia—Major General George Crook suffered a battlefield rout that eventually swept his entire army out of the belly of the Shenandoah Valley and opened a path for Confederates to invade Pennsylvania and burn the town of Chambersburg nearly to the ground.

This left Sherman and his 94,000 Westerners to meet their objective before summer's end and thereby justify the bloodiest twelve-week stretch of the Civil War, a period during which the Union had endured more than 110,000 soldiers stripped from its ranks (killed, wounded, captured, or missing) across Virginia and Georgia. Leading the only major offensive outside the state of Virginia, the home of the Confederate capital, Sherman had achieved the most success and stood less than three miles from the object of his campaign—the city of Atlanta.[2]

Atlanta's rail systems distinguished it from all other cities within the Confederate interior. Although its 10,000 citizens rendered it unremarkable in size, those rail networks carried troops and supplies from the uncontested Deep South to all contested theaters within the Confederacy. By the end of July's third week, Sherman controlled two of the four railroads leading to and from Atlanta. He craftily kept control of the Western and Atlantic (W&A) Railroad to continuously supply all two- and four-legged members of his army group with over two hundred tons of foodstuffs per day as he marched his men, mules, and horses from Chattanooga to the crossings of the Chattahoochee. Beginning on July 18, Sherman's men gained control of the Georgia Railroad (also called the Augusta Railroad), which blocked all supplies to the "Gate City" from the east. Six days of U.S. ownership produced a fifty-mile swath of destroyed railroad, the iron in several places heated and then twisted around tree trunks to form "Sherman's Neckties."

As his infantry gained control of the Georgia Railroad, Sherman's horse soldiers removed a third railroad from immediate Confederate use. Major General Lovell H. Rousseau led 2,500 Union cavalry on a sweeping mission into Alabama and then eastward to strike the Atlanta & West Point Railroad one hundred miles southwest of Atlanta. Rousseau's men destroyed the depot at Opelika and tore up thirty-three miles of this vital line on July 17, as well as three additional miles of a connecting railroad, before returning to Marietta on July 22. Although Union troops had no continuous presence on this line as they did the Georgia and W&A railroads, Sherman believed Rousseau's extensive damage "cut[ ] off Alabama for a month."[3]

This left but one unobstructed railroad into Atlanta: the Macon & Western line, a ribbon of iron running eighty-five miles southeastward from Atlanta to Macon, Georgia, where other Southern lines ran east, west, and south. If Sherman was unable to capture Atlanta by direct advance, his next objective would be to seize control of the remaining two Confederate rail lines (including the Atlanta & West Point), either most efficiently at East Point, where the two Southern rail lines conjoined four miles southwest of Atlanta, or on a wider arc by capturing the southwest and southeast lines separately.

Over the previous three days Sherman had attempted to penetrate Atlanta with his three armies. On July 20 Major General George H. Thomas and his Army of the Cumberland withstood aggressive Confederate attacks north of Atlanta near the bank of Peachtree Creek. Thomas and his men successfully parried those charges, but lost 2,100 officers and men in the vicious contest. Although Thomas won that battle, the aggressiveness of the Confederates caused Sherman to resist continuing a full army advance from the north. On July 21 Sherman tried to take Atlanta from the east by advancing his former command, the Army of the Tennessee, and overwhelming what he thought would be meager resistance. The Confederate defense proved much stronger than expected, stopping Sherman's army after a brief advance, then surprising it with near lethal attacks the next day.[4]

Sherman's men hung on strongly enough to rightfully claim victory on July 22, but, just like the action at Peachtree Creek, Sherman would not attempt a direct penetration into Atlanta from this direction. The result of the three consecutive days of battle was 8,500 casualties inflicted upon his opponent (Sherman erroneously thought losses were much higher than this), but at a cost of 6,500 officers and men in blue uniform, including an army commander. Sherman's seven infantry corps—76,500 foot soldiers and their officers—covered a four-mile arc from three miles due east of Atlanta to three miles due north of the city, and for the next two days they remained in place with nowhere to go. The infantry was flanked by most of Sherman's 12,000 cavalrymen and buttressed by 5,500 artillerists manning 250 guns.[5]

Sherman moved his headquarters to center himself safely behind his force. Through July 23, he had occupied the two-story home of Augustus Hurt, which crowned a knoll one mile north of the Georgia Railroad, but on Sunday Sherman relocated to a large white house on the road to Marietta. There he devised a new plan of maneuver to get to the railroads south of the city. He revealed the outlines of his plan to Major General Henry Halleck in Washington. "As soon as my cavalry rests," Sherman explained, "I propose to swing the Army of the Tennessee round by the right rapidly and interpose between Atlanta and Macon, the only line open to the enemy."[6]

Throughout the campaign for Atlanta, Sherman reserved the role of rapid movement to his former command, the Army of the Tennessee. For the first month of the campaign, this army was lighter, with only two of its three corps in the field. Less than half the size of Thomas's Army of the Cumberland at that time and more substantial than the single corps that composed Major General John Schofield's Army of the Ohio, the Army of the Tennessee was large enough and compact enough for flanking maneuvers in northern Georgia. After the XVII Corps arrived at the end of May, Sherman still used it on wide swinging maneuvers, such as crossing the Chattahoochee River in mid-July, solidifying the army's nickname as "The Whip-snapper." By July 24 the Army of the Tennessee was so thinned by battle losses that the three corps composing it numbered 23,000 infantrymen—smaller in

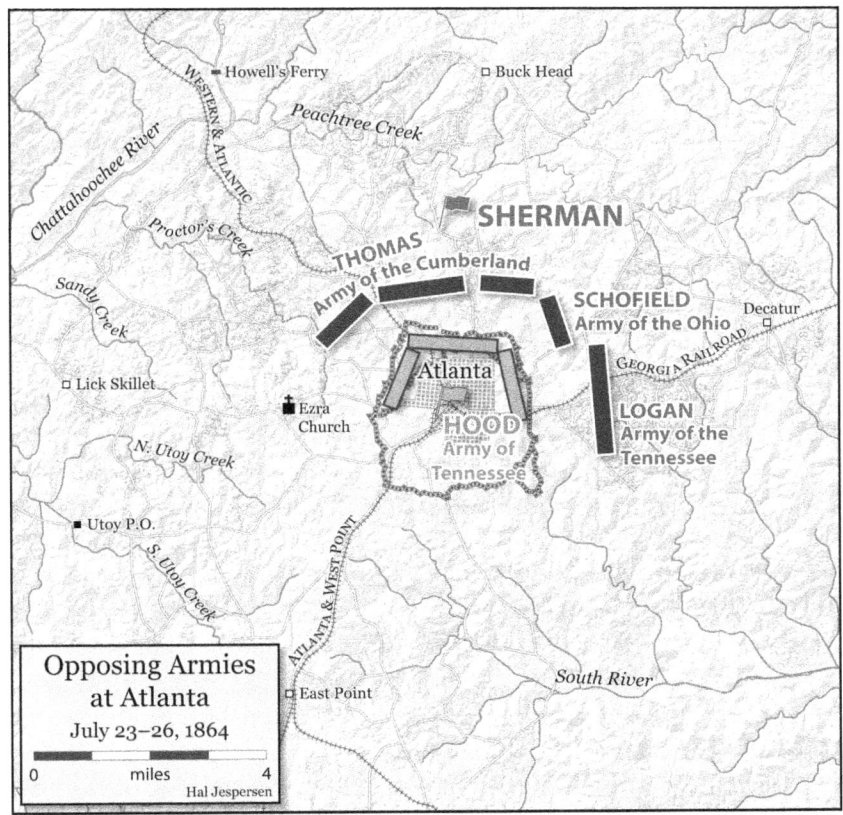

Copyright © 2016 University of Oklahoma Press

size than the two corps that had begun campaigning eleven weeks earlier.

The army suffered a Civil War rarity in its victory east of Atlanta on July 22—the loss of its leader. Major General James B. McPherson's 150-plus-pound body was stilled by an ounce of rebel lead in the early afternoon of that battle. General Sherman thus lost a steady presence and a dear army friend. "History tells us of but few who so blended the grace and gentleness of the friend with the dignity, courage, faith and manliness of the soldier," wrote Sherman in announcing McPherson's death to the U.S. War Department; "those whom he commanded loved him to idolatry, and I, his associate and commander, fail in words adequate to express my opinion of his great worth." McPherson was the only major general in command of a Union army to be killed in battle during the entire Civil War.⁷

McPherson had led the Army of the Tennessee for all but the latest forty-eight hours of the Atlanta Campaign. Major General John A. Logan was its newest commander and the first leader since U. S. Grant to claim a birthright to the force stemming from the summer of 1861 when the nucleus of the army occupied the southern tip of Illinois. "Black Jack" Logan (his nom de guerre derived from his swarthy complexion) was thirty-eight years old in the summer of 1864, and until the early afternoon of July 22, he had ridden at the helm of the XV Corps, which Sherman himself had led through the Vicksburg Campaign the summer before.

Logan entered the war as a fighting politician in the most literal way. As a U.S. congressman representing Illinois's Ninth Congressional District, Logan was viewing a skirmish preceding the First Battle of Manassas in July 1861 when the action forced him to act. He took a rifle from a shirking soldier and peeled away from the gaggle of politicians watching the battle with him. Rushing to the banks of Bull Run, he crouched and fired in the clothes of a congressman. One month later he donned Union blue with a colonel's insignia on his shoulders. Logan commanded the 31st Illinois Infantry, a regiment consisting of several hundred of his former political constituents from southern Illinois. A severe shoulder wound received in the fight for Fort Donelson in the winter of 1862 forced Logan to miss the Battle of Shiloh, but he returned to Grant's army (which had not yet been named for the Tennessee River) as a brigadier general. A year later, in February 1863, Grant successfully won a new commission for Logan, this one as major general in charge of a division of his army. "There is not a more patriotic soldier, braver man, or one more deserving of promotion in the Dept. than Gen. Logan," wrote Grant to Lincoln to seal Logan's promotion.⁸

Major General Logan earned Grant's faith in his leadership in the subsequent campaign for Vicksburg in the spring and summer of 1863. He was the field commander of record for the Union victory at the Battle of Raymond on May 12, and he led the shock troops that turned the tide of the Battle of Champion Hill in favor of the Union four days later. Grant was so impressed with Logan's performance on the Champion Hill battlefield that he told an aide in the midst of Logan's division-sized assault, "Go down to Logan and tell him he is making history today." On the Fourth of July, when the Confederates surrendered Vicksburg to Grant, he awarded Logan the post of honor to lead victorious Union troops into the newly captured city. Logan's leadership throughout the campaign could not elevate his rank, but it did gain him more responsibility. When Grant moved east with his promotion to lieutenant general in March 1864, Sherman immediately ascended from command of the Army of the Tennessee to assume Grant's former role at the helm of the Military Division of the Mississippi, and Logan rose to corps command to head the XV Corps in McPherson's army. (McPherson had led the XVII Corps during the Vicksburg Campaign.)[9]

Logan's performance commanding Sherman's former corps during the first two months of the Atlanta Campaign could be assessed as competent at its worst and spectacular at its best. At Resaca, on May 14, he superintended an efficient and daring assault to capture and hold the only real estate Union troops took from the Confederates after two hard days of battle. Two weeks later, at the Battle of Dallas, he single-handedly overturned a rout of a large portion of his corps by racing his horse into the maelstrom, a feat that inspired his men to bravery and ultimate victory. The foot soldiers reversed their retreating steps to reclaim their lost ground, recapture lost cannons, and punish the reeling Confederates, who could not absorb the counterstrike. The rebels suffered over 1,000 casualties to the resurgent XV Corps, which suffered one-third as many losses in their surprising victory.

The Battle of Dallas brightened Logan's star, both in the eyes of his troops and in those of the Northern populace. The latter saw Logan in this battle through the work of a sketch artist for *Harper's Weekly Illustrated Newspaper*. Logan's troops maintained that the artist could not do Logan justice. "No one can describe how Logan looked in battle any more than he could describe the raging sea," raved an Iowan who watched Logan's exploits in that battle, adding: "I am satisfied that the biggest coward in the world would stand on his head on top of the breastworks if Logan was present and told him to do so."[10]

Logan topped the Dallas exploit eight weeks later at the Battle of Atlanta. Barely an hour had elapsed from the time that Logan replaced the martyred McPherson on the battlefield when the XV Corps, manning the northern sector of the Union defense, came under a withering assault from General John B. Hood's old corps, commanded that day by Major General Benjamin F. Cheatham. Logan, atop a pitch-black warhorse he named "Slasher," raced to the scene from the middle of the battlefield, rallying dispirited infantrymen in the same fashion as at Dallas. Together they sealed the breach in the XV Corps line by outmuscling Confederate troops and forcing them westward, leaving four cannons they had captured behind to be reclaimed by Ohio troops. (It was a moment that would be captured for posterity twenty years later in what was then the world's largest oil painting, the Atlanta Cyclorama.) Logan's exploits and his troops' reaction also secured the hard-won Union victory at the Battle of Atlanta.

In the simplest terms, Logan was a force of nature. His inspirational leadership not only produced positive results on battlefields; it created and strengthened a unique bond with his men that had not existed with previous commanders of the Army of the Tennessee. At the beginning of the Atlanta Campaign, an Illinois soldier told his diary, "I have never heard a general cheered in my life." The soldier emphasized this as a point of pride in the reserved demeanor of the Western soldier. That all changed when they saw Logan in battle. "You should have heard them cheer him," admitted the same soldier.[11] Brigadier General Mortimer Leggett explained Logan's captivation of his troops more definitively and with years of hindsight after the war:

> When General Grant would ride down our line he commanded the most thorough respect and confidence from all of us, and it was the same when General Sherman rode down our line. But when General Logan rode down the line, every voice was heard in a shout. He seemed to have the power to awaken the enthusiasm that was in the troops, to the extent

that no other officer in our army seemed to possess. He would stir up their blood in battle. The manner in which he sat his horse, the manner in which he would hold his hat . . . seemed to have the power to call out of the men every particle of fight that was in them.[12]

By no coincidence he had built a solid record of battlefield success as a division commander in 1863, a corps commander in 1864, and now an army commander. He was the field commander for three battle victories (Raymond, Dallas, and Atlanta) with his division and corps major contributors in several others over the past fifteen months. To label him the best political general in the Union army is also a disservice, for based on his record of achievement in the field, Logan exceeded every other corps commander in the Western or Eastern Union armies.

In his third calendar day in army command, on July 24, Logan received Sherman's orders to initiate the first phase of the plan to cut off Atlanta from its supply line. Sherman desired that Logan would create a diversion to the southeast. Once Sherman's cavalry forces were united from their independent missions, Logan was to cut off his demonstration. Sherman's instruction certainly simplified the next part of the mission: "I propose to give you timely notice to send your wagons behind General Thomas and then to move your army behind the present line to the extreme right, to reach, if possible, the Macon [railroad], which you know to be the only road by which Atlanta can be supplied." A brief study of the map Sherman enclosed showed that the counterclockwise encirclement of Atlanta to reach the railroad would compass twenty-five arduous miles, and any such motion toward the Confederates' sole remaining lifeline was certain to be contested by the bold Southern general who had already assaulted two of Sherman's armies in two days.[13]

Sherman did not indicate to Logan what he intended to do with the cavalry, and he was yet to reveal his intentions with this arm to Halleck. But on July 24 he did notify his superior of an intention of which Logan was totally unaware. "The sudden loss of McPherson was a heavy blow to me," Sherman wrote Halleck at 3:00 P.M.; "I can hardly replace him, but must have a successor."

Sherman had considered Logan a mere interim army chief. "Black Jack's" command of the Army of the Tennessee would not last the week.[14]

Few decisions by Sherman during the Atlanta Campaign were more important and controversial than this one, as evidenced by the paper trail of explanations Sherman left over the next twenty years. The variance in Sherman's stated reasons bears evidence of his discomfort with the decision as well as his displeasure at being questioned about it for decades afterward. One explanation dates to a postwar discussion with General Dodge in which Sherman claimed that he intended to keep Logan at the helm but that General Thomas threatened to resign in protest if he carried that decision through. Although Thomas was not alive to comment on the claim, common sense alone dismisses it. Why would General Thomas quit on his 50,000 men simply because he (supposedly) objected to the successor of command in an entirely different army? Modifying his "Thomas reason" years after this in a newspaper interview, Sherman claimed Thomas was overly concerned that Logan, who was known to sprawl his corps beyond reasonable boundaries, would disrupt formations of the Army of the Cumberland and the Army of the Ohio with this same tendency. This explanation, like the first, appears too flimsy for serious consideration.[15]

Sherman dug into Logan in his postwar memoirs, denigrating him and Major General Frank Blair as "volunteers" who "looked to personal fame and glory as auxiliary and secondary to their political ambition, and not as professional soldiers." Just as revealing in his memoirs was his claim that because Logan was a politician by nature, he was "mistrusted by regular officers like Generals Schofield, Thomas, and myself." This reasoning highlights the pride of professional soldiers as well as their ingrained jealousies. Logan's uncanny battlefield successes had been achieved without a military education and no battle experience prior to the Civil War. His ostentatious performance in the heat of battle grated on the West Pointers. Complaints flowed early in the campaign over the disproportionate amount of press Logan was receiving; one derided the reporters as suffering from "Logan on the brain."

One West Point–trained general grew increasingly irritated while watching Logan mount his horse "with a great flourish" during the Battle of Dallas and observing him ordering his staff to hoist ammunition boxes upon their shoulders to deliver to the front rather than use more traditional means. The professional soldier dismissed this unconventional style of generalship: "Logan always played to the gallery."[16]

Although the war well into its fourth year, General Sherman continued to place a premium on West Point training—prewar education—over actual wartime experience. In Logan's particular case, Sherman had convinced himself that Logan lacked two of the essential ingredients for successful army command. Sherman named these in yet another explanation for his decision: logistics and grand strategy. While praising Logan as "perfect in combat," he claimed that Logan "expressed a species of contempt for the other two branches." In fact, Logan's toils as a division and corps commander for all but two days of his past fifteen months in the field precluded any opportunity to conduct grand strategy that he might display contempt for it; he was, by necessity, forced into handling logistics at very important points in the campaign for Atlanta, particularly concerning ammunition. Although logistics did not thrill him like combat did, no evidence exists outside Sherman's claim that Logan loathed this necessity of war.[17]

Sherman's clearest explanation for favoring a commander with the best military education to head the Army of the Tennessee focused on the immediate plan for movement and not for battle:

> At West Point they teach tactics in the midst of strategy, if they teach anything. They do get it right into the systems of the boys there. You cannot stop in the enemy's face to show how these tactics are to be exercised on the field. That was one of the things I thought about when the question of McPherson's successor came up. The movement was to pass the army by defile in the rear from left to right. The way to do it was to draw the army to be removed out to a place in the rear by detachments and then move it compactly in fighting position the whole length of the investing army, and transfer it to

the right so that it will come into position in fighting order again, tactically moving with reference to both the army and the transfer.

Why, you see, the death of McPherson was caused by the enemy coming out of his works and encountering a movement of ours to manoeuvre him out. Each side was to a degree surprised. The Confederates had defended Atlanta in a very elaborate way. They had high ramparts, ditches, salients, plenty of abatis, fraises, and whatever would make their sixty thousand men inside of these works equal to my one hundred thousand men on the outside. Besides, they were a brave garrison. My business was to see how I could trick them to give up those defences and fight me on the outside. As soon as McPherson was dead my mind came to that problem: "How am I going to get them out and neutralize their advantages?" That involved a shifting about of the army in order to make them uneasy. It was one of the things which determined me to put a trained officer in command of the army I meant to transfer.[18]

By midafternoon of July 24, Sherman kept his decision from Logan, a decision likely hashed out and solidified that very morning at the latest and likely the day before. His long dispatch to Logan that day regarding the expected counterclockwise advance to the Macon railroad never hinted at someone other than Logan leading this all-important movement. At the same time Sherman decided to demote Logan, he had already chosen a successor to head the Department of the Tennessee. At 3:00 P.M. he revealed the identity of Logan's replacement to General Halleck. "After thinking over the whole matter," wrote Sherman, "I prefer that Major General O. O. Howard be ordered to command the Army and the Department of the Tennessee."[19]

Oliver Otis Howard, a thirty-three-year-old corps commander, had been active throughout the Atlanta Campaign. Howard had proven his bravery on battlefields, as had Logan, and was down to one arm because of it—his shattered right arm having been amputated at the Battle of Seven Pines in 1862. At Gettysburg, Howard preceded Logan by one year when he was thrust temporarily into multicorps command upon the death of Major General John F. Reynolds. Both Howard and Logan also shared the same date of commission: their volunteer rank of major general dated from November 29, 1862.

There the similarities ceased. Howard was a New Englander, born and raised in Maine. He began his Civil War career with the Army of the Potomac, where he fought in most of the major battles in the East, from the First Battle of Manassas through Gettysburg. Transferred to the western theater to partake in the Chattanooga Campaign, Howard latched on to the Army of the Cumberland, to which he remained attached into the last week of July 1864. While Logan presented himself as an earthy, often profane commander, Howard exuded piety. He was called the "Praying General," whose efforts to imbue Christianity into the ranks met with mixed results within the IV Corps of the Army of the Cumberland and would not prove to be any more successful in the Army of the Tennessee.

Howard's battle performance was marked by courage, but beyond that it was a most suspect record. Perhaps no Union general in the Civil War consistently found himself in such predicaments on battlefields than Oliver Otis Howard. His misfortunes were so notorious that "O. O." could be equally known as "Uh Oh" Howard. His woes began on Chinn Ridge near Bull Run on July 21, 1861, where his brigade was overwhelmed and routed from the field to essentially close the First Battle of Manassas. After returning to duty from his Peninsula Campaign wound, Howard was restored to brigade command for the Maryland Campaign. Again, his troops were surprised and routed from the West Woods at the Battle of Antietam. He was elevated to division command and took part in the Union disaster at Fredericksburg on December 13, 1862—and then came Chancellorsville. Promoted to XI Corps command for this spring 1863 campaign, Howard posted his corps on the extreme right of the Union line. Failing to adequately protect his flank, Howard was surprised by Stonewall Jackson's famous flank march and assault and was summarily rolled up with his men in yet another rout.

Howard somewhat acquitted himself in the subsequent Gettysburg Campaign. Replacing the killed General Reynolds near the beginning of the first day of the contest, Howard was credited (perhaps overly so) for choosing Cemetery Hill as the strong defensive position for the troops of the I and XI Corps to fall back to. Where Logan was reflexive and decisive during the rout of his corps and was able to restore it, Howard at Gettysburg allowed his two corps to fight without his presence until routed. He displayed no overt leadership for the command until after it had fallen back to Cemetery Hill. Thus, it cannot be overlooked that his command was indeed routed at Gettysburg. Few commanders North or South had been routed from more battlefields in twenty-four months of war than General Howard.

Changing theaters did not reverse Howard's misfortunes on the battlefield. His generalship was found wanting in the Atlanta Campaign. He failed to secure his corps's position at Resaca on May 14, at Pickett's Mill on May 27, and at Kennesaw Mountain on June 27. The latter battle, Sherman's worst defeat to this point in the entire campaign, serves as a sound point of comparison of the corps command styles of Logan and Howard, whose forces together represented nearly two-thirds of the Union attack that day. Logan on the Union left attacked five brigades (complying with Sherman's orders) with three of them advancing *en echelon*. He breached, albeit temporarily, the Confederate defenses but was unable to sustain his offensive and suffered a literal decimation of his engaged troops in the fight. Howard's corps occupied the center of the Union line. He complied with orders to attack one division of roughly the same number of men employed by Logan. Howard specifically ordered his men to attack in column by divisions in an effort to limit the exposure of his charging men to the Confederate defenders. Unfortunately for his troops, the packed column formation severely curtailed their firepower and the attack was an utter failure. Howard's tactic backfired as he lost more men than Logan without advancing nearly as far, producing the weakest threat to the Southern defenses that day.

Sherman may have been unaware of Howard's battlefield shortcomings prior to the Atlanta Campaign. For example, from what Sherman knew about Gettysburg he was more likely to appreciate that Howard received the thanks of Congress regarding his identification of Cemetery Hill as the key to defense and knew little or nothing about his indecisive leadership of his two corps in advance of that ridge line. Sherman was, however, a witness to Howard's repeated failures in battle during the Atlanta Campaign. While he proclaimed Logan as "perfect in combat," the antithesis applied to Howard, who was not as lucky a battlefield commander as Logan, but even more clearly was not nearly as skilled. The difference in outcomes could also be attributed to the quality of division, brigade, and regimental officers of these two corps commanders. Regardless, no objective observer of General Howard and General Logan from May 5 through July 23 could rate Howard as the better corps commander to this point of the campaign.

This mattered not at all to Sherman. He did not equate the ultimate success of an army commander with how well he performed in subordinate roles in previous battles and campaigns. Sherman needed only to look at his own career path to appreciate this. Sherman's record from brigadier to army commander surprisingly mimicked Howard's much more than Logan's. His first action as a brigade commander resulted in the rout from Henry House Hill at the First Battle of Manassas just before Howard and his brigade were forced to abandon an adjacent hill. At Shiloh, Sherman's exposed division line was surprised and overwhelmed at the opening action of the battle. As a corps commander, Sherman's expedition to Chickasaw Bluffs in the winter of 1862 as well as his assault at Vicksburg on May 22, 1863, failed—miserably so. His brief stint as commander of the Army of the Tennessee was marred by repulses against the Confederate right at Missionary Ridge, and his superior numbers could not overwhelm a Confederate stronghold in the Meridian expedition of February 1864.

Too proud to admit his own shortcomings as a tactician, Sherman excelled in strategy and logistics, strengths that came to fruition once he left a single army and took control of the army group. From the moment he led the Military Division of the Mississippi out of Chattanooga, Sherman successfully fed it, supplied it, and maneuvered it over the rough and rugged terrain in northern Georgia. Convinced that he needed a military-educated army man at the helm of his former army, Sherman looked to a West Pointer to replace McPherson, who was also a graduate of the military academy. Ironically, the army McPherson had led—and the one Sherman wished Howard to lead—was nearly devoid of West Point–educated leaders. None of the corps commanders of the Army of the Tennessee had matriculated there, and only one of seven division commanders claimed the words "West Point" in his past; yet this army still fought magnificently on July 22 after being decapitated by the death of McPherson.

Perhaps out of appreciation for the skill of the Army of the Tennessee corps generals, division commanders, and brigadiers, Sherman worried less about the tactical acumen of the army commander. He deliberately and often employed the title "Department of the Tennessee" when referring to this army, partly due to the fact that two divisions were detached at the start of the Atlanta Campaign with one division remaining out of theater for the entire summer of 1864. Because of this, he sought a department commander more than an army chief. Sherman maintained "that a permanent department commander had to be appointed at once, as discharges, furloughs, and much detailed business could alone be done by a department commander." This reason, combined with Sherman's postwar "tactics in the midst of strategy" explanation, did not vanquish the controversy of his not choosing Logan, but it served as a more powerful justification for desiring a West Point–educated, Old Army–trained commander over a proven battle winner.[20]

Sherman's plan to promote General Howard to army command was destined to cause a controversy with another commander in addition to Logan, for Howard was not the senior corps commander in Thomas's Army of the Cumberland. That honor belonged to Major General Joseph Hooker. Not only did Hooker outrank Howard by date of commission, he had previous army experience as commander of the Army of the Potomac, possessed excellent upper command organizational skills, and had a more impactful fighting record than Howard. Certainly, Howard's promotion over "Fighting Joe" would not only aggravate Hooker, it might instigate his resignation over the slight (he had resigned from the Army of the Potomac a year before over a grievance about his role).

Sherman disliked Hooker, immensely so it seems, and harbored no qualms about how Howard's promotion would affect the XX Corps commander. The die was cast. Sherman formally applied for Howard's promotion with the U.S. War Department. President Abraham Lincoln, as commander in chief, needed to act upon Sherman's request before any further action could transpire.

No evidence exists to indicate that Howard, Logan, or Hooker knew about Sherman's request to the U.S. War Department on July 24 or on Monday, July 25. The Army of the Tennessee had moved little since Friday's big battle, and soldiers had spent the day resting, writing letters to loved ones at home, and compiling official reports of what corps, divisions, brigades, regiments, and companies did on July 22. McPherson's death and the 3,721 other casualties made this the most devastating battle suffered by the army since it was named back in October 1862. Two batteries and one entire infantry regiment, the 16th Iowa Infantry, had been led away as prisoners of war. Twelve regimental commanders had been killed, wounded, or captured that day. Two brigade commanders, Brigadier General Manning F. Force and Colonel August Mersy, had been wounded and another, Colonel Robert K. Scott, had been captured. Surprisingly, all division and corps commanders had escaped the casualty list on Friday.[21]

This battle, however, inflicted an upper-level casualty three days after it was fought. On Monday, July 25, Brigadier General Thomas W. Sweeny—born on Christmas Day forty-three years earlier in Ireland—was in his headquarters tent handling the duties of his XVI Corps division, which he had commanded throughout the campaign. Sweeny's men had been struck first in the surprising Confederate assault at noon on July 22 and had firmly held their ground. Their commander would not allow any other alternative. "Fightin' Tom" Sweeny's battle persona never weakened in a career that took away his right arm in Mexico, put an arrow through his neck in an Indian clash in 1852, and left his battered body embedded with bullets and scarred throughout his three years of service in the Civil War.

Sweeny's greatest fault went hand in hand with his feistiness. He was a very harsh and verbally abusive commander who was notorious for delivering his orders in three languages: "English, Irish-American, and profane." His crudeness also stood in the way of true friendships within the officer ranks of the army. On this particular day, Sweeny received two important visitors to his headquarters: Major General Grenville M. Dodge, Sweeny's corps commander, and Brigadier General John W. Fuller, a fellow division commander in the XVI Corps. Sweeny despised both men—and they likewise were not particularly fond of him.

Sweeny was looking for a fight this particular afternoon, verbal or otherwise. He got both. Dodge and Fuller took the bait and argued with him about the facts regarding the XVI Corps in the Battle of Atlanta, Sweeny accused both men of not protecting his division and supporting it effectively. When Dodge challenged him about his accusation, Sweeny faced his superior and called him "a God-damned liar," followed by "a cowardly son of a bitch," and finally "a God-damned inefficient son of a bitch." Dodge responded to the insubordination by smacking Sweeny in the face. Sweeny then punched Dodge in the nose, and a short-lived scuffle ensued before other officers intervened to break it up. Sweeny was arrested and his war career ended right then and there in his tent. Dodge immediately replaced him with the senior brigade commander of the division, Colonel Elliott W. Rice. Two days later Dodge assigned Brigadier General John M. Corse, Sherman's acting inspector general, to take over Sweeny's division.[22]

The squabbles within the Army of the Tennessee were not isolated to the XVI Corps. The XVII Corps was more unified, but it was also the most crippled Union corps of Sherman's seven in his army group. The corps was down more than 2,500 officers and men from hard fighting from the night of July 20 through the battle two days later, leaving the two divisions comprising the corps at a total of only 6,000 officers and men—the size of a single division at the beginning of the campaign. One division commander, Giles A. Smith, was new to his command (he was a former brigadier in the XV Corps), having replaced Brigadier General Walter Q. Gresham, who was wounded in action on July 20. Colonel George E. Bryant and Lieutenant Colonel Greenberry F. Wiles handled brigades now after immediate promotion to replace lost brigadiers on July 22.

Every other XVII Corps brigade was led by a colonel; one of them was so disgruntled that his days became numbered in the service. Colonel William Hall commanded the once formidable and always proud Iowa brigade. He had temporarily led Gresham's division until replaced by Giles Smith—and stewed because of it. Losing an entire regiment to capture the very next day (July 22) further soured his mood. A small man given to bouts of irritability and always appearing nervous, Hall resented losing his division helm to a noncorps member. To make matters worse, chain of command bypassed him during the Battle of Atlanta when General Smith personally instructed Hall's regiments. The latter's disgruntled nature and perhaps his quiet performance on July 22 had set him up to be replaced before month's end by a subordinate in his brigade—Colonel William Belknap of the 15th Iowa, who had gained notoriety for horse-collaring an Alabama colonel and hauling him over the earthworks to captivity during the fight for Atlanta. In his after-battle report written on July 25, Hall detailed a total of 664 officers and men killed, wounded, and captured in his brigade. "My loss is very severe," he lamented. It was the last official report Hall ever filed.[23]

The Battle of Atlanta arguably adversely affected the XV Corps most of all, notwithstanding the fact that it was numerically the strongest corps on the field after the battle and one that lost only three regimental commanders and no officer of higher rank than colonel. On July 25 the XV Corps was handicapped by a slate of promoted officers who failed to excel in their new roles on the Atlanta battlefield. After Logan's on-the-field promotion to army command, the corps was directed by Brigadier General Morgan L. Smith. Brigadier General Joseph Andrew Jackson Lightburn took over Smith's division, and Colonel Wells S. Jones took over Lightburn's brigade. Of those three, only Jones performed admirably on July 22. Smith and Lightburn failed to secure a strong defense of their earthworks at the Georgia Railroad and allowed portions of four Confederate brigades to overrun their position, temporarily capture ten guns, and rout much of the infantry from the field. Logan's return with a brigade of reinforcements from the XVI Corps initiated a resurgence within the XV Corps ranks of this division in spite of the lack of leadership from Smith and

Lightburn, strengthening and inspiring it to recapture half of the cannons and restore the line before the battle's end.

One of the more talented XV Corps brigadiers throughout the Atlanta Campaign was Giles A. Smith (Morgan's brother), who had commanded a brigade of his sibling's Second Division until July 21. His talent was no secret; back in 1863 when he was a colonel, the assistant secretary of war evaluated Giles Smith and declared, "There are plenty of men with general's commissions who, in all military respects, are not fit to tie his shoes." Brigadier General Smith was thought of so highly to be tapped as the top candidate for promotion within the Army of the Tennessee, and on July 21 he transferred from brigade command in the XV Corps to division command in the XVII Corps. His loss further weakened the talent in the officers' ranks of the XV Corps, particularly in the division he left.

Brigadier General Charles R. Woods led the First Division of the XV Corps. He was a big and burly commander trained at West Point, where he was saddled with the cringe-worthy nickname of "Susan." Woods was competent but not spectacular. Sherman was irritated to learn that Woods would soon return to brigade command because Brigadier General Peter J. Osterhaus, who started the campaign in charge of the division but had taken sick leave on July 17, was promoted to major general and soon would reunite with his command. Sherman suspected Osterhaus's leave of absence had more to do with seeking a second star on his shoulder than with recuperating from illness. "I do not object to his appointment," explained Sherman within hours of the Dodge-Sweeny tussle, "but I wish to put on record this my emphatic opinion, that it is an act of injustice to officers who stand by their posts in the day of danger to neglect them. . . . Osterhaus, who left us in the midst of bullets to go to the rear in search of personal advancement. If the rear be the post of honor, then we better all change front on Washington." Sherman's caustic opinion reached President Lincoln and Lieutenant General Grant, who both were unaware that Osterhaus had not been in command during the Battle of Atlanta. Grant replied, "Osterhaus has proven himself a good soldier, but if he is not in the field I regret his promotion."

Sherman's regret magnified when he learned that the newly christened Major General Osterhaus would remain out of action for three more weeks.[24]

The Third Division of the XV Corps was in Alabama, totally detached from the Atlanta Campaign. The Fourth Division of the corps started the campaign as the most suspect division, but by the end of the Battle of Atlanta it challenged the others as the most dependable and efficient of all divisions of the corps. Commanded by Brigadier General William Harrow, a rigid disciplinarian and transplant from the eastern theater, the three brigades of this division fought well at the Battle of Dallas, soldiered bravely and efficiently throughout the weeks leading up to and including the Battle of Kennesaw Mountain, and were stalwarts on the Atlanta battlefield protecting the northern face of Bald Hill from Confederate capture. The latter achievement was led by the rising star of the division, Charles C. Walcutt, one of three colonels leading Harrow's brigades.

Sherman finalized his plans throughout the remainder of July 25 and 26. He issued Special Field Orders No. 42 in seven parts. Sherman attempted to counter all options available to the Confederates defending Atlanta, including the possibility of retreat, as specified in section I. "Should the enemy remain as now, on the defensive, inside of the fortifications of Atlanta, the Macon [rail] road must be attacked by cavalry," instructed Sherman to begin section II, before going on to delineate the role of each army in his department. Section IV specified exactly what the Army of the Tennessee was tasked to do: "Major General Logan will to-morrow send all his trains, and sick, and impediments, to the rear of General Thomas to any point near the Peach Tree Creek, and during the early morning by moonlight of the next day, viz, Wednesday, July 27, withdraw his army, corps by corps, and move it to the right, forming on General Palmer, and advancing the right as much as possible."[25] The instruction reveals that Sherman was not going to delay the grand counterclockwise movement even though his request to install a new commander for the Army of the Tennessee had yet to be granted—or denied. Sherman received news of that decision from the U.S. War Department late in the day on July 26 when General Halleck notified him, "General Howard is assigned, as requested, to command the Army and Department of the Tennessee." Sherman relayed the order to General Thomas specifying, "I want him in his new command at once."[26]

The decision and order transformed the Army of the Tennessee on the eve of one of its toughest challenges.

2

Hood and His Army

On Sunday, July 24, 1864, General John Bell Hood spent most of his sixth day as commander of the beleaguered Army of Tennessee in the home of John S. Thrasher—his seventh headquarters in less than a week. He had convalesced in the Thrasher house the previous autumn to recuperate from his total leg amputation after the Battle of Chickamauga. On the night of July 22, Hood returned to this "pretty gothic cottage" (as described by a newspaper reporter) on Whitehall Street in the southwestern sector of Atlanta after occupying four other buildings during the daylong Battle of Atlanta. Considering the heavy fighting and casualties endured by his army between Wednesday and Friday (July 20 to 22), little or no news was good news as far as the Confederates were concerned in and around Atlanta. They welcomed the light activity as much as the cooler weather that settled in over the weekend. Hood's only known message to the Confederate War Department in Richmond on July 24 was a brief one: "All has been quiet today except a little picket-firing and occasional shells thrown into the city."[1]

But all was not quiet within Hood's army. The cacophony that had resonated throughout the course of the campaign sounded louder still when Hood ascended to command of the army on July 17, replacing General Joseph Eggleston Johnston, whom President Jefferson Davis fired because he had "failed to arrest the advance of the enemy to the vicinity of Atlanta, far in the interior of Georgia." Furthermore, Davis expressed to Johnston that he had "no confidence that you can defeat or repel him."[2]

Adherents to Johnston and to Hood appeared to be mutually exclusive; this was particularly true within the ranks of the generals and staff officers. One who carried both distinctions was Brigadier General William Whann Mackall. He had served as assistant adjutant general of the Army of Tennessee since April 1863. His run as chief of staff was an interrupted one; he first served for Braxton Bragg—a fellow and former West Pointer from the same class of 1837—until granted his own request to be relieved of command after the Battle of Chickamauga after becoming hopelessly disillusioned by Bragg's leadership. Mackall was urged back and accepted his reappointment in the same role by Joseph Johnston in January 1864.

Mackall was not fond of Braxton Bragg, but he did develop a closer, more loyal relationship with Johnston throughout the Army of Tennessee's campaign in northern Georgia as it attempted to repel Sherman's advance. Mackall had written to Johnston during the last weeks of Bragg's tenure with the army, had commanded a brigade in the Department of Mississippi and East Louisiana in the field (with Johnston as his superior) in the interim between Bragg's and Johnston's commands, and defended and lauded Johnston's leadership in his personal letters written during the spring and summer of 1864. When Davis fired Johnston, Mackall remained as chief of staff of the army, this time under General Hood, the third commander for whom he had served in less than one year. Mackall's personality did not endear him to Hood's loyalists; one of the general's staff men revealed that Mackall was coined "the owl of the army" and criticized Mackall for pessimistically predicting doom for every battle offensive Hood had planned.

General Hood surely recognized Mackall's value as an experienced chief of staff, but he must also have been sensitive to Mackall's past devotion to Johnston, which clashed with Hood's style of command. As it turns out, the situation came to a head with the intervention of Braxton Bragg himself, who came to visit Hood at his headquarters that Sunday, July 24. When Bragg stepped onto the porch of the Thrasher house and thrust out his right hand for Mackall to grasp and shake, the chief of staff refused to do so. The snub gave Hood the opening to get rid of Mackall, whose dismissal was accomplished "at his own request," according to the official record. Mackall promptly left the Atlanta headquarters, apparently secreting army headquarters records with him as he headed eighty-five miles southeast to Macon and a reunion with General Johnston the following day.[3]

This incident underscores the unique and somewhat surreal circumstances surrounding the high command of the Army of Tennessee in the midsummer of 1864: the current army commander, John B. Hood, purged himself of a loyalist to the previous army commander, Joseph Johnston, with the unintended help of the army commander (Braxton Bragg) who preceded them both. Bragg thus served the role ascribed to him by President Jefferson Davis in February, to be "charged with the conduct of the military operations in the armies of the Confederacy."[4]

John Bell Hood was apparently President Davis's most logical choice to change the fortunes of the Army of Tennessee. Davis had grown increasingly anxious throughout the late spring and early summer as Johnston and the army continuously ceded prime territory in northern Georgia to Sherman's army group. Although Johnston had adeptly sparred with Sherman throughout the campaign, he gave his commander in chief and War Department little if any assurance that he would prevent the Union capture of Atlanta; he never concretely declared that he would wage battle for the most vital city of the Confederacy outside of Richmond. This, more than anything else, is what induced Davis to dismiss him.[5]

Johnston's departure angered his subordinates and shocked many soldiers of his army. "Johnston has so endeared himself to his soldiers, that no man can take his place," wrote a Texan in July 1864. The soldier went on to claim that scores of men openly discussed deserting the army and resisting all military authority. Hood's promotion stirred further resentment over Johnston's having been replaced, as many soldiers considered Hood unsuitable. Although the anti-Hood voices in the army left the impression that they spoke for the vast majority of the Confederates defending Atlanta, no evidence exists that they represented even half, but their opinions easily outweighed those of Hood's more muted supporters. "Hood is the most unpopular Gen'l in the Army and some of the troops are swearing they will not serve under him," declared a Mississippian in the ranks who christened him "Hood the butcher"; a fellow soldier from Tennessee told his diary on Hood's first day of command, "Hood's fighting quality, as demonstrated by his total disregard for human sacrifice, does by no means suit his men." The animus toward Hood may have been tainted by a realization why Hood specifically was chosen to replace Johnston. "Gen. Hood will probably teach the army other tactics than fortifying," recorded the Tennessean in his diary.[6]

Actually, fortifying was one of Hood's favored tactics; he continued to expand and strengthen the massive earthworks that ringed the city. He issued a direct call for his army to spend the weekend fortifying the city, and the army responded with alacrity, aided by the reduction in skirmish and artillery fire from Sherman's men. Earthwork expansion ran smoothly while the army was in the midst of transitioning to a new chief of engineer. By Monday morning, July 25, Brigadier General Daniel H. Reynolds, one of Hood's brigade commanders, assessed the works as "almost impregnable against any direct assault."[7]

As he strengthened Atlanta's fortifications, Hood took stock of the outcome of the vicious contests that had initiated his first week as army commander. Three consecutive days of battle had been waged by Hood between July 20 and 22, from north of the city at Peachtree Creek to the east between Decatur and Bald Hill. The outcome of those battles was ambivalent. Clearly, Hood lost all three contests because he failed to dislodge either of the Federal armies he attacked while suffering 3,000 more Confederate versus Union troop losses. Nonetheless, a significant side effect of Hood's assault, which could not be overlooked at the time, was that he not only brought an abrupt halt to both prongs of Sherman's dual penetration directly into Atlanta, but also wreaked enough havoc on Union infantry to slow down Sherman's offensive to allow his department to lick its wounds and restructure commands due to the casualties inflicted by the Confederate attacks. These results induced Hood to notify the Confederate War Department of a quiet day on the war front surrounding Atlanta on July 24.

Hood continued to interpret the July 22 Battle of Atlanta as a Confederate victory. He did downplay his earlier gains from the contest by informing the War Department that his army had captured thirteen cannons instead of the twenty-three that he first reported (the actual number captured was ten); however, he revised the captured colors to more than double the first report. Hood's "victory" was dutifully trumpeted to Richmond by Braxton Bragg, who wrote directly to Jefferson Davis within a day of returning to Atlanta. Bragg lauded the "brilliant affair of the 22d" and the positive effect it had on Southern troops. Additionally, Bragg assured his president that "our loss was small in comparison with the enemy's" and the enemy "was badly defeated." The trump card played routinely in correspondences was the death of General McPherson, Hood's former classmate at West Point. The mention of McPherson implied this reasoning for Hood's assertion that the Union lost the Battle of Atlanta: How can an army possibly claim it won a battle if its commander was killed in the midst of the bloody affair? Robert E. Lee was not in direct contact with Bragg at the time, but he had already received the sanguine news of what Lee now called "the glorious victory at Atlanta." If this was true, a hopeful but cautious Lee predicted, Alabama and Mississippi would be free to train in supplies and troops to him at Petersburg, Virginia. Lee's optimism was evidence of how impactful Hood's and Bragg's spin on the battle had become.[8]

Letters, diaries, and reports from Confederate soldiers in the days following the battle acknowledged the treacherous losses they had suffered, but few recognized that the battle had actually been a defeat. Hiram Smith Williams of the 40th Alabama Infantry spoke for a distinct minority with his diary entry regarding the battle of the 22nd: "We charged the enemy's lines, and although we have cheering reunions, yet I do not think we have accomplished much.... Hood will soon ruin his army at that rate. It will not do for the weaker army to charge the stronger."[9]

What the Alabama soldier failed to understand is that Hood had not planned to charge headlong into a numerically stronger army on July 22 or in future operations around Atlanta. The primary problem taunting and haunting Hood was Sherman's big blue noose beginning to tighten around him. A close second among Hood's primary concerns was the size, structure, and condition of his command: the Army of Tennessee.

Size was the army's asset early in the campaign. Less than two months earlier, that army massed 77,582 officers and men present for duty—one of the largest Confederate armies ever placed in the field. Six weeks of battles, skirmishes, and consequent desertions sapped manpower from the ranks. On July 24 Hood's army that was present for duty at Atlanta numbered no more than 58,000 infantry, artillery, cavalry, and Georgia militia—still a formidable force in overall numbers. It was larger than Robert E. Lee's Army of Northern Virginia facing General Grant across the siege lines at Petersburg, five hundred miles to the northeast. It also kept Sherman's numerical superiority at a ratio less than two to one. This prevented Sherman from even considering mass assaults against a force that was dug in for over a week and was still strengthening its position.[10]

The Atlanta Campaign had stripped more than 24,000 Confederates from the ranks between May 6 and July 24. Nearly 9,000 killed, wounded, and captured Southerners had been crossed off duty rolls since Hood took over the army on July 18. The losses reflected the consequences of heavy offensive fighting, particularly between July 20 and 22, during which time Hood tried unsuccessfully to knock out General Thomas's Army of the Cumberland at Peachtree Creek, and rapidly followed up with a grand attempt to roll up the Union Army of the Tennessee while dislodging Sherman's other two armies. Hood succeeded in stopping Union momentum toward Atlanta while removing 6,500 Union soldiers and ten artillery pieces from the Military Division of the Mississippi.[11]

The cost of those battle accomplishments, however, was exorbitant. All but about eight hundred of Hood's losses in his first week of command came out of his infantry, leaving him with 39,000 officers and infantrymen—sans militia—remaining in his three corps on July 24. By comparison, Sherman boasted seven infantry corps totaling 70,000 present for duty on the same date. Hood's artillerists, horse soldiers, and militia added another 19,000 to his totals, which was closer to Sherman's 24,000 in the same two branches, but the primary fighting regiments of infantry were considerably less formidable than they had been a month before, or even one week before.

The quality of Hood's infantry was becoming as troubling as its quantity. Unlike any other battle of the campaign, the Battle of Atlanta cruelly tore the fabric of Hood's ten infantry divisions by removing an appalling number of commissioned officers from their respective division, brigade, and regimental commands. Upwards of a hundred of these commanders were rendered hors de combat on July 22; sixty from Lieutenant General William J. Hardee's corps alone. Reflecting on this, Hardee's assistant adjutant general proclaimed, "The loss of officers, especially field officers, was [unparalleled] and irreparable." One of Hardee's division adjutants lamented, "This day was the most disastrous as to casualties in the career of the division, not so much as to the loss of numbers, but that of officers, which was exceptionally heavy, and irreparable, amounting to 30 general, field, and acting field officers alone, not to count company commanders." The reliability of Confederate company officers from this day forward was more critical than ever. Twenty-three of them, by attrition of their superiors, commanded regiments in Hood's army at the beginning of July's final week.[12]

The combination of quality and quantity battle casualties wrecked one of the army's divisions beyond repair. Major General William H. T. Walker was the highest-ranking loss for Hood on July 22; he was killed within the first hour of the eight-hour battle. His division of Georgians and South Carolinians suffered so severely throughout the rest of that day that it was ruined. One brigade of Walker's division cycled through four commanders, while the original commanders of the other two brigades of the division also went down with wounds. Close to five hundred gun-toting soldiers were killed, wounded, or captured that day. Walker's division had boasted 6,000 officers and men present for duty early in the campaign; on July 23 that numerical strength had dipped well below 4,000 with an acting commander, Brigadier General Hugh Mercer, remaining as the only general still standing within the entire division—barely standing, however. So physically ailing was General Mercer that it became obvious to anyone paying attention that the fifty-five-year-old was not strong enough to continue as a field commander. Hood sent Mercer to Savannah for duties more commensurate with his physical abilities and then broke up the division by dispersing each brigade to the remaining divisions of Hardee's corps. By July 25 "Walker's Division" was defunct.[13]

Hood's decision to deal a death blow to Walker's division underscored his dissatisfaction and distrust of subordinate leadership throughout the Army of Tennessee. Walker's proud division could have remained intact even without General Mercer by the promotion of a general commanding a brigade from any of the other nine divisions to cross over to helm the leaderless unit. Either General Hood felt he could not spare a brigade general or, more likely, he felt none were capable of handling three brigades in battle, particularly since those brigades all had suspect fighting ability due to new commanders who lacked brigade leadership experience.

Division and corps leadership continued to concern General Hood on July 25, as it had from the day he took over the army a week before. Those concerns multiplied after the battles at Peachtree Creek and east of the city. It was becoming clear that Hood was most satisfied with upper command in the corps commanded by Major General Alexander P. Stewart, who took possession of the three divisions formerly commanded by Major General Leonidas Polk three weeks after he was killed in action at Pine Mountain on June 14. Stewart's three divisions were led by experienced major generals who had been in command of those divisions since the beginning of the campaign in May. Stewart's first and only battle at the helm of the corps was Peachtree Creek, an action that had engaged two of Hood's three infantry corps by design. Although Peachtree Creek was a defeat, Hood expressed no dissatisfaction with Stewart's leadership or any of his division commanders in his official report regarding the battle. Because the corps had suffered 1,657 battle losses on July 20, Hood assigned it a reserve role for the planned battle two days later. Stewart's command—initially reduced to fewer than 13,000 soldiers after Peachtree Creek—was not activated on July 22.[14]

Hood was obviously most knowledgeable about the leadership of the corps he had led for more than two months of the campaign, and he sought outside help for that corps within a day of ascending to army command. One of Hood's division commanders, Major General Carter Stevenson, instigated a response from his superior when he issued special orders on July 18 staking his claim to the helm: "Being the senior officer present with it, the undersigned [Stevenson] hereby assumes command of Hood's corps." Hood's intervention was swift: before that day's end, he replaced

Stevenson with Major General Benjamin Franklin Cheatham from Hardee's corps, the most senior division commander available in the army. Hood explained the move to the secretary of war, "I have no major-general in that corps whom I deem suitable for the position." This certainly was an overt rebuke of Stevenson, a forty-six-year-old Virginia native, West Point graduate, and Mexican-American War veteran who had commanded divisions of Confederate western theater troops since the end of 1862.[15]

Although Hood commended Stevenson in his reports throughout the Atlanta Campaign, he was unimpressed enough with him to deny him even temporary corps command. The interim role was exactly what General Cheatham held (although Cheatham may never have been aware of this), for Hood solicited the Confederate War Department to appoint Major General Mansfield Lowell as the permanent corps commander, with two other options of generals in other theaters if Lowell was not awarded the assignment. The other two division commanders within Hood's former corps were new to command. One of them, John C. Brown, was a brigadier general with only two weeks of division command experience. The other, Henry D. Clayton, was a commissioned major general who also had led a division for less than three weeks. Both of these newer commanders performed well east of Atlanta on July 22 by deploying an appropriate number of troops for their respective attacks and leading them adeptly. By contrast, Major General Stevenson did not perform well that crucial day.[16]

General Cheatham had followed Hood's orders obediently and competently as a new corps commander at the Battle of Atlanta, swiftly adapting to an abrupt change of orders in the middle of the fighting. By July 25 General Hood was aware that his request for an outside general had been granted, which would restore Cheatham back to division command with the all-Tennessee division he had led since the spring of 1862. This inevitability would be doubly satisfying to Hood, for he would be awarded the corps commander of his choosing while simultaneously restoring a solid division commander to his former helm. The latter proved necessary as a result of the July 22 battle. Cheatham's division command replacement, Brigadier General George E. Maney, had allowed his four brigades to become separated during the battlefield offensive and thus attacked disjointedly in unsupported formations. General Maney would return to brigade command to make Cheatham's division a top-notch fighting unit again.

The Tennessee troops under General Maney (soon to be back under Cheatham) fought within Hardee's corps. Generals Hardee and Hood had become a volatile mix throughout Hood's first week of army command. The animosity between the two escalated in the wake of the two big battles fought on July 20 and July 22. Hood lambasted Hardee and his corps in his Peachtree Creek report, with some justification. Despite Hardee's tardy deployment that afternoon and also allowing a division (Bate's) to get lost without making contact on the extreme right of the Confederate line, Hardee's corps fought bravely in their assault against Thomas's Army of the Cumberland on July 20—and paid the price for their forlorn hope of success. Based on his reports, communications, and subsequent memoirs, Hood did not seem to appreciate that Hardee suffered seven hundred casualties in that battle or that one division of his corps (Cleburne's) lost another three hundred killed and wounded soldiers the following day in the failed contest to hold and secure Bald Hill.

Before the last gun had fired its rounds in the July 21 action at Bald Hill, Hood had Hardee's corps marching overnight through darkened woods that loomed over the Union left flank to initiate battle the following morning against the Army of the Tennessee. The Battle of Atlanta that followed used up Hardee's corps unlike any other battle of the campaign, removing at least 3,300 officers and men. Hardee's losses in nearly nonstop action for three days approached 4,500 rank and file, severely weakening his corps to fewer than 12,000 infantry by July 25, reduced to three divisions instead of the customary four.

Hood rightfully recognized the sacrifices made by the foot soldiers in Hardee's corps and commended them for their gallantry. "His troops fought with great spirit and determination," lauded Hood of their effort on July 22. Hood clearly drew a distinction between the corps members and the corps commander, however, when he criticized Hardee for "failing to entirely turn the enemy's left, as directed." Hood's documentation of those disparate views took place two months after the campaign; ten years later he expanded on those views in his memoirs.[17]

Hardee had been dubbed "Old Reliable." Respected as a master tactician—he wrote the manual of tactics that neophyte captains, colonels, and generals devoured and regurgitated to their troops at the beginning of the war—Hardee evolved by necessity as the war entered a realm that no textbook could explain. He had been ubiquitous in the Army of Tennessee and respected as its top corps commander. That was part of the problem with Hardee's relationship with the War Department. When offered the command of the army after General Bragg was sacked after Chattanooga, Hardee refused it, agreeing only to lead it in the interim, and thereby forcing Jefferson Davis to swallow his personal animus and turn to Joseph E. Johnston as the only logical option remaining in the winter of 1864. When Johnston disappointed his president and was dismissed to follow in Bragg's footsteps, Hardee warmed up to the notion of heading the army, but Davis selected Hood. This left Hardee to stay pat with his corps, subordinate to a general fifteen years his junior whom Hardee outranked by fifteen months.

By Tuesday, July 26, after nine days with Hood at the helm and Hardee as his subordinate, both generals were of one mind that they could not continue in the same capacity. Bragg mediated between them, bringing both to an agreement, as he explained in a confidential letter to the president: Hardee should be transferred out of the region to another theater. No one was suggesting that this had to transpire immediately; three full days had passed without any movement from General Sherman opposing them, but the likelihood that three more days would pass under the same conditions were remote.[18]

That day, however, Hood's army severely altered its command structure when the Confederate War Department completed Hood's request for his replacement at corps command, originally made before the Battle of Peachtree Creek. Hood had asked for Mansfield Lowell to replace him, but Jefferson Davis denied that request as he did for Hood's second choice, Major General Wade Hampton (then in charge of the cavalry corps in the Army of Northern Virginia). Hood's third choice for corps commander was approved six days earlier, and he arrived at headquarters on July 26 to report for duty. He was Stephen Dill Lee, the youngest lieutenant general in the Confederacy at the age of thirty years.[19]

Lee's arrival received very little fanfare. Most existing diary entries and letters fail to mention him for at least two days after his official appointment. What was unwritten was likely not unspoken, for the selection of General Lee would have turned the heads of subordinate division commanders who had commanded larger bodies of infantry than Lee had, had done so for much longer in the war, and had been wed to the Army of Tennessee since its infancy. Lee's commission was certain to be a source of jealousy or even disdain rather than respect, despite the fact that the youthful Lee was one of the few generals in the Confederacy with battle experience as an artillery commander, a cavalry chief, and an infantry brigadier. A South Carolinian by birth, Lee graduated in the middle of his 1854 West Point class, transitioned in the first year of the war from a captain and aide de camp to a colonel and artillerist. (His guns and dead cannoneers in front of the battle-damaged Dunker Church at Sharpsburg became the subject of one of the most iconic photographs of the entire war.) Promoted to brigadier general, Lee transferred to the west and served in the defenses of Vicksburg in charge of several infantry regiments. He and his men were captured and subsequently paroled in the summer of 1863. President Davis promoted Lee again to major general and placed him in charge of cavalry in the Department of Alabama, Mississippi, and East Louisiana. Lee commanded the entire department—albeit a small one—when Leonidas Polk took much of that force with him when he transferred to the Army of Tennessee early in May 1864.

Lee was credited with competent management of the department for repelling Union forays into his theater. Just prior to his promotion and new assignment under General Hood, Lee was the Confederate field commander at the Battle of Tupelo, Mississippi, on July 14. There he sent nearly 10,000 Confederate troops into uncoordinated, headlong assaults against a well-defended 14,000-man Union line. Lee suffered 1,300 losses in the ill-fated attacks, twice as many as his opponent. Lee admitted his attacks were repulsed but called the loss a draw; Southern reporters turned it into a victory for Lee and the Confederacy, basing their verdict on the withdrawal of Union forces from the theater days later. Although Tupelo was fought less than a week before Hood made his request for a corps commander, President Davis likely chose Lee for his availability to Hood rather than how Davis interpreted the Tupelo fight. Even in hindsight, most of the troops based their opinions of Lee less on his past performance than the fact he had never been associated with their army. "Stephen D. Lee was a new comer among us, whose rapid promotion was thought by us to be above his deserts, especially when it placed him above several tried leaders such as Cheatham and Cleburne," recalled an artillerist in Hardee's corps, who believed the camp rumor that Lee's ascension was brought on by favoritism from the top: "The talk in camp was that President Davis was partial to him."[20]

Dark eyed and fully bearded, the six-foot "new comer" perhaps appeared very young to his peers and subordinates, but he carried himself well. A reporter's description of him two years after the fact most certainly applied to General Lee in the summer of 1864: "tall and commanding in appearance, and with the soldierly bearing and polished address and grace of manner peculiar to the Southerner of the best type, added to a strikingly handsome face and a stalwart physique." A distant cousin of Robert E. Lee, Stephen D. Lee paled in comparison to his kin's military prowess, but he was still regarded as a successful member of that talented military family.[21]

General Lee's assignment was to take over the duties of the corps temporarily held by Major General Cheatham, who held the command for merely a week and guided it through two very brutal battles within that span. Perhaps Lee's immediate benefit to the army was restoring Cheatham back to the command of his Tennessee division in Hardee's corps and putting Brigadier General George Maney back to brigade command within that all-Tennessee force. Although it was debatable whether Lee's generalship was an improvement over Cheatham's at the corps level, very few could argue that Cheatham was *the* general to command the division he helmed and that bore his name for more than two years, while Maney was still better suited as a brigade commander rather than a division chief, as evidenced by his suspect leadership at Peachtree Creek and subpar command performance at the Battle of Atlanta.

Stephen D. Lee was one of several officers who assumed new roles in Hood's army. Brigadier General Francis A. Shoup, serving throughout the campaign as chief of artillery, accepted a new headquarters assignment as Hood's chief of staff, replacing General Mackall. Major Kinloch Falconer had temporarily filled this role for a day and remained as assistant adjutant general after Shoup's appointment. Shoup had earned a solid reputation throughout the Atlanta Campaign, particularly in his river-line defenses. In fact, the small fortresses positioned along the banks of the Chattahoochee River were called "Shoupades." His background rendered Shoup one of the most unlikely of prized officers in the Army of Tennessee. Born, raised, and college educated in Indiana, Shoup had no particular ties to the Confederacy except for having moved to St. Augustine, Florida, to practice law months before the start of the war.[22]

Shoup's reassignment created a void at chief of artillery. Hood appointed Colonel Robert F. Beckham to fill that role, recommending his promotion to brigadier general (a request the Confederate War Department denied). No other personnel arrived for duty on July 26, but the other major facelift for the army was an important name change. Throughout the campaign to this point, the troops originally belonging to the corps commanded by Leonidas Polk had retained the name "Army of Mississippi" even though they had served as a third corps in the Army of Tennessee (and not an independent one). Hood officially made these troops "Stewart's corps" via special field orders to identify them as belonging to the command of Major General Alexander P. Stewart. Additionally, Walker's division of Hardee's corps was officially terminated with the late commander's brigades dispersed to the other three divisions of the corps. "No material change in affairs today," reported Hood to the War Department on the 26th, a day on which several such changes were made to his army.[23]

Hood had not yet completed the personnel changes he desired for his army, but he received assurance that others were still in the works and en route. Hood welcomed the suggestion and efforts of General Bragg to bring Major General J. Patton Anderson from what Bragg considered an "unimportant" command in Florida to take over the division currently led by a brigadier general, John C.

Brown. This transfer was approved, and General Anderson was on his way to Atlanta. Hood was also promised a quality chief engineer to replace his current, less effective one, Colonel Stephen W. Presstman. To Hood's delight, President Davis informed him that Major General Martin L. Smith—Robert E. Lee's chief engineer in Virginia—would be transferring to the Army of Tennessee to serve under him in the same role. All of these changes bore strong evidence not only of Davis's faith in General Hood's leadership—despite the two recent battle defeats—but of the premium the president placed on the continued defense of Atlanta.[24]

Ironically, most of these changes came to fruition on July 26, the very day Hood reported as stagnant to the Confederate War Department. He was, of course, referring to the fact that his army and Sherman's entire department opposing him had spent a third consecutive uneventful day following three days of atrocious battle. The inactivity disappeared with Tuesday's sun. General Shoup recorded in his journal that "about dark enemy commenced moving toward our left."[25]

Ever vigilant, General Hood immediately prepared to put an authoritative end to this movement.

3

Prelude to Battle

At 10:00 P.M. on July 26, 1864, the Army of the Tennessee took on its third commander in four days, the newest being the first who was not indigenous to this colorful and successful army. Major General Oliver Otis Howard, commanding the IV Corps of the Army of the Cumberland, received his assignment for promotion to take the helm of General Sherman's old army. Howard waited for his new army to come to him. At daylight on Wednesday, July 27, the vanguard of the Army of the Tennessee struck Buck Head Road near Sherman's headquarters. From there General Howard took over from General Logan, so quietly as to escape the notice of the rank and file.[1]

The transition, however, created mayhem in the upper ranks of Sherman's department. Most adversely affected by Howard's ascension was General Logan, who appears to have been oblivious to the machinations to replace him with Howard until Sherman summoned him to headquarters after Logan successfully transported his command in the first phase of the grand counterclockwise movement. Logan protested the decision, claiming he deserved the command until the end of the campaign. Sherman naturally disagreed, explaining to Logan that all of the necessary behind-the-scenes duties of a department commander—including paperwork—needed to be addressed immediately, and he wanted Howard in place to take care of these duties.[2]

Logan sulked. He sat dejected on the porch of Sherman's headquarters. That's where Major General Grenville Dodge, the head of the XVI Corps, found him before entering the building to request an explanation. Sherman, however, would not provide it. Unsatisfied, Dodge returned to the porch to console Logan. "There is something here that none of us understand," offered Dodge to Logan. "It makes no difference," Logan responded; "it will all come right in the end." Logan virtually disappeared from view for the rest of the day, but Sherman diplomatically wrote him, "I assure you in giving preference to General Howard I will not fail to give you every credit for having done so well." The letter failed to pacify Logan; several days removed from his demotion, Logan characterized Sherman as "an infernal brute."[3]

Howard's promotion certainly stung General Logan, but the most dramatic response came from General Hooker, the commander of the XX Corps of the Army of the Cumberland, who was adamant that if Logan was to be replaced, he should do it since he was senior in command to Howard. Sherman's slight of Hooker was not clandestine. "He talks of quitting," remarked Sherman about Hooker later that day in a dispatch to the U.S. War Department; "If Genl. Thomas recommends I shall not object. He is not indispensable to our success. He is welcome to my place if the President awards it, but I cannot name him to so important a command as the Army of the Tennessee." Hooker did resign, explaining that Howard's promotion was "an insult to my rank and service." Hooker correctly perceived the injustice; nevertheless, his decision represented the second time in thirteen months that he quit on his troops in the midst of an ongoing campaign.[4]

At daylight on Wednesday morning, the first troops of the Army of the Tennessee reached Buck Head Road. General Howard was given no time to become acquainted with his new command, for General Sherman, accompanied by some of his staff, summoned Howard to join him on a westward ride. The two trotted to the line of entrenchments constructed by Major General John M. Palmer's XIV Corps of the Army of the Cumberland. Palmer's troops occupied a position running east to west at a point north of Proctor's Creek, a northwestward-flowing tributary of the Chattahoochee River.

Sherman and Howard ascended a high hill that Sherman dubbed "Davis's Hill" for the troops of Brigadier General Jefferson C. Davis, whose XIV Corps division occupied the area. Sherman pointed out to Howard a north–south ridge a mile southeast of them, running perpendicular to Palmer's line. "I propose to extend on a ridge due south," explained Sherman, "so that by facing left the right of our line will be a strong threat to East Point." The ridge, two and a quarter miles west of the center of Atlanta, was designated to Howard as the point "along which [Sherman] desired my column to move." Howard later recalled that the ridge ran substantially parallel to the western ring of Confederate works protecting Atlanta. According to Howard, General Sherman "believed that my lines would be long enough to enable me to get a hold of Hood's railroad before Hood could extend his trenches to guard it effectually."[5]

What Howard and Sherman both observed from Davis's Hill was a heavily wooded countryside typical of the landscapes they had been passing through and fighting for since they embarked on this campaign in early May. A day before the July 27 reconnaissance, Sherman characterized the region as a major blind spot for fighting men: "dense woods fill all the ravines & hollow, and which little cleared ground there is on the Ridge levels, or the alluvium of Creek bottoms. The hills are all Chestnut ridges with quartz and granite boulders & gravel. You Cant find an hundred acres of land clear ground between here & Chattanooga, and not a day passes but what every Genl. Officer may be shot as McPherson was."[6]

General Howard appeared more concerned about his troops and their mission than about suffering the same fate as General McPherson. He concurred with Sherman's description of the region, particularly in regard to the land features they observed from Davis's Hill. "In general," he explained, "there was more rough woodland than open ground. Some of the woods had troublesome undergrowth, but for the most part it was not difficult to push a skirmish line from road to road." He countered Sherman's belief that the Army of the Tennessee could advance and deploy on the ridge unmolested. The ridge they viewed was covered by trees while thicker woods sprawled east of it on the low ground—ample protection to conceal a clandestine attack by the Confederates. Rather than quickly hustle southward down the ridge line, Howard convinced Sherman to approve a more methodical southward advance of the army by unfolding it in a way that each successive division of the three corps would protect the previously deployed one by covering its flank. Sherman disagreed with what Howard deemed a necessity, but indicated he would allow it and rode away, leaving Howard to await the arrival of the army's vanguard to begin the southward advance along the ridge line.[7]

Artillery fire had slackened but never ceased since the Battle of Atlanta. On the morning of July 27, as Howard's army circled around Atlanta's northwestern environs, Brigadier General Matthew D. Ector, a commander of a brigade of Texas and North Carolina infantry in Stewart's corps, sat on a parapet and directed cannon fire from the outer perimeter earthworks crossing Turner's Ferry Road west of Atlanta. Captain John J. Ward's Alabama battery of Napoleons commanded this position. A brief exchange with Yankee artillerists—presumably from Palmer's XIV Corps—turned ugly for Ward and Ector. Ward was severely wounded by an exploding round, while a shell fragment nailed General Ector through the lower left thigh. The damage was severe (his fractured femur was visible in the gaping wound); the limb required immediate amputation, which removed Ector from the campaign and virtually out of the war. Colonel William H. Young of the 9th Texas Infantry immediately succeeded to Ector's position. For Major General Samuel D. French, the division commander to which Ector's brigade belonged, the loss of Ector deprived French of his sole subordinate general, as his other two brigades were temporarily commanded by colonels.[8]

The Union artillery barrage on the Confederate left was clear confirmation of the threat to Hood now posed by Sherman from this direction. Hood had known of this since the night of the 26th, confirmed it early on Wednesday, the 27th, and proceeded to react. At the same time, scouts confirmed the inauguration of Sherman's cavalry raid. Learning of the grand movement of Major General George Stoneman's cavalry force toward Flat Rock, Hood determined that their ultimate goal was to cut the Macon and Western Railroad, and he correctly deduced that the Confederates overseeing the prison at Andersonville would need to remain vigilant. Hood considered the threat substantial enough to send out Major General Joe Wheeler to end it. Wheeler's command of

8,500 horse soldiers rode out on Wednesday afternoon, leaving behind just one cavalry division in the vicinity of Atlanta for Hood and his army.[9]

Before the close of the second hour of Wednesday afternoon, Hood dispatched orders to each corps commander regarding troop positions to counter the new Union movement. Through his new chief of staff, General Francis A. Shoup, Hood ordered General Stewart to arm his corps with sixty rounds per man and prepare them "to move at a moment's notice." General Lee received Hood's orders to shift Brown's and Clayton's divisions westward and to conceal that shift from any and all of Sherman's observers. Hardee obeyed his instruction to replace Lee's withdrawn divisions with his own troops, his left extending to Peachtree Road.[10]

Hood ordered two of his infantry corps commanders, General Stewart and General Lee, to headquarters early that evening at the Thrasher house.[11] Informing them of Sherman's attempt to attack their left, Hood devised a plan to not only counter and thwart Sherman's effort, but to cripple a substantial portion of his department. Hood's battle plan contained some elements of his ambitious and ultimately failed plan for the Battle of Atlanta on July 22. Hood had detailed the council he held at headquarters for the Battle of Atlanta, both in his official report and again in his memoirs. Curiously, he left no equivalent paper trail for how he planned to attack Sherman's bluecoats west of Atlanta. In his report and memoirs, he mentioned only briefly his objective for one corps (Lee's). The plan, therefore, can only be hashed out from a combination of Hood's writings and those of General Lee and General Stewart, the two chief Confederate leaders of the ensuing battle.[12]

Hood had ascertained Sherman's massing of troops on his left to the northwest of Atlanta, but he had yet to confirm Sherman's goal. Throughout July 27 Hood seemed more concerned that Sherman was positioning troops in order to attempt an assault against Atlanta's western ring of defenses, not realizing yet Sherman's true design of heading toward East Point to threaten the railroads. "It became apparent almost immediately that he would attempt our left," revealed Hood in his report discussing what he knew at the time and never mentioning the railroads as Sherman's infantry objective. Ironically, the plan Hood relayed to Lee and Stewart was designed to disrupt Sherman's attack or even his deployment to assault the Confederate defenses, yet it was also destined to impede Sherman's true intent.[13]

Hood revealed to Lee that on July 28 he would order him to march his new corps out onto Lick Skillet Road, one of the east–west thoroughfares leading from Atlanta. Two roads were known as "the Lick Skillet road." One ran due west from Atlanta and was likely the original or "old" Lick Skillet road. The other road—to which Hood and every other Confederate referred as the Lick Skillet road—was actually the Green's Ferry road for the first two and a half miles west of Atlanta. This road ran adjacent to the railroad leaving Atlanta's southwestern environs up until the point where both thruways cut the Confederate earthworks protecting the city; from there, the railroad diverted southward while the road swung westward. One mile from the ring of works, the road bent from west to northwest; a mile from there it emptied into Lick Skillet Road in a broad, smooth elbow. Now oriented due west, the road traversed four miles of Fulton County woods and fields until it ran through its namesake village of Lick Skillet (six road miles from Atlanta). From the western side of Lick Skillet, the road led northwestward two more miles to the Chattahoochee River.[14]

Since Lick Skillet Road existed as the major (and ostensibly most reliable) thoroughfare west of Atlanta, Hood considered it vital for the protection of the Gate City. Not only did Hood strive to keep Lick Skillet Road out of Federal control; he wanted to possess it for a Confederate infantry offensive he spelled out to his corps commanders. Hood had a two-day battle plan employing six divisions of infantry, two out of the three divisions from Lee's corps, and all three from Stewart's corps, plus an additional unnamed division. After massing inside the Confederate works near Lick Skillet Road for the rest of Wednesday, July 27, General Lee's men would move out westward on Thursday to interpose 8,000 men south of Sherman's troops.

Knowing that Sherman had accessed the wooded ridge line near the north–south Chapel Road that afternoon (Chief of Staff Shoup's journal entry for July 27 revealed skirmishing contact with those moving troops), Hood rightfully expected the threat to Lick Skillet Road to be near its northwestward bend three miles west of Atlanta. While Lee's corps (more exactly, 60 percent of it), confronted the vanguard of Sherman's attempt to mass troops due west of the city, General Stewart would march out all three divisions of his corps plus "one from some other corps" (Stewart's characterization) from their rendezvous point at the junction of the Confederate line of works and Lick Skillet Road and remain there until Friday morning. On July 29, "at an early hour," Stewart would march out the four divisions, pass behind Lee's two divisions, and gain Sherman's right flank. Once this was attained, Stewart would turn right off Lick Skillet Road, pass to the rear of Sherman's army, and attack him in flank.[15]

This was Hood's intention, at least as Stewart—and, to a lesser extent, Lee—understood it. Hood himself revealed almost nothing about his plan in his after-action report and in his memoirs.

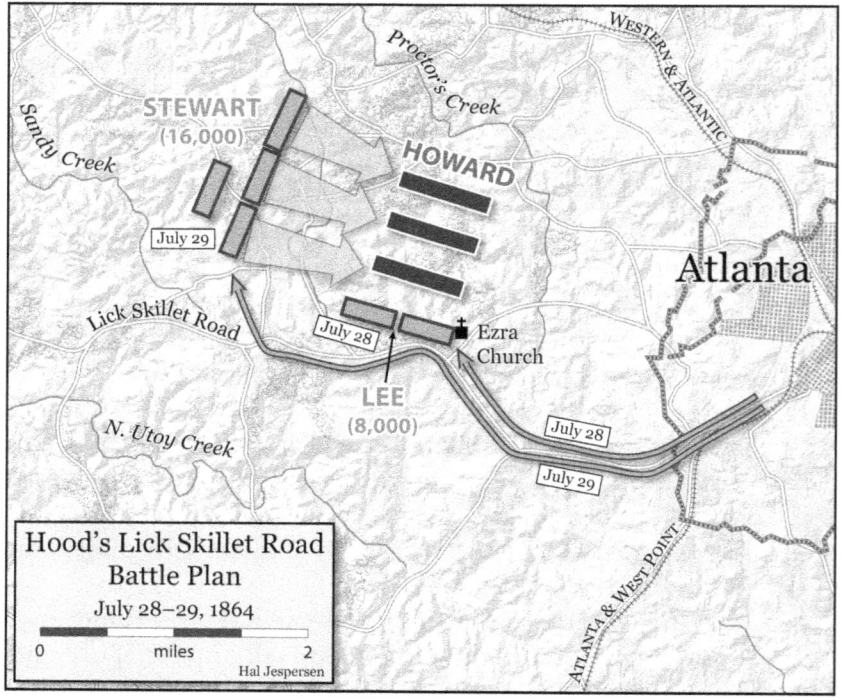

Compared to his battle plan crafted for the Battle of Atlanta and provided to his subordinate commanders on July 21, Hood's plan for the fight on the west side of the city was much less ambitious. By engaging six divisions of infantry—two in front and four in flank—Hood was using only half of his understrength force to surprise the head of Sherman's massive force. The Confederates would number upwards of 22,000 infantrymen in Hood's plan of battle, a force heavy enough to inflict damage on an unsuspecting foe sufficient to stop him in his tracks, but not likely numerically strong enough to annihilate or rout a force exceeding 70,000 infantry and end the campaign. Unlike in his plan for July 22, Hood did not expect to destroy Sherman's army group or even one army in it. At best, Hood's battle plan for July 28 and 29 was to disrupt whatever force was oriented eastward by firing into the right flank of those would-be attackers; or if that Union force was heading farther south to use Lick Skillet Road for that eastward advance, to inflict enough damage upon Sherman's infantry to buy valuable time for the Confederates to build a stronger line of protection in the southwest sector of Atlanta's defenses.

Hood's choice of Alexander P. Stewart to launch the flank attack was, in his mind, his only available option. Under normal circumstances, General Hardee ranked as the most experienced commander for such a large-scale operation; less than a week earlier, he conducted a similar flanking maneuver of three times the distance and without the benefit of daylight. However, his corps was nearly wrecked by three consecutive days of battle at Peachtree Creek, Bald Hill, and Atlanta from July 20 to 22. The loss of nearly 4,500 soldiers and more than sixty line officers in the previous week's battles north and east of Atlanta severely weakened Hardee's corps and forced its reconfiguration from four divisions to three. Most problematic to Hood regarding Hardee's corps was its commander. The very day Hood relayed his battle plan, Braxton Bragg spent his last day in Atlanta writing President Davis that General Hardee should be sent elsewhere.

Since General Stephen D. Lee was new in town and an unknown commodity, Stewart was the only officer left to head the force of impact for the pending battle west of Atlanta. His three divisions had withstood 1,657 casualties in their fruitless assaults at

Peachtree Creek, but since then they were the most rested troops in Hood's army with the most stable cadre of line officers. Stewart's present-for-duty infantry strength after Peachtree Creek barely exceeded 12,000 infantry officers and men, with artillerists adding another 1,100, which prompted Hood to place a fourth division under Stewart's command for the attack. Stewart's total force ostensibly numbered 16,000 to 17,000 for the planned July 29 offensive. Its nebulous fourth division was never identified.[16]

Regardless of what constituted his fourth division, the likelihood that Stewart would be able to march his corps and this division undetected for three or four miles across the front of an enemy army, while quietly deploying those twelve to fourteen brigades against an unsuspecting Federal flank, and then attack was extremely slim, based on Civil War precedent. Stewart had never handled so many troops before. His previous attack with three divisions on July 21 was not nearly as complicated and had ultimately proved unsuccessful. No evidence exists to suggest that Hood provided Stewart with any specific instructions on how to manage the assault. Was it to be launched en echelon or in concert? Was Stewart expected to attack with three divisions and one reserve, two in front and two behind, or all four deployed and attacking at once? Was the attack designed to move from west to east or on an angle from that direct axis. Considering that each brigade would consume nearly a third of a mile when all the regiments were deployed in a double line of assault, the tactics chosen for such a mass assault were critical and required considerable preplanning, including a reconnaissance, for it to be carried out with any considerable expectation of success. Unless Hood had intended to powwow with Stewart on July 28 for intense battle planning for the next day's action, Stewart was apparently given full discretion for the tactics of this offensive.

Timing created a very puzzling challenge for Confederate planning. Why was Hood stretching this plan into two calendar days? July 28 would have fourteen hours of adequate light for Lee to march out two miles early in the morning and ensconce on the high ground, force the unidentified Union force to react to his threatening position while Stewart advanced no more than five miles on the same road, and then clandestinely slip off to the west from behind Lee. Stewart's attack could commence as early as noon on July 28 if an enemy force confronted Lee almost immediately after the Confederates reached their designated point. Alternatively, if the Union reaction was unusually slow, using up all of the afternoon or early evening hours to reorient and challenge Lee's position, Stewart's flank-crushing assault by his four divisions could then be postponed until early morning light of July 29—the day Hood had designated for the mission.

If Lee or Stewart sought a reason from Hood for the unorthodoxy of a two-day mission so close to the initiation point of both forces, no evidence exists that either ever asked him. Hood remained tight-lipped about the answer, never spelling out his reasons in writing. Subsequent events on July 28 would provide the only feasible explanation for a two-day plan, including the decision to hold one of Lee's divisions from the mission. Regardless of the reason, Hood's desire to draw out a second corps into the second calendar day depended on the initial success of the first prong of the plan—Lee's maneuver—as well as his obtaining and holding the endpoint of his mission. Ideally, Lee's 8,000 men would have to be in position very early on Thursday morning to confront the Union advance. Based on the assumption that Lee would beat Sherman to the point of confrontation, Hood apparently expected two divisions to hold off mounting Union pressure for most of the daylight hours on July 28 and at least four more lit hours on July 29. Hood's best-case scenario would be for Lee's position to threaten the Union right flank as it was advancing eastward to challenge Hood's western ring of defenses late on Thursday, July 28, and disorient this portion of Sherman's army enough to force it to reorient from east to south to confront Lee directly, a maneuver that would consume too much time and daylight, allowing Stewart time to work his way to the flank before it overwhelmed Lee on July 29.

The portion of Lick Skillet Road including and surrounding its big bend was the intended segment that Lee was ordered to protect; both Hood and Lee were in sync regarding Lee's instructions. Lee reported that his orders were to "check the enemy" in order to maintain a Confederate hold of that road. This part of the road, however, did not run on a dominating height. Ridges of higher ground loomed above this road. The ambiguous directive "check the enemy" needed a specific endpoint named to accomplish that check, for if Lee simply deployed his troops on the road, he not only assured ultimate and potentially swift failure to hold off even an equal-sized body of troops, but his position potentially interfered with Stewart's mission to use the same avenue to work his way past Lee and deploy west of him.

Hood did provide a specific endpoint to define what "check the enemy" meant; he most likely reviewed those instructions by showing Lee a map of the region three miles from where they stood and defined the exact place where he wanted him to deploy. Hood pointedly ordered Lee to "check the enemy" on the high ground aligned "nearly parallel with the Lick Skillet road" but nearly half a mile above it, not by positioning his troops on the road near its bend three miles west of Atlanta. Lee's defense of these heights and position facing northward would assure two outcomes: (1) Union forces would be held at bay too far from Lick Skillet Road to seriously threaten it with Lee staunchly in place between them, and (2) Lee would be off the road to allow Stewart an open path to march behind and beyond Lee's troops and deploy to the west.[17]

Did Hood not consider the possibility that Sherman would beat Lee to Lick Skillet Road? Stewart maintained that Hood did indeed cover this contingency. "As I understood the instructions," explained Stewart, "General Lee . . . was to move out on the Lick Skillet road, attack the enemy's right flank and drive him from that road." Stewart also maintained that the objective of Lee's attack was to clear enemy troops from the same heights Hood assigned for Lee to occupy in an effort to "check the enemy." Whether he had intimate knowledge of this region of Lick Skillet Road or simply a map, Hood understood the necessity to remove the Union threat from the road and ostensibly to place Confederate troops on those heights, an understanding that appears was effectively conveyed to his two corps commanders. Hood had clearly plotted more than one scenario for this plan to be carried out. Experience from three years of bloody war and the compact size of Lee's intended force together told Hood that Lee would be vastly more successful as a holding force by reaching those heights well before Sherman did.[18]

Notwithstanding Lee's undersized holding force, Hood's plan was hampered by long odds for success due to the assumption that Lee and Stewart could accomplish what Hood expected of them. On its face, it appeared that Hood was attempting to repeat the intricacies of his July 22 battle using less-experienced corps commanders, battle-wearied troops, and less knowledge about the ever-changing position of his opponent and the ground that opponent occupied. Part of the reason for Hood's defeat on July 22 was the nearly last-minute deployment of a Union corps at the point where Hood's attack initiated; those Union reinforcements thwarted an easy panic and rollup of the Union left. Five days later Hood appears not to have considered a contingency plan for a certain repeat of the Union's fluid flank alignment. Hood's plan was bold; it was not foolhardy, but it was too dependent on previous accomplishment within its framework to guarantee success.

While Hood anticipated and contemplated Sherman's movements on July 27, General Howard was fretting over compliance with his superior's orders. His deployment was delayed until the middle of the afternoon when Major General Grenville Dodge's XVI Corps arrived at the foot of Davis's Hill. At 3:00 P.M. General Howard directed Brigadier General John M. Corse's division (the force formerly commanded by General Sweeny) of the XVI Corps to cross Proctor's Creek and scale the height 1,500 yards south of it. This they did, negotiating through thick underbrush to claim the ridge. They spent the remainder of the afternoon entrenching on the elevated ground and building a six-gun battery redoubt on one of the more prominent knolls. It is these men and their isolated activity that Confederate skirmishers confronted and notified Hood's headquarters of, close to the time Lee and Stewart arrived to ostensibly learn Hood's two-day plan.[19]

Unfortunately for General Howard, Corse's division essentially acted alone for nearly two hours, but this was not by design. Brigadier General John Fuller's brigade had halted well north of Corse's men, which delayed the entire movement behind them. By the time Fuller's brigades crossed the creek and reached the right of

Corse's division late Wednesday, daylight had all but disappeared. Major General Frank Blair's XVII Corps, reduced to 7,000 men as a result of their staunch, multidirectional defense at the Battle of Atlanta, came in on Dodge's right and extended its four brigades southward.

The XV Corps was forced to tarry most of the afternoon. "Frequent stopping is almost as wearisome and far more annoying than if the movement was a steady one with no hindrances whatever," surmised a XV Corps colonel of the day. He added, "The standing around with a knapsack on one's shoulders, momentarily expecting to hear the order to move is very annoying and tiresome." The entire corps had run out of daylight on Wednesday to march into position south of the remainder of the Army of the Tennessee. A soldier in the 30th Ohio complained about the wagons and troops that blocked their path: "The column moved by 'jerks' as the men called it, a most aggravating, tedious style of marching."[20]

They moved in fits and starts throughout the moonless hours of the night. When they did enjoy a protracted march, it was often cut short to allow the ammunition and supply wagons to close up. According to a member of the 70th Ohio, the soldiers became adept at snoozing during the respites. "At this time of the campaign it did not require much of an effort for us to go to sleep when we were still," he claimed. "We could sleep in any position—standing, sitting, lying down; or we could sleep while marching." Very little marching and considerable sleeping had commenced between midnight and 3:00 A.M.[21]

Rearward XV Corps soldiers were treated to a spectacle of the numerical power of Sherman's department. As they slid behind the Army of the Cumberland, 76th Ohio soldiers from Woods's division of the XV Corps could not help but be awed by the sight of XIV Corps soldiers standing on high ground, their forms lit by dozens of campfires. "We could see forty thousand men stretching for miles before us," raved one of the Buckeyes (embellishing the numbers), "their blue figures standing out in relief on the glimmering horizon. It gave us a feeling of confidence and strength to look upon such a mighty host." Ironically, as the Army of the Tennessee troops glided past Thomas's impressive army, they were relegating "the mighty host" to a mere supporting role for the next infantry battle.[22]

Skirmish fire slackened considerably into Wednesday night. During this lull Sherman wrote a dispatch to General Schofield, whose Army of the Ohio continued to occupy the grounds where much of the Battle of Atlanta had been fought near the Georgia Railroad (also called the Augusta Railroad). Sherman advised him to "burn that big brick house" near the railroad, ostensibly to prevent Confederate pickets from occupying it to harass the left of Sherman's army group. At 9:00 P.M. Schofield replied: "The brick house you refer to was burned this evening." This was the Troup Hurt house, the most identifiable human-made structure of the Battle of Atlanta, now reduced to a pile of smoldering bricks and ashes.[23]

According to General Howard, the moon did not appear until 3:00 A.M. on Thursday morning, July 28. The moonlight marked the return of the XV Corps to its original command structure. General Logan resumed corps command after four and a half days in charge of the army. In doing so, the corps' Second Division underwent a series of command changes while the other two divisions of the corps remained pat in their respective command structures. Brigadier General Morgan Smith returned to the helm of the Second Division; Brigadier General Joseph A. J. Lightburn took back his brigade of Smith's division from Colonel Wells S. Jones, who in turn returned to the command of his 53rd Ohio, which briefly halted Lieutenant Colonel Robert A. Fulton's short tenure as a regimental commander.[24]

Morgan Smith was the first to move on Thursday, shifting his division to the extreme right (south) of the Army of the Tennessee beginning at 3:00 A.M. Once Smith reached the flank, he kept his brigades off the road to cover the entire force as it extended southward beginning at 7:00 A.M. The Army of the Tennessee continued from where it left off at nightfall on the 27th, edging southward about two miles down Chapel Road from its intersection with Turner's Ferry Road. By 9:00 A.M. Grenville Dodge's XVI Corps was the northernmost corps on the road, followed southward by the XVII Corps and then Logan's XV Corps extending to near the southern terminus of Chapel Road and its namesake—a ten-year-old frame Southern Methodist Episcopal (M.E.) house of worship identified in this campaign as Ezra Church or Ezra Chapel. Proudly, members of Logan's corps took to calling themselves "Sherman's racers" to commemorate their rapid-marching abilities.[25]

Breakfast for the XV Corps was interrupted by its first contact with Confederate soldiers. Rebel cavalry covered Lick Skillet Road, fanning out in an arc northeastward from the big bend in the road toward Chapel Road. The Confederates belonged to Brigadier General Frank C. Armstrong's brigade of cavalry, half of Brigadier General William H. "Red" Jackson's 4,000-man division. They were the only significant body of horse soldiers left to serve Hood's army since General Wheeler had taken the remaining 8,500 cavalry to counter the Stoneman-McCook raid.[26]

Red Jackson remained with the brigade, rendering General Armstrong obsolete this particular morning. Jackson directed his force from Lick Skillet Road. He stood at the big bend of the road near the Fulton County Almshouse, known by the locals as the Poor House. Built four years earlier, the Poor House actually consisted of three small wooden structures, one of them used as an office building and the others, segregated by race, for long- and short-term residents. They sheltered the poor and infirm for as little as a night for some, and for several months for others. Before July 28, 1864, all the buildings had been emptied of their otherwise luckless inhabitants, who were fortuitously relocated to another facility. These frail noncombatants would not be subjected to battle this day.[27]

The cavalry were all Mississippians, led by Colonel R. A. Pinson's 1st Mississippi. Pinson ordered three companies to dismount and fan out toward Chapel Road to replace some Georgia state troops deployed in the area during the early morning hours.[28] "I sent, or rather started a picket over the field," recalled Lieutenant Colonel Frank C. Montgomery, who was in charge of the cavalry companies:

> They got about half way when they were fired on, and before they could get back to me, the woods on the other side were

full of bluecoats, who seemed to be advancing in line of battle with skirmishers in front, who however halted awhile at the fence on the other side. We did not yield the post without a show of resistance, for it at once occurred to me that this was an advance in force, for as far as I could see to my right, the enemy were advancing, and from the noise made which I could hear at a greater distance than I could see, I was sure there was a large force. It was therefore necessary to make as good a fight as I could to delay the advance, and to give warning to the rest of the brigade which I knew could not be far from me on my right, though up to that time I heard no firing in the direction I supposed it to be. I was on the extreme left as I knew, of any force we had at the time on the Lick Skillet road, and as far as I could judge at the time or afterward, was engaged with the extreme right of the advancing enemy.[29]

The Mississippians were decent marksmen, hardened by experience to delay enemy advances. Forced to give ground by superior numbers, they drew back toward Lick Skillet Road. According to one Southerner, "We retired slowly through the woods, firing from every stump and tree, and prostrate log into the ranks of the enemy." Upon reaching Lick Skillet Road, the Mississippi veterans retrieved their horses upon the hill from where they began their mission and mounted them. They fell back to a defensive line created by the 2nd Mississippi Cavalry, who stood behind works of rails, logs, and stumps—"anything that could stop a bullet" claimed one—and waited for an attack. Fortunately for the overmatched Southern horsemen, they exchanged skirmish fire only; the attack never came.[30]

The XV Corps skirmishers had driven the Mississippians nearly half a mile southwestward toward Lick Skillet Road. This cleared the heights north and northeast of the road for Union troops to occupy. This was the same elevated ground Hood identified for Lee to deploy his troops. But Lee and his Confederate infantry were nowhere in sight, leaving uncontested hills for blue-coated infantry to align upon.

Three signal stations were immediately established in trees along the Union main line and on the high ground between the

XV Corps line and its skirmishers to the west. Lieutenant John H. Weirick, a signalman perched in one of the makeshift outlooks, caught site of large bodies of Confederate infantry moving up Lick Skillet Road from the southwest defenses of Atlanta, likely alerted by the dust kicked up by several thousand men advancing en masse. Weirick notified Logan of the large-scale Confederate approach.[31]

The signalmen were not deceived; two divisions of Confederate infantry hustled toward the ground heretofore contested by XV Corps infantry and Red Jackson's cavalry. Lieutenant General Stephen D. Lee led the two divisions from Hood's former corps westward on Lick Skillet Road. Lee got a late start this day, apparently held back by Hood until Confederate cavalry reports pinpointed where Sherman's infantry was moving. Hood sent Lee out at 10:30 A.M. on a two-mile trek from the outer works of Atlanta to the Poor House.[32] Leaving one brigade behind, Lee ordered two divisions consisting of 7,000 officers and men to march in seven available brigades. Marching four abreast on Lick Skillet Road, each brigade took up nearly half a mile of roadbed as they marched toward the big bend. By the time the first Confederate infantrymen came within sight of the Poor House at 11:00 A.M., only the four brigades of one of Lee's divisions had been on the march; the other division had yet to start out from the southwestern edge of Atlanta's ring of earthworks.

The main body of XV Corps troops behind the Union skirmishers also steadily advanced in a formation described by one of its brigade commanders as "in the nature of the left wheel of the Army of the Tennessee" to deploy on advantageous ground, heights they could defend against a Confederate charge. The XVI and XVII Corps formed a parallel line within a hundred yards west of Chapel Road and began fortifying their position with hasty breastworks along this eastward-facing defense. The first division of the XV Corps completed this transition by fish-hooking around Ezra Church. Colonel Hugo Wangelin's brigade of Union Missouri infantry completed the left-hand formation a few paces beyond the church by wrapping troops around each side of it. Colonel Wangelin received confirmation that this was the "permanent" line, and after seeing the rest of the first division fortify its position to his left, he ordered the same for his brigade. Missouri troopers entered the church and then exited with pews. Soldiers filled these benches with knapsacks to create the most solid breastwork of any in the corps, given that no entrenchment tools were at hand.[33]

Ezra Church and the ground occupied by Army of the Tennessee troops north of it stood on elevated terrain. Directly west of the church the ground dropped to a creek valley then rose to a ridgeline again four hundred yards southwest of the church. Brigadier General William Harrow's division shifted toward this next range of hills, leaving a considerable gap in the "fishhook" line. As skirmishers commenced their southward work across Lick Skillet Road, General Harrow deployed his three brigades to the right of Ezra Church, west from where Brigadier General Charles Woods's division had begun to dig in. From three hundred yards off Woods's right flank, Colonel John Oliver's line was anchored by the 70th Ohio Infantry. According to a Buckeye in the regiment, they formed their line "on and along a hard gravel road." This road originated from Lick Skillet Road running northwest for a thousand yards to Ezra Church and extending another two miles beyond, terminating in the western environs of Atlanta.[34]

The 70th Ohio formed a salient in the broken Union line, bending it from southwest to northwest. The rest of Oliver's brigade and Colonel Reuben Williams's brigade nestled in the high ground running northwest of the chapel, while Charles Walcutt's brigade held a reserve position behind them. Continuing northwest from Williams's brigade was Morgan L. Smith's division troops. Colonel James S. Martin's infantry brigade of Ohio, Illinois, and Missouri soldiers stopped their forward progress to align with Harrow's brigades. They were satisfied to cease moving toward their opponent, savvy through experience to understand the expected disparity of casualties between a defensive force versus one on the offensive. A regimental officer explained, "We could proceed no farther without becoming the attacking party, which we did not propose to do."[35]

The entire Union line in position between 11:15 and 11:30 extended 1,500 yards, but it was not yet prepared to fend off the Confederate troops marching toward it. In all, the four front-line brigades should have numbered approximately 4,500 men, with

Walcutt's force adding another 1,500 in reserve and another brigade moving in position to deploy on the Union right. However, the actual number of Union troops in the front line likely dipped closer to 2,500 men due to excessive straggling from the intense Georgia heat this particular late summer morning.[36]

Williams's brigade was down a quarter of its usual strength because one of the four regiments, the 100th Indiana Infantry, was on detached service in Marietta. Williams's front-line regiments, from southeast to northwest, arrayed with the 90th Illinois on the left and the 26th Illinois on the right, the latter perched on the tallest hillock of the line. In reserve stood the 12th Indiana (Williams's original regiment before he took over the brigade), directly behind the 26th Illinois.[37]

Harrow's other front-line brigade covered Williams's left flank on that timbered hill. Colonel John M. Oliver extended the line southeastward from the 90th Illinois in the following order: 48th Illinois, 15th Michigan, 99th Indiana, and 70th Ohio. The flank of the 70th Ohio was uncovered except for a hundred-yard gap beyond this regiment's left flank where Wangelin's Missouri brigade bent the XV Corps line northeastward toward Ezra Church. Walcutt's brigade covered the gap in a reserve role by forming the apex of a triangle formed at the base by Oliver's and Wangelin's brigade.[38]

As the Union line nestled into position, General Sherman rode to the extreme right of his army group, resuming his activity from twenty-four hours earlier, again followed by an entourage of staff As he approached Ezra Church, Sherman and his orderlies came under fire from a battery near Lick Skillet Road, guns ostensibly attached to Red Jackson's cavalry. One cannonball barely missed Sherman as it seared over his shoulder and passed through the horse of an orderly behind him, separating the mount from the man atop it. Sherman terminated his southerly course and turned westward. After trotting across the creek valley, he dismounted, and accompanied by General Morgan Smith, he scaled the height occupied by Martin's brigade from Smith's division. There they found General Howard and Logan, who were also paying close attention to the fire from the opposing battery.[39]

Under directions from either General Logan or General Howard, General Smith ordered two regiments from the nondeployed portion of his division to drive out the skirmishers three hundred yards in front of their hill in an attempt to silence the Confederate battery. The response started as a single regiment from Brigadier General Joseph A. J. Lightburn's brigade. Lightburn turned in a shaky performance as a temporary division commander in the July 22 battle, but he returned to familiar territory as a brigadier for action at Ezra Church. Lightburn arrived on the high ground to the right (north) of Martin's flank, with the rest of the second division and the fourth division positioned southeast down the ridge line toward the chapel. Receiving Smith's order, Lightburn sent out one regiment, the 53rd Ohio.[40]

The region in which the XV Corps had deployed was part of Cook's District of Fulton County. The Coursey family owned most of the property, with at least three different homesteads between Lick Skillet Road and Turner's Ferry Road. James Coursey donated the half acre for the construction of Ezra Church in 1853, a mere four hundred yards west of his homestead. Charles P. Coursey's home stood on the south side of Turner's Ferry Road, at the southern base of Davis's Hill. William Coursey's farm stood half a mile north of the heights upon which the Union high command (Sherman, Logan, Howard, and Morgan Smith) conferred regarding deployment of XV Corps troops (Howard would choose William's home for his department headquarters). The 53rd Ohio descended the heights toward a home recently occupied by the Benjamin Touchstone family, who had moved from Campbellton, Georgia, after 1860.[41]

At 11:15 A.M. General Sherman was cognizant of General Howard's entrenching and the heavy resistance the troops had been fending off for the past hour. Regardless, he dismissed the opposition as insignificant. "During this time," Sherman admitted with several weeks of hindsight, "there was nothing to indicate serious battle save for the shelling of one or at most two batteries from beyond the large field in front of the Fifteenth Corps." He voiced this opinion to General Howard, who quickly and decisively corrected him: "General Hood will attack me here." Sherman acquiesced to his subordinate's assessment, reminded him to look for XIV Corps troops expected to arrive from Turner's Ferry, and then rode off toward Davis's Hill to ensure that those troops were en route to aid Howard and Logan's XV Corps. Sherman's oblivion to an imminent battle is beyond mystifying for so experienced a commander. Incredibly, by the time Sherman left the environs of Ezra Church and trotted northward, Stephen D. Lee was deploying a division in line of battle a mere 1,200 yards from where Sherman had stood.[42]

As the infantry regiments of the XV Corps hustled into position to prepare for battle, General Logan ordered artillery to work its way into the defense line. Unlike any other battle line of the campaign, the Ezra Church defensive position offered few advantages for artillery deployment. Although the ridge for the infantry was elevated, it was wooded at the topographical crest and at the military crest on the downslope. The trees concealed and protected the foot soldiers; however, artillerists found great difficulty in finding open space to unlimber a battery. The growing inevitability of a considerable Confederate assault—destined to be sooner than later—limited the ability of Major Thomas Maurice, less than two months into his job as chief of artillery of the XV Corps, to locate prime positions for his batteries.

Major Maurice commanded considerably fewer gunners, and guns, on July 28 than he did six days earlier. Reduced to twenty-seven cannons due to the losses at the Battle of Atlanta, Maurice had been forced to shift a two-gun section of twelve-pounder smoothbores from the 1st Iowa Light Artillery to Battery A, 1st Illinois Light Artillery, in the interval between the two battles, to replace the guns captured on July 22. This transplanted section was called into action shortly after 11:00 A.M. on July 28. Battery A started the day without a commander, as one lieutenant had been killed in the Atlanta battle and the other was captured. Captain Francis De Gress, the commander of Battery H, 1st Illinois Light Artillery, received orders to lead the section. De Gress ordered the two guns to unlimber in open space thirty-five yards in front of Colonel Martin's brigade line; another two-gun section from the 4th Ohio Light Artillery rolled into position southeast of De Gress's position.[43]

At 11:30 A.M. the entire defensive line of the Army of the Tennessee formed a somewhat jagged "J" shape with the XVI and XVII Corps aligned in the straight edge of the shape while Woods's and Harrow's XV Corps divisions turned the formation with a semicircle concave to the south. Martin's brigade of Smith's divi-

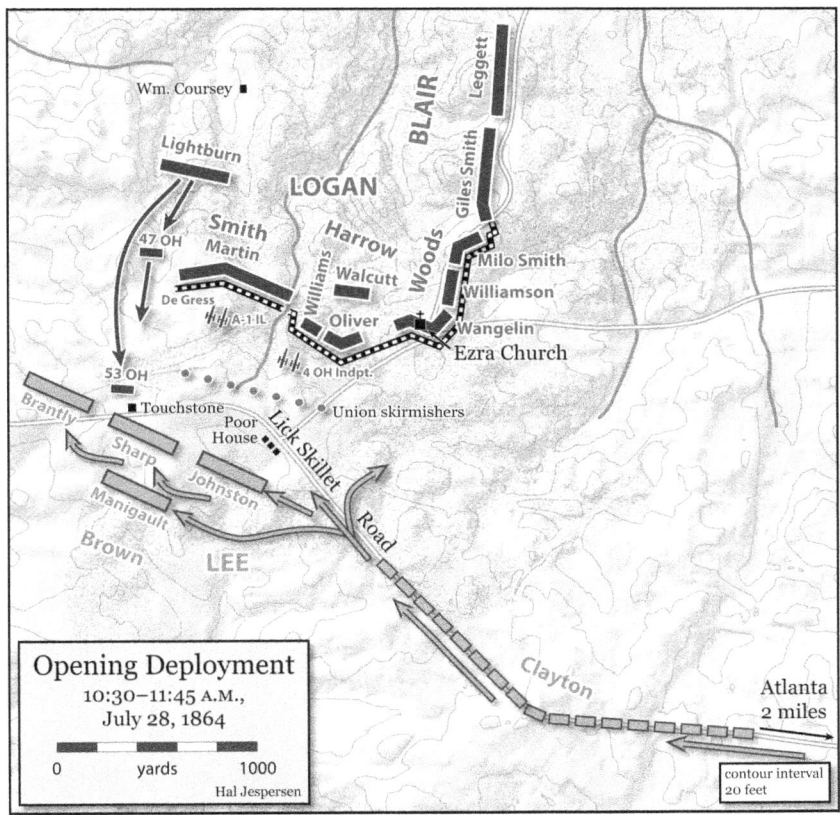

Opening Deployment
10:30–11:45 A.M.,
July 28, 1864

Hal Jespersen

Copyright © 2016 University of Oklahoma Press

sion put the short tail of the "J" in place. Meanwhile, Lightburn's brigade had not yet deployed to complete the army's formation and transform the formation from a "J" to something closer to a "U." The strength of the line was the right (eastern) side where the troops were more numerous and strengthened with reserves, artillery, and time to build up defensive works.

By contrast, the southern and western side of the Union formation was not yet ready to do battle. A considerable gap between the two southernmost brigades with no infantry or artillery to cover the gap highlighted its vulnerability to attack. The weakness of this position was matched by the continuation of the XV Corps line to the northwest where three of the four available brigades crowded at the edge of the tree line on the contours of the height. These brigades, and the fourth one yet to be locked in place, were buttressed by only four cannons. The vulnerability of the brigades' defense was magnified by their performance in their previous battle six days earlier. All four of those brigades had been overrun on July 22, when most of the men were absolutely uprooted and routed from defensive works comprising three times as many cannons as were available at Ezra Church.

Within minutes those vulnerable troops would be put to the grandest test. "Here," pointedly claimed Brigadier General Morgan L. Smith, "commenced the most persistent and bloody attempt to dislodge us and turn our right that I have ever witnessed."[44]

4

Vicious Volleys

Three miles east of the Poor House at the John S. Thrasher house, General Hood had toiled most of Thursday morning strengthening the defense of Atlanta by positioning his troops surrounding the city while fielding intelligence to determine where Sherman was and what he was doing. Hood had become increasingly uncomfortable about an attempt to breach Atlanta's defenses at points north and northeast of the city, but more recently from the west and northwest where Sherman's greatest activity had been detected since late Tuesday night and continuing all day Wednesday. When he collected General Lee and General Stewart at his headquarters the previous evening, Hood was aware that the western threat to the city had broadened beyond Turner's Ferry Road and extended from the northwest to more directly west. Hood's battle plan for Lee and Stewart carried an ultimate mission of securing Lick Skillet Road, but as that plan was ostensibly being discussed on Wednesday evening, Hood remained uncertain as to where Sherman planned to place his right (southern) flank for this apparent eastward assault against Atlanta's outer defenses.

Hood withheld sending Lee to the heights above the big bend of Lick Skillet Road at first morning's light of July 28. That decision held past 6:00 A.M., then 7:00 A.M., then 8:00 A.M., and even 9:00 A.M. The delay carried great risk, but Hood felt it necessary as his intelligence had yet to define where the Union right flank stood or intended to stand. Hood may have believed that for Lee's 8,000 soldiers to rush out at sunrise and occupy the intended high ground while Sherman's right flank stood exactly where it was late the previous afternoon would have jeopardized the safety of Atlanta and ultimately accomplished nothing except to strip his defenses of valuable, experienced troops. This could, after all, be Sherman's intent: to purposely goad Hood into overreacting to a feint in order to improve his own odds to penetrate the city.

The defining intelligence Hood sought most assuredly arrived from Red Jackson's cavalry shortly before 10:00 A.M. Jackson's cavalry had been skirmishing with Howard's Army of the Tennessee since midmorning. Unable to identify which of Sherman's three armies he had made contact with, Jackson more importantly realized that they threatened Lick Skillet Road as they continued moving southward on Chapel Road, just west of it on a parallel ridge. Hood divined the information and quickly decided where Sherman intended to end the march that day: "on the 28th it became manifest that the enemy decided to place his [flank] on Utoy Creek," Hood reported.[1]

This had to be the most alarming piece of news for Hood. The waters of the North Fork of Utoy Creek, a westerly-flowing tributary of the Chattahoochee River, ran from a point one mile south of the big bend of Lick Skillet Road. Until this moment Hood was defending against Sherman's attempt to charge into Atlanta, but the possibility of Sherman extending down to Utoy Creek was much more ominous, for that destination placed a flank of his army within two miles due west of the remaining railroad Hood possessed. Having previously anticipated that Sherman would attempt to capture that railroad with a cavalry operation, Hood realized Sherman was going to make a grand infantry sweep to claim the final ribbon of iron north of East Point (from where the line branched southeast and southwest). Knowing that all Union armies were still north of Lick Skillet Road at 10:00 A.M., Hood finally determined that Lee's force had a clear mission to accomplish.

Lee had his troops at the ready that morning at the junction of the outer works and Lick Skillet Road, where his men had tarried overnight. Hood's order left headquarters at 10:00 A.M. or shortly after, heading one mile westward on a fast-paced horse into Lee's hands. Lee's men commenced marching between 10:15 and 10:30 A.M. "General Lee is now moving against the enemy to our left," penned Hood's chief of staff in a 10:30 A.M. note sent to General Hardee.[2]

Stephen D. Lee had an urgent and tremendously important decision to make—one for which he had been given an unusual degree of discretion based on the fact that he had taken the helm of his corps only one calendar day before and was completely foreign to his troops and subordinate officers. As he led his two available divisions from the outer works of Atlanta to the big bend of Lick Skillet Road, Lee arrived at the Poor House nearly simultaneously with the vanguard of his leading division. The division's commander, Brigadier General John C. Brown, was already there in conversation with General William H. "Red" Jackson, whose leading brigade had been driven behind (southwest of) the bend in the road by Union foot soldiers.[3]

The moment that the corps commander trotted up to the cavalry general, the Fulton County Almshouse formed the scene of the first Lee-Jackson meeting site since a much more famous surname pairing met for their last time during the Chancellorsville Campaign nearly fifteen months earlier. According to Hood's plan, Lee's role was to secure Lick Skillet Road for the duration of that Thursday to allow General Stewart to negotiate behind him with four divisions and strike the Union flank on Friday. The current situation facing Lee jeopardized Hood's plan, but it did not ruin it. According to the information fed to Lee by Red Jackson, Union infantry had rapidly pressed Jackson's cavalry back to Lick Skillet Road, but the enemy force was "small." At that point, only one regiment—the 53rd Ohio infantry—would reach the road at about the time of Jackson and Lee's meeting.

Hood's instructions to Lee, either specified at the headquarters meeting the previous evening or delivered to him earlier in the morning, defined exactly where he wanted Lee to deploy to successfully "check the enemy" to secure this specific region: "on a line nearly parallel with the Lick Skillet road, running through to Ezra Church." Hood's inclusion of the chapel bore evidence of his knowledge of the line of heights on which Ezra Church stood, information he shared with Lee by verbal description and perhaps by a map. Likely unappreciated by Hood, however, was a special advantage that line of hills held for the Confederates, for the heights aligned in a semicircle with wooded ground south of the lip and more open ground north of it. Confederate defenders on the ridge could lay a plunging fire with artillery and infantry upon any attempt to attack and dislodge them. "Inside the ridge was a kind of basin," remarked a Union soldier observing it from the north. "Where [the Confederates] had gained the ridge they could have used artillery to great advantage upon us and they well knew it." Unfortunately for Hood, he probably did not know it, for if he did his suspect delay in sending Lee to those heights could only be characterized as derelict and inexcusable.[4]

Lee could not see those heights from his vantage point as a much closer but less dominant rise of ground interfered with his view. Red Jackson's interlude with Federal skirmishers indicated that the body of Union troops behind them was either on those heights or closing in upon them. If Lee vacillated or took even an additional half hour or so to reconnoiter the area, those heights would more likely be lost to the Confederates—so would Lee's mission and Hood's plan.[5]

Lee swiftly decided to clear whatever was up on those heights with the strength of his complete available force—a seven-brigade attack, five in front and two in reserve, thus deploying 7,000 infantry. (One of the eight brigades originally intended to participate in this mission was left behind to man Atlanta's defenses.) The full-scale commitment is strong evidence of Lee's aggressive nature—"always prompt and energetic," recalled General Howard, who knew him from West Point before the war—and his likely suspicion that his opponent was a more sizable force than Red Jackson had believed it to be. General Brown summarized Lee's 11:15 A.M. decision by reporting: "I was directed to drive the enemy to Ezra Church and hold that position." The fact that this portion of Brown's report matched identically with what General Stewart interpreted from Hood's instructions to Lee—"attack the enemy's right flank, and drive him from [Lick Skillet] road and the one leading from it by Mount Ezra Church"—was too uncanny to be a coincidence. Lee's decision to attack was one that he (and clearly Stewart) understood as necessary to comply with their commanding general's orders.[6]

The ensuing battle is known to history by five common names: the Battle of Ezra Church, the Battle of Ezra Chapel, the Battle of the Poor House, the Battle of Lick Skillet, or more simply, the Battle of the 28th. This was a battle with a mysterious and misleading impetus. General Lee eventually reported that his decision to launch the assault was due to his discovery "that the enemy had gained the [Lick Skillet] road." This of course was not literally true at the time, and when the 53rd Ohio reached the road to the west of the big bend, Lee would remain oblivious to this fact. General Lee may have meant that the enemy had gained a firing range upon the road—although no Union artillery fire had yet been offered by the four cannons deploying within that range—and Lee also failed to report the actual opposing position. Regardless, the intelligence sent three miles east to General Hood must have led the army commander to believe that Lee attacked to recover the road already in possession of Union forces, a very misleading scenario. What was not misleading was the real threat to the line of heights running through to Ezra Church that Hood had directed Lee to occupy.[7]

As the sun scaled upward toward its peak in an overcast forenoon sky, General Brown aligned his division for its second assault against the XV Corps in six days. From a point five hundred yards behind the big bend in Lick Skillet Road, three brigades of 3,000 veteran Southerners aligned from the roadbed and extended northwestward at a forty-five-degree angle from the road in a double line of battle nearly three-quarters of a mile long; another 1,000 Confederates from the division aligned behind them as a reserve brigade. It was an awesome attack line, one formed by veterans of three years of hard campaigning in Kentucky, Tennessee, and Georgia.[8]

Anchoring the formation on the Confederate right was a brigade of five Alabama regiments and a battalion of sharpshooters under the command of thirty-two-year-old Brigadier General George D. Johnston. Johnston was a North Carolinian by birth, an Alabaman in childhood, but a Tennessean for his adult life. He fought at the First Battle of Manassas as a second lieutenant three years earlier, and rose through the ranks to lead the 25th Alabama throughout the Atlanta Campaign as its colonel. Johnston performed so well at the Battle of Atlanta—credited for capturing more men than he led in his gallant charge—that he was rewarded with a commission of brigadier general in Richmond on July 26, an honor he received a few hours before the pending action of July 28. For the upgrade in rank, Johnston took over Colonel John G. Coltart's brigade. This chain of events surely did not set well with Coltart, who had led his men nobly and efficiently in that big battle on the other side of Atlanta the previous Friday and yet somehow lost his command. Coltart returned to the helm of his former regiment, the 50th Alabama, for this battle.[9]

The Alabama brigade marched forward 1,143 strong on July 28, but several hundred men lighter than one week before. Officers in particular had been thinned from Johnston's ranks from the Battle of Atlanta and the bloody campaign preceding it. A mere 101 commissioned company, regimental, and brigade officers in this brigade aligned with the right on Lick Skillet Road at 11:30 A.M. in a force that should have fielded eighty more ranked men. Regimental officers still led all but one of the regiments; however, most of these regiments had but one of its commanders rather than the requisite three (colonel, lieutenant colonel, major). Should Johnston's men get into another fight, discipline would suffer if the house of cards representing each regiment collapsed with the fall of the lone officer in charge.[10]

Johnston's men aligned from four hundred yards south of the big bend of the road and extended northwestward for five hundred yards, nearly touching the east–west portion of the road by forming the base of a triangle with the road. Brigadier General Jacob H. Sharp's Mississippi brigade aligned to the left of Johnston's brigade, crossing the east–west portion of Lick Skillet Road and extending into the woods northwest of the road. This brigade mirrored its Alabama neighbor in size (1,020 officers and men) and structure with five regiments and one battalion of sharpshooters. From right to left General Sharp positioned the 44th, 10th, 7th, 9th, and 41st Mississippi regiments. Two hundred yards in front of them his skirmish line—consisting of the 9th Mississippi Battalion of Sharpshooters buttressed by a company from the 10th and 41st Mississippi—advanced. Like the Alabama brigade, the Mississippians enjoyed an all-too-brief success on July 22 by penetrating the line of the XV Corps. The 41st Mississippi was conspicuous as some of the first troops to have captured (albeit temporarily) the four twenty-pounder Parrotts of De Gress's battery in that battle before being forced to withdraw without those prized guns.[11]

The final brigade in the front ranks of Brown's impressive battle line was another unit of Mississippi troops, commanded by Brigadier General William F. Brantly. Like General Johnston, Brantly was commissioned general on July 26 in Richmond and received the promotion two days later. Brantly's promotion had been earned for conduct becoming a general starting with the Chattanooga Campaign through the Atlanta Campaign. His brigade had a tough day during the Battle of Atlanta as the only brigade of Brown's division that failed to pierce the Union defensive line. This had been mainly due to the mortal wounding of Colonel Samuel Benton at the Federal earthworks. (Benton died on July 28, shortly before his brigade marched upon Lick Skillet Road.) Brantly, who immediately took over for Benton, had been unable to rally his new brigade that day and was forced to call a retreat from its position. More than any other brigade on the field, The Mississippians of Brantly's brigade had something to prove six days later on July 28.[12]

Brantly's force was five regiments reduced to three due to the consolidation of the 24th and 27th Mississippi, as well as the 29th and 30th Mississippi (the 34th Mississippi remained as a single unit). Brantly had been marching his regiments in customary columns on the road within a mile of the bend from northerly to due west. Receiving orders from General Brown to file off west of the road and pass behind General Sharp's brigade, Brantly's command bisected the arc created by the road and aligned off Sharp's left flank.[13]

Behind Brown's mile-long battle line stood the Alabama and South Carolina brigade as the reserve force. Manigault's men shed more blood than any of the other three brigades of the division on July 22 when they lost four hundred killed and wounded soldiers while penetrating the XV Corps line, temporarily capturing ten guns, and routing the Union defenders protecting those cannons. It would be clear by the end of July that Generals Brown and

Manigault did not see eye to eye, a disagreement perhaps stemming from Brown's promotion from colonel and transfer from Stevenson's division to head Major General Thomas C. Hindman's division after its namesake commander left in mid-July to recover from an eye injury. Manigault had been a commissioned general since 1862; to see a man he outranked now serve as his superior officer must have rankled him, but it also showed the lack of faith Manigault's superiors held in his abilities to prevent his ascension from brigade to division command. Regardless, the reserve role for this pending battle was satisfactory to Brown and Manigault. Both men must have realized from experience that the reserve position was likely to be temporary once the battle heated up.[14]

General Lee was hampered by the normal but underappreciated tactics necessary to deploy a corps for a battlefield assault. Desirous to trap his opponent by the element of surprise, General Lee ordered Brown's attack before his other available division had any chance to deploy. Major General Henry Clayton and his three brigades tarried at the outer ring of works of Atlanta until approximately 11:15 A.M., when General Brown commenced deploying his marching column from the roadbed into line of battle near the Poor House. As each brigade shifted northwestward to bisect the arc caused by the big bend of Lick Skillet Road, the section of the road between Brown's column and the outer works finally opened enough for Clayton to fill with his men. Heading out the requisite two miles to the Poor House, he anchored the left of his division near the buildings and deployed in line of battle eastward from there. Clayton needed at least half an hour after Brown's deployment to complete the march and deploy his line, but—in Lee's decision process—this was too costly in precious time. The result would be a huge assault by Brown's division, but one that could have been nearly twice the size had Lee taken more time to deploy his available force.

The assault commenced shortly before 11:45 A.M. with 4,000 Southern soldiers steadily marching northeastward. They likely had no idea which of Sherman's three armies they were facing even after initial contact was made by the skirmishers. Not only did they face off against the Army of the Tennessee again, but against the XV Corps—the same body of troops that they had routed, albeit temporarily, from the trenches they had constructed east of Atlanta six days earlier. Perhaps because of their inability to turn the batteries they captured onto the Union corpsmen on July 22, General Brown's attack added a unique feature to the clash at Ezra Church: Confederate artillerists were spliced into the infantry line ostensibly in the hope that they could immediately man the Union batteries they expected to capture.[15]

The heady placement of Confederate gunners in the infantry line quickly became a moot point. Captain Frances De Gress had opposed the approaching line with two twelve-pounders. Another section of artillery from the 4th Ohio Battery had deployed south of De Gress, but had fired only a few volleys before retiring under orders from Major Clem Landgraeber, the First Division artillery chief, who deemed the position too tenuous to maintain it. De Gress lasted longer, but after his artillerists belched out merely twenty total rounds from those two guns, he came to the same conclusion as Landgraeber, ordered his guns to be limbered, rolled them up and over the infantry and tree-lined hill, and retired to the rear. The harrowing experience De Gress had endured at the Troup Hurt house north of the Georgia Railroad on July 22 would not be repeated this day.[16]

The swift removal of the four Union cannons made the battle unique not only for the campaign, but for the entire Civil War up to this point. No engagement of this size had been waged without artillery support for the defenders. Since the Union ridge line dropped to a creek valley behind (east of) it with only wooded heights farther east, no artillery batteries could easily be deployed to provide cover for the line, thus leaving the Union infantry to fight alone. Confederate attackers had more open field and hillocks, but the nonwooded patches of terrain were limited enough to prevent deployment of more than two of their batteries. As the Southern infantrymen closed in upon the defenders, their supporting artillery silenced their pieces to prevent friendly fire.[17]

At 11:45 A.M., as the advancing Confederate attackers put the road to their backs, the weight of Brown's advance smoothly drove back the Federal skirmishers. Brown's troops followed a half-mile trajectory that would sweep the region at and above Ezra Church. Brigadier General John C. Brown had been wounded twice in previous campaigns, and cited for bravery more recently at Missionary Ridge and Dalton. He had held division command for less than three weeks, but he demonstrated competence at the Battle of Atlanta as his men briefly breached a strong Union defense. The Union defense at Ezra Church was much shakier than east of Atlanta on July 22. Brown's success depended on the number of men that could be positioned in front of his impressive attacking column.[18]

General Brown had no idea of the numbers he opposed as his infantry line entered an open field in front of the wooded hill topped by blue-clad soldiers. Johnston's Alabamans faced the southern end of the crest on which two brigades of General Harrow's division were ensconced. Colonel Reuben "Reub" Williams frantically worked to protect his brigade. "I immediately instructed the command to secure themselves by throwing up a protection of whatever could be found," explained Williams, "and afterwards procured a few shovels, and ordered that they be used without delay." A few members of each company were sent out to find anything that could be used to build a line of protective works. The Yankees had precious little time to entrench with the spades, but those who found wood, stones, and knapsacks constructed a barrier that barely rose above their knees. Essentially defenseless and without artillery support, they gripped their guns to await the onrush of Johnston's charging brigade.[19]

Although Brown's entire line was outnumbered in its attack, two of his brigades were pitted against only six front-line Union regiments, 2,200 Alabamans and Mississippians versus a nearly equal number of soldiers hailing mainly from states of the Old Northwest Territory in Harrow's two brigades and Martin's brigade from Morgan Smith's division. No overwhelming mismatch presented itself; however, Brown had a chance for success here as those Union soldiers were not dug in, had absolutely no artillery support, and were reduced to battalions due to the limited space they occupied. Understanding his tenuous position, Colonel Oliver had sent out four companies of each regiment as skirmishers. His position consisted of three lines, a standard skirmish line of four companies out nearly two hundred yards west of his main line attempting to hold the Alabama attackers in check, and another line of twelve companies between the skirmishers and the main line. This middle line attempted to entrench, as did the remaining six companies of each of the remaining four regiments in Oliver's main line.

The first clash occurred within ten minutes of noon. After reforming its ranks and lying prone two hundred yards from the Union position, General Johnston ordered his brigade to attack, as did General Sharp to his left. An officer in the 22nd Alabama reported that the entire brigade charged "in gallant style, driving the enemy from their skirmish line and from another and stronger position protected by rails and earthworks" as they beelined to Oliver's main line. The Alabamans enjoyed swift success pushing back Oliver's two advanced lines of protection, closing to within seventy-five yards of the Union brigade. But they could advance no farther as Oliver's men held firm.[20]

General Johnston was intrepid in the saddle, urging his men onward toward the Union defenses. Eighteen months earlier, a shell fragment careened into his thigh at Murfreesboro and removed him from that battlefield. At Ezra Church his lower body took another wound. Before his Alabamans struck the Union line northeast of the bend in Lick Skillet Road, a bullet nailed him in the leg and broke one of its bones. Johnston used his bridle reign to immobilize the fractured leg and keep as much pressure off of it as possible. He continued to command his men, but the wound prematurely ended his first day as a commissioned general.[21]

Johnston's left-side regiments rushed headlong into Reub Williams's two front-line regiments. "The enemy surged like a vast wave upon our lines," recalled a member of the 12th Indiana, the reserve regiment in Williams's brigade; he was awestruck at their tenacity as they rushed toward them "yelling like demons and firing as they came." Within ten minutes, Johnston's entire battle line of Alabamans was heavily engaged, but their general was suddenly out of the action. General Johnston could no longer keep the saddle; his shattered leg forced him from the field. At nearly the same time, Colonel Benjamin R. Hart cheered on his 22nd Alabama, but before he could reach the Union works with his regiment, a bullet seared through his body and ended his life.[22]

Colonel John G. Coltart immediately took over the brigade, a responsibility he held the last time they attacked Williams's brigade six days earlier six miles east of Ezra Church. His regiment, the 50th Alabama Infantry, was without another field officer to replace him, leaving Captain George W. Arnold as the senior company officer to take over the regiment (as he had also done on July 22). Coltart started his brigade command with a handicap: he had been wounded when the brigade commenced its advance twenty minutes earlier. Coltart's tenure as brigade commander lasted only several minutes; he was unable to continue due to the debilitating effects of his wound.

Lieutenant Colonel Harry T. Toulmin began the advance at 11:45 A.M. as second in command of the 22nd Alabama Infantry. After Colonel Hart was killed, he briefly took over the regiment but learned minutes later that with Coltart's wound having forced him out, he was the ranking officer within the brigade—no other colonels led regiments within that brigade, and Toulmin happened to be the only lieutenant colonel in the brigade this day. Once Toulmin took over the brigade, the only regimental officer remaining in all five of his regiments was Major Solomon Palmer, who had a tenuous hold of his 19th Alabama after he was struck by a XV Corps bullet.[23]

The Alabamans suffered from bad luck with this high attrition rate in officers during the first fifteen minutes. The loss of these leaders dissipated their punch; Toulmin called off the charge and pulled the regiments back into the line of temporary works left by Harrow's skirmishers where they went prone and exchanged rifle fire with Oliver's and Williams's brigades. Perhaps fifty foot soldiers were struck during this opening advance, which was repulsed methodically by Harrow's two front-line brigades. The result did not help this Confederate brigade's reputation. Like several brigades in the Confederate army, the Alabamans were known as "Deas's Brigade," or "Deas's Alabama Brigade," named for Brigadier General Zachariah Deas, who had been out of action since May due to illness. By the time of this battle, at least one member of Hood's army derided them as "General Deas's Racehorses" for their infamy of running swiftly from battlefields. Although they did not run from Ezra Church, their perceived penchant for pusillanimity combined with their inability to sustain the assault in the opening attack garnered them no sympathy for the incredible handicap that no fewer than four different commanders had to lead this brigade in less than fifteen minutes of action.[24]

While the Alabama brigade was weakened by leadership casualties, Sharp's brigade on its left was enjoying more success against the center of the westward-facing Union line. Sharp's brigade was opposed by six regiments from the brigade of Colonel James S. Martin, a subordinate commander in Brigadier General Morgan L. Smith's division of the XV Corps. Martin's brigade line was formed by the contours of the ground they protected. The 55th Illinois anchored the left end of the brigade, its left formed at right angles with the right flank of Williams's brigade of Harrow's division. Aligned more north than west, the regiment faced a crooked brook (a northward-flowing feeder to Proctor's Creek) with waters running from left to right in front of the Prairie State soldiers. The right flank company ("A") angled away from the rest of the regiment on the other side of the brook. Extending from this company and continuing at ninety degrees from the 55th was the rest of Martin's brigade, now resuming a westward-facing position like Harrow's men to their right and one hundred yards southwest of them. Next in Martin's brigade line was the 116th Illinois and 111th Illinois, followed to the north by the 57th Ohio, 30th Ohio, 83rd Indiana, and 6th Missouri, all but the Missouri regiment belonging to Lightburn's brigade. The sixth and final regiment of Martin's brigade, the one hundred members of the 127th Illinois, took a reserve role behind Martin's line.

Martin's defensive line had a makeshift breastwork of logs and stones "only eighteen to twenty inches high," according to the estimate of Lieutenant Colonel Samuel R. Mott of the 57th Ohio infantry. Not only were they poorly protected; they were undermanned, mainly due to temperatures likely exceeding ninety degrees before noon. "The day being very hot, maneuvering through thick underwood, over fences and [rocks], . . . was anything but 'light duty,' and many of the men were obliged to fall out," revealed one soldier of the brigade. Heat consumption and sunstroke downed XV Corps soldiers before any Confederates fired a shot at them. The conditions reduced at least one regiment, the 30th Ohio, to fewer than one hundred rank and file and visibly affected soldiers in all of the regiments.[25]

The 44th Mississippi anchored Sharp's right flank and charged toward Martin's center. Two members of Company C, 55th Illinois, Corporal Oscar Johnson and Orderly Sergeant John Quincy Adams Curtis, stood out with their company mates in advance of the brigade line, attracting the first volley of Sharp's Confederates. The bullets pierced five members of the company; both Johnson and Curtis were struck in the head and killed instantly. Curtis was the third brother of his family killed in the war—one sibling from the same company had been struck down at Kennesaw Mountain a month earlier.[26]

The 44th Mississippi pressed on. This was Colonel Sharp's former regiment, commanded by Lieutenant Colonel Robert G. Kelsey when Sharp rose up to brigade command. Kelsey's men rushed eastward in two lines, the 10th Mississippi keeping pace with them on their left flank. "It was a grand sight to see that line come marching down the hill, with their officers riding ahead," remarked Elijah Coombe of the 116th Illinois, who faced them directly. The soldier recalled one of the officers on a gray horse (likely Lieutenant Colonel Kelsey), waving his sword above him, and "as he turned to give an order, down went their guns and here they come at double-quick with a yell."[27]

As the 44th Mississippi charged in toward the center of Martin's line, they rushed by the two hundred officers and men of the 55th Illinois, who faced the flank of the attackers. Another Illinois soldier in the ranks was mesmerized by their approach:

> The two charging lines came steadily on, at first without firing, the sergeants behind with fixed bayonets keeping every man up to his work. Exposed to our fire at long range, scores were dropping under the cool aim of marksmen who had not lost the skill acquired by their practice at Vicksburg. But the gaps were quickly closed, and the rapid step quickened. Alone and on foot, an almost exultant expression lighting up his dark face, General Logan passed along behind the line with words of cheer on his lips: "Hold them! Steady, boys,

we've got them now." Yet that desperate wave, though gradually growing thin and weak, is getting too near; it is scarce eighty yards from the regiments on our right. Encouraged by their general's presence these regiments increase the rapidity of their fire.[28]

Kelsey's command melted away before his eyes due to the small-arms barrage from flank and front. In less than fifteen minutes his command was down to half of its starting strength, dozens upon scores of Mississippians killed and wounded between the brook and the 55th Illinois. In turn, the Mississippians nearly decimated the 55th Illinois, killing and wounding fifteen members of the regiment. All of their casualties were isolated to five companies, with most of the bullet wounds striking them above the waist. Most unfortunate was John Funk, a new recruit who was helping the surgeon in the ravine that had separated Company A from the rest of the 55th Illinois in the rear of the line when a bullet tore into his left side and killed him. Funk was the regiment's drummer, a mere boy.[29]

The 44th Mississippi protected the 10th Mississippi from the wicked volleys delivered by the 55th Illinois on their right. They charged directly against the right flank of the 116th Illinois and the entire front of the 111th Illinois. Their casualties mounted to nearly half of their engaged numbers. Five Mississippi color bearers of the regiment were cut down in front of the Illinois troops. As the battle entered the noon hour, the entire right half of Brown's attacking division had been checked by blue-clad defenders.[30]

The left of Sharp's attacking brigade threatened the entire XV Corps line by penetrating the right flank of Martin's brigade. The Mississippians rent the air with their version of the rebel yell as they charged within a hundred yards of Martin's northernmost defenses. The shocking approach of the butternuts terrorized and broke the right regiments of the brigade. The 6th Missouri anchored the right flank, and they broke first, exposing the right flank of the 83rd Indiana, a hard-luck regiment that lost its colonel in front of Kennesaw Mountain one month earlier and its lieutenant colonel at Dallas, Georgia, a month before that when that

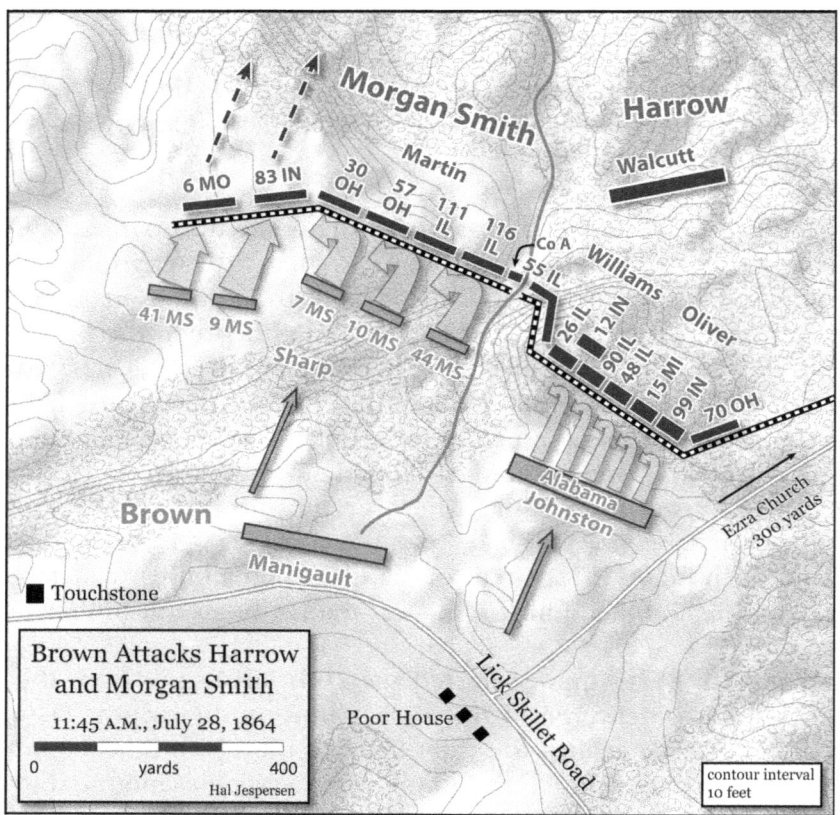

overly intoxicated officer raced out in front of his skirmish line and was immediately cut down and killed. Led by a captain at Ezra Church, the 83rd Indiana was now considered a suspect fighting unit. The Hoosiers dropped back rather than face the oncoming 7th, 9th, and 41st Mississippi.[31]

To the left of the Indianans stood the 30th Ohio, which immediately adjusted to the unexpected loss of its flank protection by swinging back its right-hand companies to position the regiment perpendicular to the main line—much like the 55th Illinois had done some three hundred yards south of them. Carrying a mere ninety-four soldiers into the battle, the 30th Ohio was undermanned to be positioned as the left anchor of Morgan Smith's division, but since an interval existed between the left and right of Sharp's Confederates, the Ohioans were not concerned about flank or rearward fire as they waited for the Mississippians to enter the trap in front of them. Their greatest concern was their meager protection. Neither spade nor pick was available to them. Lieutenant Colonel George Hildt recalled that by "hastily" aligning in position, "we grabbed up a few rails, but before we had the line fairly marked with them, they were upon us."[32]

Mississippi attackers on Sharp's left entered the trap and found themselves under an enfilading fire from the 30th Ohio. "Some of them jumped over our works," admitted an Ohio soldier, "but [they were] killed or taken prisoner." The Magnolia State soldiers dished out considerable punishment as well, killing and wounding nearly a third of the Ohio regiment opposing it. Colonel Theodore Jones commanded his regiment this day, aided only by his lieutenant colonel, George Hildt (the major was out sick). Hildt assessed the weakness of his regiment's protection by the location of the bullet wounds on his soldiers' bodies. "We had men wounded in limbs as low as the knee, so you can form some idea of how much service our works were," he told his parents in letter.[33]

The efforts of the 30th Ohio held the 7th Mississippi and part of the 9th Mississippi in check, but the rest of the 9th and 41st Mississippi watched the Missourians and Hoosiers fall back in front of them and gravitated toward the abandoned flank. "We charged and drove [the Federals] in great confusion," railed Colonel J. Byrd Williams of the 41st Mississippi, "capturing 9 prisoners, 3 of whom were wounded." Martin's flank was gone. Making matters worse for the Federals was the approach of another brigade of Mississippi troops to extend the Confederate attack line to the north, but these Confederates were still several minutes away from strengthening the Southern attack line.[34]

Noon passed on the battlefield with Johnston's and half of Sharp's brigades held in check by the troops brigaded under Oliver, Williams, and Martin. Two Mississippi units, however, were about to position themselves to break the stalemate against the Confederate regiments on their right. The 9th and 41st Mississippi regiments rushed to the ground abandoned seconds earlier by the Missouri and Indiana defenders. Once they gained a toehold on the Union flank, the complexion of the Ezra Church fight was transformed.

Black Jack Logan had moved northward behind Martin's brigade to prevent the catastrophe. Logan's inspirational leadership had developed into the hallmark of XV Corps battles throughout the Atlanta Campaign, beginning at Resaca, blossoming at Dallas, and burgeoning in the Battle of Atlanta on July 22. At Ezra Church, General Howard noted that Logan was ill on July 28.[35] This, in combination with his demotion from army to corps command, would be enough to neutralize this ostentatious commander. However, since the first exchange of skirmish fire in midmorning, Logan was omnipresent to his troops. As Sharp's right-hand regiments assaulted the left flank of Martin's line, one of the Union defenders recalled the intensity of the moment and the fear that their line would break:

> The suspense is almost beyond endurance, for we expect a break on our right. Pen fails a description here of those awful moments as they pass. To our right, at the angle of the Fifty-fifth and One Hundred and Sixteenth Illinois, a rustling in the leaves and a firm step is heard. We anxiously look in that direction to see if our boys are running away. But no. A whisper goes up the line: 'It is General Logan.' On foot and alone, passing up the line, saying: 'Steady, boys: hold them!' Confidence is restored in a moment.[36]

In the region behind the 116th Illinois was Logan's position when he learned of the collapse of the 6th Missouri and 83rd Indiana on his right. Logan sent an aide back to General Harrow to order up two reserve regiments to shore up the flank. In the meantime, Logan galloped northward to restore the flank, accompanied by Major John R. Hotaling, a loyal member of his staff. Hotaling had been conspicuous in battle six days earlier when he created a hodgepodge force of routed XV Corps soldiers and organized them to rush and retake the works they were forced from thirty minutes earlier. Hotaling's face bore evidence of his bravery in battle, a long saber scar from the Mexican-American War still visible upon his visage. Hotaling had a uniquely Union-loyal family with five brothers also fighting for the North.[37]

The general and his intrepid aide stopped the retreat of more than one hundred panic-stricken men by personally blocking their escape route and turning them around with choice, profanity-laden sentences. Several Missouri and Indiana soldiers were treated to the flat of Logan's sword as he attempted to swat more courage into them. According to an Ohioan in Martin's brigade, Logan was the only corps commander he ever saw on a battlefield. "He knew this was a crisis," continued the Buckeye, "and he also knew that his personal appearance at this moment would endear him to his command and make the assault a failure to the Confederates." A member of the 55th Illinois concurred: "The question may be asked: Did the timely presence of General Logan save the day and the turning of the flank of his army? I emphatically answer yes."[38]

The wayward members of the 6th Missouri and 83rd Indiana reached their old position before the Mississippi soldiers had time to exploit their earlier mistake. Colonel J. Byrd Williams, taking charge of both Mississippi regiments, found their separation from the rest of Sharp's brigade too tenuous to go on without necessary adjustments. "I deemed it necessary to halt my regiment and reform," explained the commander, "as the men had become scattered owing to the dense wooded country through which they advanced." He reformed just as the Union flank was restored. There, the two sides exchanged fire, neither flinching nor moving.[39]

The battle lasted approximately twenty minutes on the height with a stalemate between three brigades of Union soldiers and two brigades of Confederates. The rapid exchange of vicious volleys between the opposing sides produced a great deal of agony among the soldiers and a tremendous and all-too-familiar sound of small-arms fire that reverberated for at least two miles. Acoustic shadows played their typical tricks this day, for Hood appears not to have heard these battle sounds three miles east of Ezra Church (partly due to the dearth of cannon fire), while Sherman—who was an equal distance from the clash north of Ezra Church—clearly did. Sherman had told General Howard there would be no battle this day, but he confessed to a XIV Corps staff officer that he knew all too well that a battle had been transpiring: "Logan is feeling for them and I guess he has found them." Shortly after this retort, one of General Howard's aides rode up from the battlefield and reported to Sherman that Logan was under attack from Hood. Sherman became so excited that he could not help repeating himself confidently. "Good! That is fine—just what I wanted, just what I wanted," he exulted in staccato phrases. "Tell Howard to invite them to attack, it will save us trouble, save us trouble, they'll only beat their brains out, beat their brains out."[40]

The Confederates had indeed answered the Union invitation, with each side beating the other nearly senseless. It was only the beginning. As Sherman belted out those phrases, more opposing troops were racing to the highest ground on the battlefield. Whoever reached the hill first—and secured it—would likely determine the outcome of the contest.

5

Battle Hill

At noon, half a mile south of Ezra Church, Henry DeLamar Clayton deployed his troops in his second battle as a major general commanding a division. A Georgia native, the thirty-seven-year-old commander had worked in Alabama as a lawyer and state legislator until the outbreak of the war when he commanded two Alabama regiments in succession before being promoted to brigadier general and ascending to brigade command after surviving a severe wound at the Battle of Murfreesboro (or Stones River). The death of Leonidas Polk at Pine Mountain in mid-June set off a chain of ascensions in his corps that raised Alexander P. Stewart to replace Polk at corps command and Clayton to replace Stewart as division commander in Hood's corps.[1]

Stephen D. Lee inherited Clayton and his troops, knowing that they had enjoyed initial success with Brown's division on July 22. The most engaged brigade in Clayton's division that day was Colonel Abda Johnson's brigade, which took the brunt of over five hundred casualties suffered by the division east of Atlanta. Perhaps for that reason, Johnson's regiments did not march out on Lick Skillet Road with Clayton on July 28, leaving him with three brigades with between 3,000 and 3,300 officers and men. Clayton had marched out directly behind Brown's division that morning, but he had only begun to deploy his troops east of the big bend of Lick Skillet Road when Brown's four brigades marched off to battle at Ezra Church.

General Lee's decision to attack at 11:45 A.M., when Brown's troops were ready but before Clayton's men were deployed, saved Lee at least half an hour of valuable time also needed by Union troops to deploy and strengthen their defenses, but cost him an additional two-brigade front line. Lee did not expect Clayton to need much more than ten more minutes after Brown's first contact. Lee expected Clayton's troops to be moving toward the battle line by 12:00 P.M. But noon had passed without Clayton's men in motion or even deployed. Unaware of the time required to deploy nearly half of his available corps, Lee was too focused on the problems confronting Brown's troops to immediately divert his attention to Clayton. Only half of Brown's men—two brigades—who had been fighting XV Corps soldiers to a stalemate, now required the commitment of the rest of the division. General Brantly's Mississippi brigade had marched out nearly simultaneously with Sharp's and Johnston's men, but they were the outer third of Brown's line and required more time to cover a greater distance. Manigault's brigade stood behind Johnston's and Sharp's troops awaiting orders to join the attack.

Brantly's command consisted of the 34th Mississippi and two consolidated infantry regiments, the 24th/27th and 29th/30th Mississippi. The entire command, rank and file, numbered slightly under 1,000, making it the weakest numerically of Brown's four brigades. Their path began about three hundred yards northwest of the Poor House. By noon their outer-line advance was about five hundred yards behind (northwest of) Sharp's brigade, the latter deployed and engaged against Martin's brigade. The 24th/27th Mississippi, led by Colonel Robert P. McKelvaine, marched on the outside (left) of Brantly's brigade; the 29th/30th Mississippi, commanded by Lieutenant Colonel James M. Johnson, held the right; and Captain T. S. Hubbard's 34th Mississippi was sandwiched between them.[2]

Brantly was delayed from reaching his destination by an aggressive skirmish force. It started as a single regiment from Brigadier General Joseph A. J. Lightburn's brigade. Lightburn had arrived on the high ground to the right (north) of Martin's flank near 11:30 A.M. and sent the 53rd Ohio several hundred yards west of the XV Corps line to chase off what appeared to him to be rebel cavalry occupying a height near Lick Skillet Road that could eventually threaten the Union defense if it were secured long enough to place Confederate batteries atop it.[3]

The cavalrymen were leftovers from Red Jackson's command, but directly behind them the Ohioans found Brantly's skirmishers. Colonel Wells Jones sent an aide back requesting a second regiment, while his own command drove off the Mississippi skirmish line. Lightburn immediately complied with Jones's request by detaching the 47th Ohio, which came in on the left (south) of the 53rd Ohio on the height the latter had just captured by the roadbed. Major Thomas Taylor led the 47th Ohio, taking over the regiment during the Battle of Atlanta at the Troup Hurt house when the colonel of the regiment was wounded. Major Taylor was beset with intraregimental troubles because three companies (A, B, and I) were teeming with three-year soldiers who did not reenlist and whose terms would expire the following day. Taylor had been noticing these men acting cowardly and shirking duties. He could not trust them to be loyal and dependable soldiers in the heat of battle.[4]

General Lightburn believed he had sent sufficient reinforcements to the skirmish line. Colonel Wells Jones had a better view from the hill than did his rearward brigadier and—likely seeing Brantly's brigade coming toward him and perhaps also spying Manigault's men in reserve—Jones sent his adjutant, Lieutenant George W. Cavett, galloping back to Lightburn to plead for two more regiments. Lieutenant Cavett returned near Lightburn's hill where he found Lightburn conferring with the division commander, General Morgan L. Smith. Smith heard Jones's request and dismissed it, sending his own aide back to Jones to tell him not to be alarmed since it was only cavalry opposing him. Colonel Jones responded with exaggerated peevishness: "Give General Smith my compliments and tell him that I am not alarmed, but that I have Hood's army in my front and cannot whip it with two regiments. I insist the reinforcements I asked for be sent at once."[5]

Before Jones's second request could be processed, Brantly's and Sharp's troops surged en masse against the two Ohio regiments. The Buckeyes had aligned a wooden fence on the north side of Lick Skillet Road, near Benjamin Touchstone's homestead. Attempting briefly to hold the Mississippi men in check, Jones could not contend with the numbers arrayed against him.

The 54th Ohio arrived at this moment providing half of Jones's request, but their journey was merely up and back; by the time they reached the two-regiment skirmish line, all three regiments were falling back under the weight of Brantly's advance. Major Thomas Taylor of the 47th Ohio described the enemy numbers as "an avalanche of bayonets," in a letter to his wife, while a private of the 54th Ohio caught a panoramic view of at least two of Brown's brigades and declared that "it looked to me as though the whole Southern Confederacy stood in compact line of battle." The Mississippians deployed in two columns to pass around a house and while doing so had temporarily entrapped the Ohioans, but they slipped through the noose of soldiers before it could choke them off from the main line.[6]

As the Buckeyes dropped back from Lick Skillet Road two hundred yards, Brantly did not immediately pursue. "Here I halted and rectified my line," reported the Mississippi brigadier, "and while doing this I received orders from the brigadier general commanding that in advancing to swing my left around, thus putting my line at right angles with the balance of the division line, which order I obeyed, and again moved upon the enemy." General Brown's adjustment orders to Brantly assured two outcomes for his division's battle against the XV Corps. It guaranteed that Brantly would fight a separated battle against the Union right flank, completely apart from the rest of Brown's division. The other result from the special realignment was that Brantly could no longer move in concert with the other two brigades; his attack against the Union defensive line was therefore delayed by ten to fifteen minutes behind the remainder of Lee's attack.[7]

After his realignment, Brantly's biggest problem at this stage was strength and cohesion. Starting his movement with more than nine hundred men, he was likely down to fewer than seven hundred gun-toting soldiers when he reached the base of the hill where Lightburn had set up his defense. This height—the northwestern end of the Union battle line—was the highest ground in the vicinity and stood just south of the property of William Coursey. It was separated from Martin's brigade by a creek ravine and had no troops between it and the flank of the 83rd Indiana and 6th Mis-

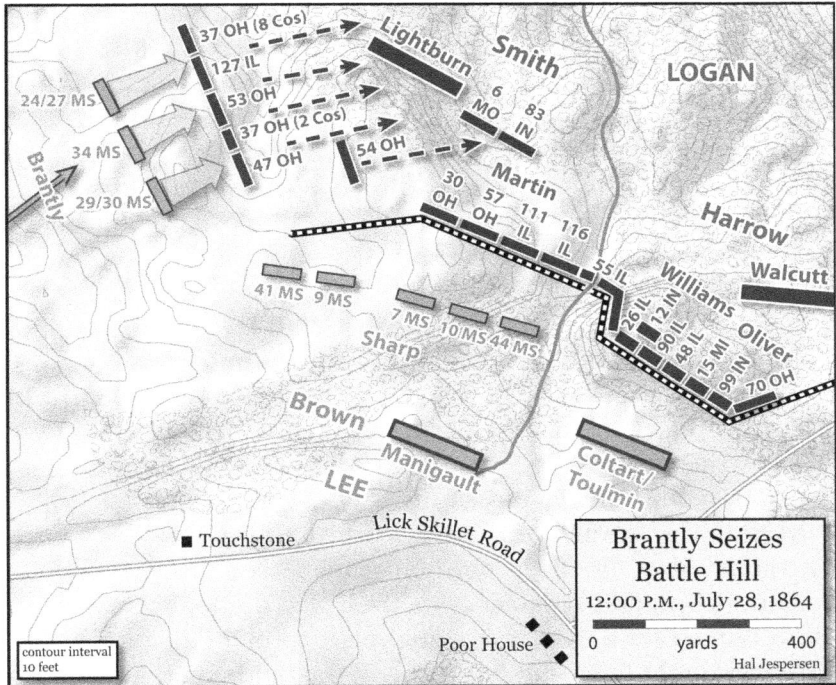

souri. On top of the hill, behind a quickly assembled defense of logs, rocks, and knapsacks, stood a mix of Ohioans from Lightburn's brigade, including the three Ohio regiments that had worked the advance skirmish line.

The other regiments on the hill were the understrength 127th Illinois, which Martin sent to the extreme right of the division from its reserve position behind his brigade line and the 37th Ohio infantry, commanded by Major Charles Hipp. They were the lone forces on the height at noon. Responding to direct verbal orders from General Howard, Hipp detached six companies to cover the right flank and soon followed by sending out two more companies to scout the byroads surrounding the hill. Within a few minutes of the noon hour, Hipp's two companies suddenly became four regiments attempting to make a stand on the hill.

Hipp attempted to shift his regiment (most of the companies had returned to him) to cover the northern approach. Sighting Colonel Jones, Hipp asked the senior commander of the height, "What shall I do?"

Jones responded: "Fight like the devil!"[8]

Hipp's attempt to follow that directive was short lived. After advancing his regiment forward into line, Hipp ordered his Buckeyes to loose a volley at the charging Mississippians. The Confederates immediately returned the fusillade, dropping a few members of the 37th Ohio. Hipp, too, was struck, with the bullet entering his breast. The shot jerked him in the saddle, but Hipp kept atop his horse. Another volley by the Confederates tore through his left arm and toppled the major off his mount. Hipp lay prostrate between the lines, a prize capture for Brantly's men creeping toward the hill from two directions.[9]

Private Ernst Torgler, the color bearer of the 37th Ohio, saved his commander. The German immigrant served in Company G. Watching Hipp fall, Torgler instinctively and immediately rushed out to him (ostensibly, a regimental mate took the flag for him). Torgler brought the wounded Hipp off the field, safely away from the Mississippians. Hipp would have to endure a surgeon's amputation blade, which removed the irreparably damaged arm. Torgler's act earned him the respect of his regiment, and later in life he would be awarded the Medal of Honor for his valor.[10]

It appeared all to have been done in a losing effort. Jones knew he could not hold the hill. Although he had the numbers, he had no time to organize them against the heavily pressing regiments of Brantly's brigade. The Ohioans abandoned the hill, and by 12:10 P.M. Brantly's Mississippi brigade occupied the height destined to be called Battle Hill.

At that moment the Confederates owned the most dominant ground of the battlefield. The Union right flank south of the Mississippians was manned by regiments that had to be rallied by General Logan and Major Hotaling to grab a tenuous hold on this part of the line. With a show of strength, Brantly's men could roll up the Union line from northwest to southeast and rout their opponent from the field. What the Confederates needed was to apply eastward pressure directly to the front of the Union line and to instill a panic from north to south in order that the Union defenders might fall like dominoes. The same XV Corps regiments had temporarily fled from the field on July 22. What would prevent them from fleeing again at Ezra Church?

Timing conspired against the Confederates on that ridge between 12:00 and 12:15 P.M. Lieutenant Colonel Toulmin's brigade lost too many leaders at the brigade and regimental level to sustain its initial assault. Having been repulsed just before noon, the brigade was relegated to exchanging fire with their Union counterparts across more than two hundred yards. Sharp's brigade lamented the loss of Confederate protection on its right with the withdrawal of Toulmin's Alabamans. Losing nearly half of their numbers in each regiment, the 10th and 44th Mississippi could not sustain momentum and fell back. According to General Sharp, "The other regiments of the brigade were advancing steadily, when they were forced to retire because the right had been repulsed." This appeared initially true for the 7th Mississippi immediately on the left of the 10th Mississippi, which had absorbed heavy losses in front and flank. A gap on the left of the 7th Mississippi widened enough for a complete separation from Sharp's remaining two regiments—the 9th Mississippi and the 41st Mississippi, on the left flank of the brigade. General Sharp hastened to the left flank to superintend the shift of the 41st Mississippi to his heavily pressed right flank. When Sharp reached his left flank, he was horrified to discover the 41st Mississippi "so scattered that it was impossible to handle it as an organization." Sharp's left—scattered as it was—remained in position, but his three regiments on the right withdrew from the field, having suffered close to two hundred casualties at the hands of Martin's and Lightburn's regiments.[11]

The retirement of more than half of Sharp's men left only five Confederate regiments in line, the 9th and 41st Mississippi from Sharp's brigade and the three regiments from Brantly's Mississippi brigade—1,000 Magnolia State soldiers pressing against the Union right. Brantly's regiments had seized Battle Hill, but merely minutes later a new threat moved in upon them from the southeast, led by the most conspicuous figure on the battlefield. Black Jack Logan led reinforcements including two infantry regiments from Walcutt's reserve brigade, the 6th Iowa and 40th Illinois.

Major Hotaling was not with Logan on this occasion, but a staff officer from Walcutt's brigade, Captain Samuel H. Watson of the 40th Illinois, took his place.[12]

Logan fed his instructions to the regimental commander and peeled away. Two majors were in charge of these reinforcing regiments: Thomas J. Ennis headed the 6th Iowa, and Hiram W. Hall commanded the Illinois troops. Logan had ordered the reinforcements when Williams's flank was being threatened half an hour earlier. Although Walcutt's detachment would arrive too late to be of much help, its presence was made even more timely and crucial when, at 12:15 P.M., several hundred yards farther to the Union right, Logan directed Majors Ennis and Hall to attack Battle Hill and reestablish the Union line on top of it. Guiding the reinforcements to the height was a most unlikely soldier—a fifteen-year-old drummer from the 127th Illinois named Robinson Murphy, who served as one of Colonel Martin's orderlies. Mississippi bullets took Murphy's horse out from beneath him, forcing the teenager to finish his mission on foot. For his work on the battlefield, the young drummer would become the sixth member of the 127th Illinois to win the Congressional Medal of Honor during the war, and the second soldier to earn the honor at Ezra Church.[13]

Brantly's Mississippians opposed Logan's plan. Sensing but not seeing the threat to his infantry's new position, Captain T. S. Hubbard, heading the 34th Mississippi, sent Sergeant Andrew J. Hamilton of Company D southeastward from the hill to determine from whence Union troops would counterstrike. Hamilton crept out about fifty yards then suddenly observed an entire regiment pop up seemingly out of nowhere mere feet in front of him. With the cover of trees protecting him, the sergeant fired several shots at the approaching regiment, aiming specifically at an officer on horseback. One of the bullets found its mark and penetrated the body and bowels of Major Ellis. The mortal wound knocked the twenty-three-year-old Iowa commander off his horse. Ennis became the first regimental commander to die in the battle and to this point, the highest-ranking Union officer to die that day. Captain William H. Clune assumed command of the 6th Iowa and continued the advance toward the hill with the 40th Illinois on his right.[14]

The two Union regiments, numbering some four hundred rifles, fired and stepped as they ascended the height, resisted by all three of Brantly's regiments struggling to maintain the hill they had just captured. Colonel Robert P. McKelvaine attempted to organize his consolidated 24th/27th Mississippi to move by the right flank. Unfortunately for the colonel, his regiment haphazardly attempted the difficult maneuver under fire before the company officers could oversee its proper execution. The result was a ripple of confusion that threatened the cohesion of the entire brigade. Colonel McKelvaine rode out to rectify the problem but was victimized by Union lead before his leadership could correct his wayward command. Struck in the left shoulder, McKelvaine was severely wounded and required immediate removal from the hill.[15]

McKelvaine's second in command, Lieutenant Colonel William L. Lyles, took over the regiment as the rest of Brantly's brigade held the hill. The Magnolia State soldiers peppered the advance of Major Hall and the two regiments he ultimately led, as the only Union regimental officer remaining from the 6th Iowa and 40th Illinois. The Union ascent from the northeast was complicated by the terrain. Walcutt's detachments were impeded by rocks, briars, and tangled underbrush. Rebel bullets tore into the Yankees, piercing Illinois and Iowa men by the dozens. Two Iowa color bearers dropped from their wounds while attempting to reach the crest with the Hawkeye flag. The Mississippi standards alone remained atop the contested height.[16]

A third, surging Union regiment suddenly entered the fray to affect the stalemate. Half an hour earlier Lieutenant Colonel William E. Strong, the army's inspector general, fulfilled General Howard's call for support at the start of the battle by leading the reserves of the first brigade, Third Division, of the XVII Corps to the contested Union right. The 12th Wisconsin advanced hurriedly with the 31st Illinois lagging behind. The Badgers suffered their first casualties during the 2,000-yard advance to the creek ravine near the foot of the hill as several men fell under the scorching sun. One of them, a late-1863 enlistee named James H. Clement, died from the intense heat.[17]

The 12th Wisconsin formed in the ravine and surged uphill toward the Mississippians. "The 12th gave a tremendous yell as they came up and poured volley after volley into the Rebel ranks," relayed Edwin Levings of Company A. Their charge immediately threatened Brantly's left flank. Simultaneously on Brantly's right, the 29th/30th lost its right-flank protection when the last vestiges of Sharp's brigade—the 9th and 41st Mississippi—fell back to reform with the rest of their brigade members. Meanwhile, Brantly's entire front was losing its contest against the Iowan and Illinois troops, which gained more ground near the crest of Battle Hill.

General Brantly's three regiments stood alone against this counterstrike—a surge initiated by two Union regiments and now supported by a third. Losses of officers and men considerably weakened Brantly, but in addition, tremendous numbers of men appeared to be shirking their duty. One of his regiments, the 29th/30th Mississippi, fielded 277 privates at the start of the advance but lost seventy unscathed men—one-quarter of its strength—from the skirmish line and flanks when these soldiers passed to the left as the regiment shifted right. The loss of two dozen more men to enemy bullets cut the regiment's strength well below two hundred.[18]

Brantly knew he should have fielded more numbers at the hilltop to defend it. He lost 126 officers and men on the 28th, a serious but not crippling blow when compared to what other Confederate brigades had already suffered (and would suffer later on this day). Still, Brantly was forced to call a retreat because of the confusion on the hill and the unexpected reduced command defending its crest. The latter factor still rankled him three days later when he reported, "Being greatly weakened by the killed and wounded and the innumerable cases of utter exhaustion among the best men of my command, as well as by the absence of a goodly number who had no legitimate excuse, I was unable to hold the works." For the second time in less than a week, this Mississippi brigade performed below expectations in battle.[19]

As the Magnolia State soldiers retrograded off the height and retreated westerly, the 40th Illinois and 6th Iowa chased them up and over the crest of Battle Hill, while the 12th Wisconsin pressed farther north on the height. Casualties mounted in the three Federal regiments attempting to penetrate a formidable line of Mississippi soldiers. Major Hall, elevated on his horse atop the hill, became a conspicuous target for the Confederates. As his regiment descended from the southwestern side, Hall reeled from a severe bullet wound and could no longer keep control of his horse or his regiment, leaving his senior captain, Michael Galvin,

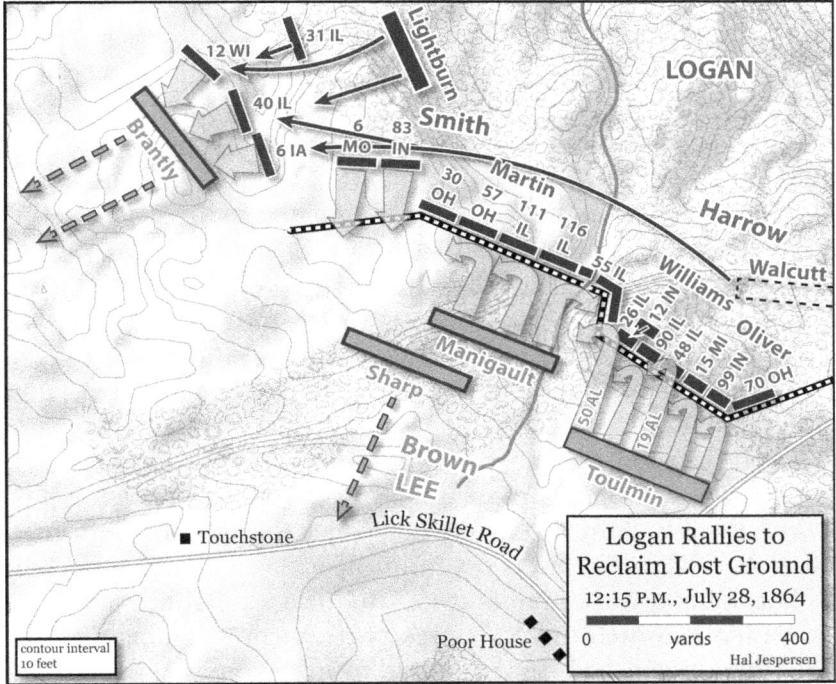

Copyright © 2016 University of Oklahoma Press

in charge of the 40th Illinois. The two XV Corps regiments lost fifty officers and men in a matter of minutes, but their achievement did not go overlooked by their brigade commander. Colonel Walcutt hailed their charge as "equal in brilliancy to anything that has occurred during the war." The 12th Wisconsin from the XVII Corps lost two men killed and seventeen wounded in their fight for the height.[20]

Colonel Charles C. Walcutt, the brigadier of the two XV Corps reinforcements, swiftly and obediently fed them into the action at the most opportune moment. The Columbus, Ohio, native had turned twenty-six years old on February 12, sharing a birthday with Abraham Lincoln, though he had celebrated fewer than half as many as had the president. Walcutt was well connected; his congressman lobbied the president that spring to grant Walcutt a brigadier's commission. Despite his age—a generalship would make him the youngest in Sherman's district—many felt Walcutt had earned it with three years of solid leadership under his belt. He was noted for his unflinching bravery and toughness. Proof of this was lodged in his shoulder—a two-year-old bullet from the Battle of Shiloh—and would remain there for the rest of his life. He had caught Sherman's attention even when he was second in command of the 46th Ohio; Sherman had described Walcutt then as "an elegant young fellow," one who was worthy of a higher command. Walcutt had taken the helm of the 46th Ohio, and subsequently he commanded a brigade in the heat of the Battle of Chattanooga after an injury to Brigadier General John M. Corse. Throughout the Atlanta Campaign, Walcutt excelled on the battlefield, most recently at the Battle of Atlanta where he made a crucial decision that overruled his superior's order but saved hard-pressed Union troops on a hill.[21]

With the loss of the two regimental majors on another contested hill at Ezra Church, Walcutt's intrabrigade leadership reflected his knack for being in the midst of the heaviest fighting in all of the battles in which the XV Corps performed a significant role. Eight line officers had been removed from the ranks in ten weeks. By 12:15 P.M. on July 28, four out of Walcutt's five regiments were led by captains, the most recent one leading the 40th Illinois, a regiment that had not even entered the campaign until June. The Confederates they faced deceptively looked more fortunate at the regimental level. Brantly's brigade had one captain in charge of a regiment, but the other four of his regiments had suffered so much in the past year that they were forced to fight consolidated as two, both led by line officers in charge of the regiments for the first time in battle.

The Union resurgence on the right reclaimed Battle Hill and opened the door for Lightburn's regiments to return to the line they had been forced to abandon just minutes before. The young men of the 37th, 47th, 53rd, and 54th Ohio advanced—bellowing "prolonged huzzas," according to one—on the heels of Walcutt's reinforcement troops and took over the hill for the second time. Colonel Wells S. Jones naturally resumed the brigade command role he had held until a few days before and organized Lightburn's brigade on the hill and covering each side of it. With the full advantage of time—a commodity he did not possess when the Buckeyes were driven off the hill earlier in the day—Jones aligned the men for a stronger defense.

General Lightburn was the true brigadier for this force, but the consensus in the ranks was that Colonel Jones commanded them on the height. Although under normal circumstances four regiments would overcrowd the hill, Major Thomas Taylor of the 47th Ohio revealed that they had retaken the hill "more by noise than numbers." This suggests the Ohio regiments were understrength enough to have discernible gaps between the regiments as their defense spanned for nearly half a mile, but Jones expertly positioned them so that every position in front of them would be struck with Union crossfire. With the men fast at work creating light breastworks by piling rails in front of their position, Battle Hill was becoming a more formidable Union stronghold by the minute.[22]

Three attacking brigades of Brown's division had all been repulsed. At 12:15 P.M. the Union line strengthened for a mile with twenty regiments from Harrow's and Morgan Smith's divisions of the XV Corps as well as the 12th Wisconsin of the XVII Corps, which were placed behind rudimentary earthworks on the ridge line. For nearly five minutes Federals faced retreating or reforming Confederates. With no direct pressure applied to the defenders, the result was the closest to a lull experienced on the battlefield.

General Brown had already rectified the inaction in his front by committing his reserve brigade into the contest. Brigadier General Arthur Manigault had maintained his reserve role and kept his brigade in place behind the center of Brown's attack line. "I suppose I had remained in my position twenty minutes, and the firing had nearly ceased," recalled Manigault, "when an order came for me to advance straight to the front." Well aware of the repulse of Johnston's Alabamans, Manigault supposed Sharp's and Brantly's Mississippians had suffered the same outcome. He could also sense, in puzzlement, that Clayton's division on the right of the road had not moved into battle—incorrectly believing they were ready and in battle formation.[23]

Manigault's brigade was the only one in Lee's Corps, and one of only a few in Hood's entire army, that was not homogeneous in state regiments. Whereas most Confederate brigades in the eastern and western theaters followed President Jefferson Davis's preference to consist of all regiments from one state, Manigault's regiments comprised Alabama and South Carolina troops. Manigault ordered them to address to the left in the following order, from left to right: the 34th Alabama, 28th Alabama, 24th Alabama, 19th South Carolina, and 10th South Carolina. They essentially followed in the footsteps of Sharp's brigade, negotiating through a thick belt of trees north of the Poor House, then through a more thinly wooded area. Manigault halted the men to realign while still protected by the woods. Ahead of them, beyond the tree line was the five-hundred-yard-wide cleared field. Beyond that was the rise that held the Union line atop it.[24]

General Lee personally superintended Manigault's deployment, a sign of desperation and an admission that Brown's assault had thus far failed. Manigault's division chief, Brigadier General John C. Brown, accompanied Lee, but it was the latter who directly instructed the brigadier of his mission. Years later Manigault was still shocked at the deceptive tactic used by General Lee and then General Brown to persuade him of his high probability of success:

> I was directed to place the Brigade in such a position that the front would be exactly parallel with that of the ridge, and pointing out to me the highest portion of it, directly in our front, which seemed for the distance of 300 yards to exceed by fifteen or twenty feet the height of any other portion, was ordered by him [General Lee] to carry it and establish myself there, remarking at the same time that I would find little difficulty in doing so, as the enemy were not in force, and only held it with a few light troops. General Brown also remarked by way of encouragement, I suppose, to myself, and the line near which we were standing, that General Sharp with his brigade had found no difficulty in executing a like order. I never yet have been able to explain to myself how it was that those officers so unblushingly made such a statement, knowing, as they must have known, that it was totally incorrect.[25]

Oblivious to the poisonous falsehood he had just been fed, Manigault inspected the region of his advance and ordered his regiments forward. The Alabamans and Carolinians paced between trees and exited the woods, pouring into the open field. Visible for the first time to XV Corps defenders, the Federals opened fire at a distance of four hundred yards, well within killing range. Yankee bullets stopped and silenced surging Southerners in an attempt to collapse Manigault's entire attack line. Dozens of soldiers dropped in the clearing.

General Lee watched the inauspicious start of Manigault's attack and was dismayed at its disorientation. The 10th South Carolina lost nearly thirty men in the clearing and were visibly lagging behind their four sister regiments. Lee galloped to the regiment, seized a stand of their colors, and personally led them into the field. Lieutenant Colonel C. Irvin Walker must have taken his corps commander's bold gesture as a personal challenge to reinvigorate his men. Walker rode to General Lee's side and cried out, "General, give me those colors." Lee handed the banner off to Walker and rode away. Within minutes of his departure, a Union bullet tore into Lieutenant Colonel Walker's neck and knocked him out of the fight. That shot essentially wounded the fragile organization of the 10th South Carolina and kept them out of Manigault's assault; they did not continue forward. The 19th South Carolina became Manigault's new right flank. With rebel yells rending the air, Manigault's four remaining regiments rushed across the field, over the ravine, and up the wooded height.[26]

Morgan L. Smith's division was ready for them. The infantrymen made good use of the time between Sharp's attack and now Manigault's coming in the same manner. They attempted to strengthen their position with "anything that can help stop a bullet," including fence rails, logs, and stumps. A soldier in Martin's brigade viewed the onrush of Manigault's troops: "Again the well-known yell; the pop-popping of the preliminary shots; the magnificent on-coming of proud lines from behind the opposite ridge, with flag-bearers seeming to dance out defiantly in their front."[27]

Nine hundred Alabama and South Carolina soldiers assaulted the same part of the Union defense where Sharp's Mississippians had attacked and failed fifteen minutes earlier. Martin's and Lightburn's intermixed brigade accepted the new assailants with more preparation and, consequently, more confidence. "The enemy reformed immediately, and rushed upon us again," wrote John G. Brown of the 55th Illinois regarding Manigault's attack, which commenced immediately after Sharp's; "but there stood the boys, in blue emblems of freedom, like that many statues." Manigault quickly realized that he had been deceived by General Lee, for he was experiencing tremendous difficulty in this advance. Under a fire Manigault described as "galling," the Confederates forced XV Corps skirmishers back to their main line. (Manigault's claim of battling a second line of skirmishers is uncorroborated.) From there the Southern storm was silenced as Union soldiers struck the unsupported brigade in front and flank simultaneously.[28]

Manigault believed he was attacking alone, but he was mistaken. Off his right flank and out of his view surged Toulmin's Alabama brigade for a second attempt at the line defended by Williams's and Oliver's brigades of Harrow's division. Toulmin had kept his men behind the temporary works erected by Harrow's skirmishers and from there had exchanged fire with the Union main defensive line for the next twenty minutes until he saw Manigault advancing across the field toward the Union center. Toulmin received the order to charge and swiftly set his men in motion, double-quicking two hundred yards to Harrow's two-brigade line.

A member of the 48th Illinois was awestruck by the thundering Alabama stampede that "came at us 3 columns deep." Colonel Reub Williams gauged that the renewed attack came at his line "with redoubled energy." As the Alabamans closed within seventy-five yards, Toulmin believed that only portions of three regiments—the 19th, 22nd and 50th Alabama, perhaps no more than five hundred men—continued the assault organized. The other Alabama regiments, the 25th and 39th, participated more likely as a mass of one to two hundred unorganized men on the right of the brigade.[29]

Toulmin's soldiers reached the Union works in a minute, attacking the right (north) flank of Oliver's brigade and the entire front and right flank of Williams's brigade. The 19th Alabama beelined to the 48th Illinois and penetrated its defense. "They charged right into our ranks," noted a Prairie State soldier.[30] Farther to the left of the 19th Alabama charged the 22nd Alabama (Hart's and Toulmin's former regiment). Captain Isaac Whitney outranked all remaining officers of the 22nd Alabama and continued forward with them as they closed in upon the 26th Illinois Infantry. Colonel Robert Gillmore of the 26th Illinois had ordered his men to limit their fire after the initial repulse of the brigade twenty minutes earlier, for although the Alabamans had remained within firing range the entire time, Gillmore maintained that "their intention was to draw our fire, until we were either out of ammunition or our muskets out of order." During the second assault he placed no restrictions on his men. "They came on again in three lines but were driven back with good slaughter," Gillmore raved in his official report. One of the Illini bullets tore into the Alabama color bearer, Ensign William R. Leary, just ten paces from the Union works. He fell with the folds of the flag covering his body.[31]

The 50th Alabama struck the right of the 26th Illinois and entered the works in a gap where the 26th Illinois and a portion of the 55th Illinois had defended. Portions of both regiments buckled under the pressure of Toulmin's charge. Colonel Williams quickly formed the reserve regiment, the 12th Indiana, perpendicular to the Union defense line and pushed forward three companies to throw an oblique volley into the Alabamans. Six days later in his official report, Williams, as diplomatically as possible, would describe the Illini regiments as displaying "symptoms of weakness." More than twenty years after the battle, the Union colonel felt less inhibited in recalling how the right of his brigade caved in to the menacing Alabamans. "I was frantic over the situation," he admitted.[32]

By the time the Indiana companies rushed into their oblique position, most of the Illinois troops on their right were gone, displaced by Alabama soldiers, particularly those from the 50th Alabama who rushed into the abandoned works and planted their flag there. Their second commander of the day, Captain Arnold, fell from a wound—likely inflicted by a bullet fired by the 12th Indiana. He was quickly replaced by the next senior captain, Archibald D. Ray, who kept his troops within the Union defense line.[33] Their position was uncontested on the left (north), as Union troops from the next brigades had followed the contours of the ridge line and formed perpendicular to the position of Williams's brigade, bending eastward and then northward again. The zigzag formation left Williams's brigade unprotected from the Union right flank.

General Logan assured that the protection for Williams's brigade would come from the rear. After Logan and Major Hotaling restored the right of Martin's brigade twenty minutes earlier, both men performed an encore to restore Williams's flank. The general and his intrepid aide stopped the retreat of hordes of panic-stricken men by personally blocking their escape route and turning them around with choice, profanity-laden and tersely delivered orders. Logan grabbed one of the regimental flags and bore it to the line, likely handing it to the now rallied members to carry toward the Alabamans. An admiring and impressed Reub Williams raved over what he saw. "Hence I have always claimed that the presence of General Logan at that point was equal to a brigade at the precise moment," he lauded. "A brigade could have done no more than to have restored a broken line than this General Logan did with the meager assistance of a single officer."[34]

The impressive breach of Williams's and Oliver's flanks by the 50th and 19th Alabama could not panic the Union line, as rearward troops rallied and quickly countersurged to restore the line. The unorganized right flank of the Alabama brigade gave way, exposing the rest of Toulmin's command to simultaneous front and flank fire. More than 150 officers and men were killed, wounded, or captured within and in front of the hotly contested works. Toulmin was forced to pull back his entire force. The two charges had bled 269 officers and men from the brigade and reduced its strength to fewer than nine hundred. This included the 50th and 19th Alabama, which retreated from their point of penetration, leaving both healthy and wounded prisoners behind. The 19th Alabama lost its colors to its opponent, the 48th Illinois, which seized the battle flag after shooting down every member of the color guard, including the unidentified private who was brazen enough to plant the flags several paces inside the makeshift works.[35]

Northwestward from where Toulmin struck, more Alabama soldiers were experiencing similar frustration. In less than ten minutes Manigault lost nearly 150 men, scores of them within forty paces of the Union line. The Confederates lay down in the death zone to escape the withering fire. The 34th Alabama, which marked the left flank of Manigault's brigade, was victimized by Union troops in front and on its left flank—a result of the contour of the ridge that had shaped the Union line into a box-shaped trap that the Confederate brigade unknowingly entered. Major John N. Slaughter, commanding the Alabamans, asserted that this battle "was the fifth general engagement in which the regiment had participated, but this was by far the most destructive fire they had ever been under." The sixty-nine casualties suffered by the 34th Alabama—close to half of its numerical strength—provided ample evidence for Major Slaughter's claim.[36]

Similar havoc played into the ranks of the 19th South Carolina on Manigault's left flank. The 55th Illinois confronted them on their right and the 116th Illinois directly in front—a defense line much like the 44th Mississippi had faced in the previous assault. Captain T. W. Getzen led the Carolinians this day, having inherited the regiment after its remaining line officer, Major James L. White, was wounded on July 22 east of Atlanta. It cannot be ruled out that General Manigault purposefully protected the inexperienced captain by positioning the 19th South Carolina inside of the 10th South Carolina before the assault. Lieutenant Colonel Walker's wound and the subsequent disarray of the 10th South Carolina forced Captain Getzen to man Manigault's flank with his command.

Captain Getzen was not experienced or talented enough to manage the 19th South Carolina—particularly when it was in the most precarious position in any battle to date. As the regiment melted away from mounting casualties from the crossfire, Getzen decided that he could not continue to hold its position on the height. He ordered his men to withdraw, thus evacuating Manigault's right flank.[37]

The loss of the 19th South Carolina reduced Manigault to his three Alabama regiments. "It was evident that retreat could only be delayed a few minutes," he admitted, unless he received reinforcements. The inevitable outcome was catalyzed by Union aggression on each flank. Sensing how vulnerable the Confederates were, Illinois and Ohio soldiers surged from their protection and poured a simultaneous fire into the flanks of Manigault's line, collapsing them toward the center. John G. Brown of the 55th Illinois remarked accurately and succinctly, "The rebels could not stand our unerring rifles, and soon broke in confusion." According to Manigault, "The rest was flight and confusion, until we reached the ground from which we started to make the assault." The retreat carried them back three hundred yards behind the protection of an intervening hillock. Thus ended the third unsuccessful attack against the XV Corps line; all completed in fewer than forty-five minutes.[38]

Another attempt by the Confederates was imminent and immediate. Manigault successfully reorganized his routed men and had them lined up again in five minutes, including both Carolina regiments. Five minutes after that, Manigault received orders to renew the attack. He advanced with five regiments, ostensibly in the same position as the first assault, including the 10th South Carolina returned to the left flank. However, the casualties and incohesion in captain-led regiments produced an attack seemingly lacking effort. The regiments advanced only 150 yards before heavy Union fire froze them in place. Manigault pulled back the troops a hundred yards from the previous rally point. Some took refuge in an old excavated roadbed while others hid behind stumps and logs and in gullies. This withdrawal gave the Southerners additional protection and an opportunity to rest and reorganize.[39]

Continuous but slackening fire was exchanged between Brown's division and the troops comprising Harrow's and Morgan L. Smith's divisions. As the time approached 12:30 P.M., the Battle of Ezra Church had yet to complete its first hour, but the contest was already characterized by three distinct attacks. The results were a Union line growing stronger and a Confederate division bloodied if not quite beaten. Brown's four brigades suffered eight hundred losses with no gain of territory. Reduced to a division of 2,800 tired gun-toting soldiers, Brown's division suffered equally in quality as it did in quantity with the loss of nine brigade and regimental commanders. The division could not be an effective fighting force without rest and reinforcements.[40]

General Stephen D. Lee initiated the Battle of Ezra Church with four brigades of his available corps and was determined to escalate it with the other three brigades. His inability to coordinate the two divisions guaranteed a prolonged contest and provided General Howard time to strengthen and reinforce his defenses. If General Lee could find and exploit a weak portion of the Union line, he could win this contest. Lee's problem was that he had but one division remaining to accomplish this feat.

Figure 1. Major General William Tecumseh Sherman. Called "Cump" by his friends and "Uncle Billy" by his men, Sherman commanded the Union's Military Division of the Mississippi, an army group of nearly 95,000 troops. Courtesy Library of Congress, LC-B813–3624A.

Figure 2. Major General John A. Logan. The head of the Union's XV Corps for most of the Atlanta Campaign, Logan was credited as the victorious field commander at the Battle of Ezra Church. Courtesy Library of Congress, LC-BH831–2053.

Figure 3. Major General Oliver Otis Howard. The one-armed, hard-luck brigade, division, and corps commander found success as the head of the Union's Army of the Tennessee beginning with the Battle of Ezra Church. Howard never lost a battle at the helm of Grant and Sherman's former army. Courtesy Library of Congress, LC-B813–3719A.

Figure 4. General John Bell Hood. Tasked by Confederate president Jefferson Davis with the responsibility of defending Atlanta against Sherman's encompassing army group, Hood planned a two-day battle near Ezra Church, but was forced to alter the mission to a single day and sent 10,000 fewer men than he originally intended. Courtesy Library of Congress, LOT 4213.

Figure 5. Lieutenant General Alexander P. Stewart. Sent by General Hood to Ezra Church with two divisions, Stewart was hit in the forehead by a glancing shot and forced from the battlefield. Courtesy Library of Congress, DRWG/US—Waud, no. 922.

Figure 6. Lieutenant General Stephen D. Lee. The youngest lieutenant general in the Confederacy at thirty years of age, Lee opened the Battle of Ezra Church with a 4,000-man assault in an effort to drive ill-prepared XV Corps troops off the heights near the chapel. Courtesy Library of Congress, LC-B813–1609A.

Figure 7. Artist Theodore R. Davis's on-site sketch of the Battle of Ezra Church. The Iowa soldiers of Charles Woods's division battle Alabama infantry from Brigadier General Alpheus Baker's brigade on the east side of the field. This image from the August 27, 1864, issue of *Harper's Weekly Illustrated Newspaper* depicts a portion of the battlefield generally neglected for over 150 years. Courtesy Western History Collections, University of Oklahoma Libraries.

Figure 8. This page from the August 27, 1864, issue of *Harper's Weekly Illustrated Newspaper* shows "Dead Brook," the northward-flowing feeder of Proctor's Creek, in the upper right, strewn with Confederate bodies. Theodore Davis's sketch of Ezra Church appears in the image in the upper left. Courtesy Western History Collections, University of Oklahoma Libraries.

6

Gibson's Attack

At the time that General Lee's second division prepared to assault the Army of the Tennessee, General Hood remained oblivious to what had transpired near Ezra Church. Hood's headquarters stood merely three miles east of the battlefield. Of the three battles waged or being waged under his helm by the Army of Tennessee, General Hood seemed least cognizant of, and less proactive in, the Battle of Ezra Church. As unlikely as it may seem, the sounds of Johnston's, Sharp's, Brantly's, and Manigault's assaults against Logan's corps did not reach General Hood; the near absence of artillery fire may have delayed the acoustic "announcement" of this prenoon start of the battle.

Two known messages that Hood sent out within the first half of the noon hour illustrate the delay in his awareness of the battle, but also a growing concern that may have prevented him from personally riding out to inspect the start of his two-day mission for Lee and Stewart. Hood had fielded a dispatch from Red Jackson and forwarded it to General Lee at noon, advising him, "If the enemy should make an assault upon our left . . . strike him in flank." The directive suggests that Hood was permitting Lee to initiate a fight that had already commenced fifteen minutes prior. The fact that Lee did not receive Hood's instruction for another hour provides evidence that couriers were inexplicably slow in completing communications between the generals, taking nearly twice as long as expected to deliver dispatches three miles on a direct road.[1]

Based on this reality, Red Jackson's dispatch to Hood likely was written at 11:00 A.M. or a little earlier, before General Lee met him at the Poor House. If so, Hood believed that Lee was close enough to assault the Union force (whose identity was unknown to Hood). Hood remained under the false impression that the enemy force had oriented eastward, in preparation for an assault against Atlanta. Hood's instructions for Lee to "strike him in flank" can only translate to a northward assault against the right flank of an attack force heading eastward "to make an assault upon our [Hood's] left." The dispatch did not reveal Hood's desire should Lee confront what he actually faced—the vanguard of the enemy force, not the flank, but given the battle plan as Hood explained it and Stewart remembered it, Lee was permitted to attack only to secure the line of heights; but Lee was not to attack if he was already deployed upon this prime defensive ground (unless that inviting flank passed in front of him from left to right).[2]

Thirty minutes after Hood fed updated instructions to Lee, headquarters followed up by notifying General Hardee, "General Lee is directed to prevent the enemy from gaining the Lick Skillet road, and not to attack unless the enemy exposes himself in attacking us." This simply rephrased the original message to Lee, but somewhat inarticulately so as to leave a completely false impression that Lee was forbidden to attack unless the enemy's right flank invited him to strike as this force attempted to pierce the outer defenses of Atlanta. Implicit in the message is the assumption that Lee had effectively checked the enemy (hence, "prevent the enemy from gaining the Lick Skillet road") by Hood's very explicit instructions to occupy the heights running through Ezra Church, half a mile above that road.

Most revealing in the dispatch to Hardee is the sentence that immediately followed the restating of Lee's orders. Hood warned, "Please inform your officers that all indications are that the enemy intends to attack us to-day or to-morrow." The dispatch revealed Hood's ever-growing concern that Hardee's sector of Atlanta's defenses was likely to be attacked within the next thirty hours and hence his attempt to alert his subordinates accordingly. The phrase "attack us" did not refer to Lee, but to Hardee and other points in the ring of works surrounding Atlanta.[3]

At the same time headquarters wrote out the warning message to Hardee, the high-intensity start of the Battle of Ezra Church temporarily waned. More than a thousand Confederate and Union soldiers had already been killed or wounded in forty-five minutes of action. Lieutenant General Stephen D. Lee had just completed his exploit to rally Manigault's brigade and returned to his observational position rearward—likely close to the Poor House. His daring gesture may have been born out of frustration and not a little desperation, for it was clear at this point that Brown's four-brigade assault had failed to dislodge the Yankee defenders and secure the road in order to carry out Hood's plan. Lee had underestimated the size of the force needed to complete the mission. What made matters worse for him was that he initially had two divisions at hand, close to 7,000 soldiers at his disposal, had he been patient to withhold Brown's attack until Clayton had successfully formed his battle line. Lee superintended Brown's attack; by noon he realized he needed Clayton's men to come up and apply pressure closer to Ezra Church. Lee issued orders for Clayton to move.

The burning sun hung at its highest point in an otherwise cloudy sky on Thursday as the third assault of General Brown's division reached its apex against the XV Corps defenders ensconced on the wooded heights northwest of Ezra Church. Aligning on the right (east) side of Lick Skillet Road, facing north toward the chapel and the U-shaped ribbon of blue forming and broadening behind it, was the division of Major General Henry D. Clayton. Like Brown's division, Clayton's force had been heavily engaged east of Atlanta six days earlier, losing several hundred men in that battle. Colonel Abda Johnson's brigade did not march out to battle and was not part of Clayton's force this day, reducing the division to three brigades totaling slightly more than 3,000 soldiers rank and file.

On the left side of General Clayton's division line and aligned first for battle was the Louisiana brigade of Brigadier General Randall L. Gibson, who had led this unit since his promotion from the helm of the 13th Louisiana in January. Gibson was thirty-one years old with a law degree earned from his studies at Yale University. He had led the 13th Louisiana from Shiloh through Chickamauga, earning brigadier status after the original commander, Brigadier

General Daniel W. Adams, was captured in the latter battle after suffering his third wound of the war.[4]

Gibson's Pelican State soldiers had shed blood on several battlefields in the western theater prior to Gibson's promotion; they continued to do so in the early months of the Atlanta Campaign. They had a reserve role in the monstrous battle on July 22 and consequently suffered the fewest casualties of all troops comprising the remaining brigades of Clayton's division. While every other Confederate brigade lost numbers from attrition over the summer, Gibson's brigade actually gained numerical strength when the 30th Louisiana Battalion and the 4th Louisiana Infantry transferred to join the other Louisianans in July. With the additional regiment and battalion, Gibson's brigade consisted of sixty-five infantry companies with identities in ten regiments and battalions. This included a two-company battalion of sharpshooters that specialized as the brigade skirmishers. Two other battalions in Gibson's brigade had begun their war service as full-sized infantry regiments when they were organized in 1861–62, but arduous campaigning weakened these units enough to force their consolidation into the 16th/25th by the close of 1863. Two other regiments, the 13th Louisiana and the 20th Louisiana, began the year 1864 consolidated but acting as separate entities since April. They still were made up of consolidated companies (one such consolidation in the 20th Louisiana numbered fewer than sixty officers and men). Regardless, the presence of sixty-five companies easily made this the largest of Clayton's three brigades—if not the largest brigade in Hood's entire army. In mid-July the brigade numbered 1,115 officers and men, ostensibly before the 4th Louisiana (and, perhaps, the 30th Louisiana Battalion) officially transferred to Gibson. No specific report accounts for its strength on July 28; a reasonable estimated range tallies 1,300 to 1,500 Louisianans present for duty at Ezra Church.[5]

The two newest additions to Gibson's brigade, the 4th Louisiana and 30th Louisiana Battalion, consisted of companies of Acadians (Cajuns). These French descendants spoke the same language as their seventeenth-century ancestors, which distinguished them from their Southern brethren in neighboring companies and regiments. Their constant Creole banter both annoyed and amused the rank and file. During the siege of Port Hudson a year before the Atlanta Campaign, a Tennessean relayed, "As we stood in line during the bombardment the frogs in a puddle kept up a constant chattering, when this boy said to me; 'These frogs have camped by the side of the 30th Louisiana till they have learned to talk French.'"[6] The Acadians in Gibson's brigade line likely kept up "the jabbering" (a term coined for their unusual banter) while they awaited their attack orders.

Unfortunately for Gibson—and by extension, Major General Clayton and Lieutenant General Lee—the other two brigades on the right of the Louisianans were not ready to fight. Clayton had intended a two-brigade battle line formed by Gibson's brigade on the left and Colonel Bush Jones's brigade on the right with Brigadier General Alpheus Baker's brigade in reserve. As Brown's second wave of attackers had begun to recede from its high tide, Clayton was struggling to finish his front-line formation. General Gibson decided he needed to lend a hand. Gibson temporarily left his brigade to help align Colonel Jones's troops so that the division could salvage Brown's waning assault by extending it to the right.[7]

Unbeknownst to General Clayton was that Lee had grown so impatient that he sent orders to move his division immediately. Lee relayed the attack orders through his assistant inspector general, Lieutenant Colonel Edward H. Cunningham, a twenty-nine-year-old Texan on Lee's staff. Cunningham, like most members of Lee's corps, was a holdover staff officer handpicked by Hood, having served in Hood's former brigade early in the war as a captain in the 4th Texas Infantry. On July 28 Cunningham fulfilled Lee's request to prod Clayton's men forward.

Cunningham likely rode eastward from behind Brown's line to reach the left flank of Gibson's brigade, anchored near the Poor House. There he found Colonel Leon von Zinken of the 20th Louisiana, whom Gibson had delegated to command his regiment and two others on the left side of his brigade. For reasons unclear, Cunningham directly relayed Lee's advance order to Colonel von Zinken, being either unaware that the colonel lacked authority over the entire brigade or unwilling to seek out Generals Gibson or Clayton.

Von Zinken magnified the mistake, upsetting Clayton's plan for a full-scale division assault, by immediately marching Gibson's entire brigade forward without permission from any of his commanding officers. The Louisianans headed northward, negotiating through thick woods as they advanced toward Ezra Church. The Southerners enjoyed no protection on either flank and were directed by a Prussian commander with no authority or experience as a brigade commander. According to General Lee's after-battle report, "Clayton's division moved forward as soon as formed, and about ten minutes after Brown's advance." His claim is unsubstantiated on both accounts: only Gibson's brigade moved forward, and based on the available evidence the Louisianans marched toward Ezra Church at least thirty minutes, not ten, after Brown's initial advance. Lee must have known this, for he sent Cunningham ostensibly due to the lateness of Clayton's involvement. Assuming a lapse time of five to ten minutes for Cunningham to leave Lee's side and reach the left flank of Gibson's brigade, it is inconceivable that Lee would feel compelled to send a staff member to encourage a stagnant force to advance unless enough time had elapsed for Lee to feel extremely uncomfortable about it.[8]

The disruption of the planned division-sized assault astonished General Gibson, who had been with Colonel Jones's regimental commanders discussing their plan of attack. "Having accomplished this," reported Gibson, "I went at once to the direction of [my] brigade, when to my astonishment I found that it had been moved forward without any order from me or notice to me." Incredulous of this unfortunate action, Gibson galloped northward through thick woods to find and overtake his command before it made contact with the enemy.[9]

Gibson did not make it in time. The aligned soldiers of Oliver's brigade had just fended off the second, more tenacious assault by Toulmin's brigade. With a mere minutes lapsing between the charges, the Hoosiers, Buckeyes, Michiganders, and Illini had held firm and took advantage of the temporary lull to buttress their thigh-high barrier. Colonel Oliver ordered spades distributed throughout his brigade. Before any significant digging could occur, however, Union skirmishers caught sight of the fresh Southern brigade rushing toward them.[10]

Colonel von Zinken had the Louisianans advancing on a path to strike obliquely the southeastern portion of Harrow's line. The gap between Wangelin's and Oliver's brigades was essentially behind the 70th Ohio and would be undetected by Louisiana skirmishers. The Louisianans' approach consisted of the two sharpshooter companies skirmishing in front, aided by an additional company of skirmishers from the 30th Louisiana Battalion. Behind them marched the Louisiana brigade in a double line of battle that stretched at least four hundred yards and likely included a reserve line marching directly behind it. The length of the Confederate assault line guaranteed that it would overlap the left flank of Oliver's brigade where Major Brown and his 70th Ohio anchored the southeast flank of General Harrow's division line. On the Confederate left marched the infantrymen of the 13th and 20th Louisiana with the 30th Louisiana Battalion marching on their right. These specific flank regiments were opposed by the Ohioans.[11]

Sensing the Union line's vulnerability, either General Harrow or General Logan corrected it with reserve troops. Colonel Walcutt had already committed half of his reserve brigade's numbers to assist Morgan Smith's division when the 40th Illinois and 6th Iowa successfully charged and regained Battle Hill. Perhaps no more than fifteen minutes later, Walcutt deployed two more regiments of his reserve brigade by sending forward the 46th Ohio (his former regiment) and the 103rd Illinois. The Ohioans moved in behind and between the 99th Indiana and 70th Ohio, while the 103rd Illinois moved to fill the gap between Wangelin's and Oliver's brigades. Several companies of the 46th Ohio carried Spencers, a repeating rifle that allowed the shooter to fire seven rounds without reloading.[12]

The 70th Ohio fired the first shots at the Louisianans. The Buckeyes blazed away at the 13th, 20th, and the 30th Louisiana directly opposing them and extending beyond their left flank. The Louisianans were the second group of attackers to strike them and the fourth wave of Confederates overall—all within one hour. Captain Louis Love was impressed at the tenacity of the Louisiana assault upon his company's line, reporting that it was attempted "with greater fury and numbers" than the Alabamans had placed on them. His perception was influenced more by the fact that the

Louisiana men were opposing the 70th Ohio more directly than did the Alabamans forty-five minutes earlier, whose assault was farther west and off the right-flank position.[13]

Lieutenant Colonel Thomas Shields commanded the 30th Louisiana Battalion on July 28. The curly-haired, clean-shaven commander had been born in Shieldsboro, Mississippi (a town founded by his ancestor), but he had lived in New Orleans for so much of his life to be considered a native.[14] Shields's battalion numbered 270 officers and men; all of them learned the harrowing consequence of marching through woods to strike an opposing line. "Unfortunately our line of battle was formed obliquely to that of the enemy," recalled one of the Southerners in the line, "with the result that the Thirtieth Louisiana, whose position in the line was near the extreme left, came first in contact with the enemy's works, which were located on the edge of the woods, concealed from our view, with an open field in their front." Major William Brown adeptly held his 70th Ohio's fire until the unsuspecting Louisianans were close enough in order to overwhelm them with destructive volleys. The order came when the 30th Louisiana marched within fifty yards of the Union position. Ohio bullets pierced the Louisianans unabated; some Confederates were struck four or five times by these aimed volleys. A member of the battalion revealed that "our men were actually mowed down without being able to do much injury to them, they [the Ohioans] being concealed by the thick underbrush in front of their works."[15]

Officers fell as quickly as did the privates. Within ten minutes, both regimental officers—Lieutenant Colonel Thomas Shields and Major Charles Bell—were shot dead. Leadership disintegrated with the loss of half a dozen company officers and close to one hundred men from this seven-company battalion. Still, the Southerners did not yield. The Louisianans got so close to the Buckeyes and their thigh-high earthworks that some were man-handled and hauled across as prisoners of war. "The fighting now became most terrific," noted a member of the 70th Ohio; "the enemy pushed forward under our destructive fire to within twenty-five paces of our lines and planted their colors."[16]

The flag of the 30th Louisiana Battalion became the focus of Union and Confederate soldiers around 12:30 P.M. on July 28. The flag was older than the standards designed by General Joseph E. Johnston and carried by most of the regiments. The 30th Louisiana was still distinguished by a flag issued from the Department of Alabama, Mississippi, and East Tennessee, which consisted of a red background bordered in "buff moiré antique" (as described by a reporter), dominated by crossed blue-silk diagonal bars trimmed in white against a red background with the name "30th. LA. REG^t." in the center and four sets of three stars spoking from the identifying name.[17]

With the loss of so many officers in the regiment, killed so early in the charge, the flag itself now essentially held the regiment together as a rally point for the Louisianans. The flag—and anyone daring to carry it—became a target for the Union soldiers firing from twenty to thirty yards away. After a succession of Louisianans were gunned down attempting to haul it, a badly wounded corporal handed it off to the lieutenant of the color company, who temporarily centered his regiment around it before turning it over to Private William Dalton with instructions to save it at all hazards and, if necessary, to detach it from the staff and wrap it around his body to conceal it. At this time, according to a Confederate witness, "the color bearer and all the color guards were shot down; only six members of the color company and only three members on the left of the color company remained standing."[18]

A reserve Union regiment sealed the fate of the 30th Louisiana Battalion. The 46th Ohio was ordered to shift from its position between the 70th Ohio and 99th Indiana to the opposite (left) flank of the 70th Ohio. This they did by hustling behind their fellow Buckeyes and extending the southeast flank of Harrow's division line. Several companies of the 46th Ohio were armed with "murderous Spencer six-shooting rifles" (as defined by one of the Louisianans; the rifle actually could fire seven uninterrupted rounds). The combination of position and enhanced firepower put an end to the left flank of Gibson's Louisiana brigade in just ten minutes. When the dust cleared in this sector, nearly two hundred members of the regiment were killed, wounded, or captured. Although the 70th Ohio was responsible for shooting down most of the officers, soldiers, and multiple flag bearers of the 30th Louisiana, the 46th Ohio would receive the credit for

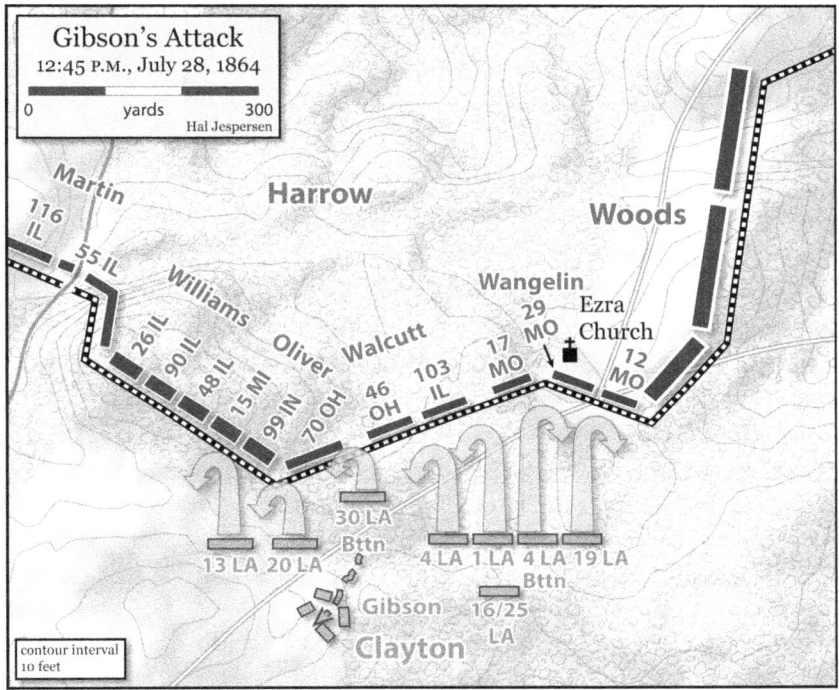

seizing the grand prize when Private Harry Davis watched the final Louisiana flag bearer (either William Dalton or the man who succeeded him) fall with his colors. Davis immediately rushed out twenty-five yards, gripped the standard, and raced back to his position greeted by cheers from his regiment. (Davis received the Congressional Medal of Honor for this feat.)[19]

The 30th Louisiana Battalion, which had boasted a strength of more than eight hundred soldiers as a regiment as late as 1862, but which was already reduced to 270 officers and men on the eve of this battle at Ezra Church, now consisted of no more than a couple of companies, having lost more than two hundred officers and men. Every member of the color guard had been shot down. Both regimental officers—Shields and Bell—were killed, as were twelve captains and lieutenants of the battalion. Only six officers and sixty soldiers stayed off the initial casualty list.[20]

The martyrdom of the 30th Louisiana commanded the utmost respect of its opponents. Major William B. Brown, the commander of the 70th Ohio, who would be killed in action six days after Ezra Church, was awed by their gallantry. He left a vivid impression in his final interview with a Cincinnati reporter that was published in newspapers throughout the country within a month of the battle: "Major Brown told me he saw the flag fall four different times and the last time there being none of its brave followers left to carry it off the field; and I must here say that the fighting of the enemy merits a better cause. They came up facing this regiment of ours, too proud and brave to be driven away by slight losses, but stood there, fighting to the last, scarcely enough to tell the sad tale to the remainder."[21]

The 30th Louisiana's annihilation was so swift—no more than twenty minutes from the first volley—that the battalion was unsalvageable by the time General Gibson galloped in from the rear to overtake his command. "On reaching the brigade I found the enemy posted in strong works," reported the brigadier, who also was there to witness the 46th Ohio and 103rd Illinois deployed to crush his brigade's left flank. Colonel von Zinken went down with a shattered hand and forearm. Dozens of soldiers in his tiny regiment could not help but be peppered by bullets from Oliver's brigade—"They mowed us down like grass," confessed a company officer of the 20th Louisiana in a private letter, himself crippled by a bullet in his knee. The consolidated companies of the 20th Louisiana withered to a total of twenty-four officers and men—the equivalent of one small Confederate company. The 13th Louisiana lost twenty-nine soldiers in the action, which reduced the regiment to fewer than one hundred officers and men. This destruction removed any continued threat by the Louisiana brigade against Oliver's brigade.[22]

Gibson's fight was not over, for the center and right of his brigade overlapped Brown's regiment and, for the first time in the battle, threatened a Union position other than the southeast-to-northwest line created by Harrow's and Morgan L. Smith's divisions of the XV Corps. Gibson had been with his men for mere minutes, but the Louisianans had already fought for more than a quarter of an hour without him. Walcutt's reserves had filled in the gap during the interval to finally connect with the right flank of the 29th Missouri of Wangelin's brigade. The additional Union soldiers and the solidified line guaranteed that the rest of Gibson's regiments would be taking severe casualties.

Indeed they did. The 4th, 16th/25th, and 19th Louisiana Infantry as well as the 4th Louisiana Battalion met pulsing volleys discharged from the guns of the Missouri, Illinois, and Ohio soldiers in front of them. An officer in Company A of the 4th Louisiana estimated that his company was "engaged with the enemy about one hour," but he must have included the time spent marching out to the Union defense and still appears to have overestimated Gibson's fight by fifteen minutes. Regardless, enough time was spent on the battlefield to result in the death or wounding of all but eight men in his company; the entire 4th Louisiana suffered sixty battle losses.[23]

Yankee bullets marred every regiment in Gibson's line as they approached within a hundred yards of the Union defenders. Like the 30th Louisiana Battalion on the Confederate left, the hardest-luck Louisiana force on the right was the 19th Louisiana Infantry, commanded this day by Colonel Richard W. Turner. Turner and his men found the woods in front of them as difficult to see through as they were to negotiate. "We that were in the ranks could see nothing," testified one soldier. The 19th Louisiana butted up against Missouri skirmishers from Wangelin's brigade who were scampering back to the brigade line west of Ezra Church. They notified Colonel Wangelin that they observed three lines of enemy troops coming toward them. Wangelin's men were better protected than the troops engaged west and north of his line. Their breastworks that had begun as church pews and knapsacks were now higher, as they had half an hour longer to prepare them and more material to use. Like the other brigadiers who had fought earlier, Wangelin ordered his men not to fire at the approaching Louisianans until they exited the woods and entered a clearing beginning eighty yards south of the Union works.[24]

If the skirmishers did view three lines, they may have been seeing a reserve regiment advancing with the 19th Louisiana and the two regiments advancing with it. Missouri defenders later insisted that they were harassed by Confederate artillery fire. One recalled "the shot and shell shrieking and crashing through the trees over our heads, and occasionally striking our works, covering with dirt those near." (This was likely enfilade fire from Captain James Hoskins's Mississippi battery at the southwest sector of Atlanta's ring of defense.) Wangelin's reserves—the 17th and 29th Missouri—had been deployed to the right (west) of the 12th Missouri; all three of these regiments were destined to receive the approach of Gibson's right. The skirmishers barely gave enough warning, but this sector of the field was quiet enough for the Missouri Unionists to hear the brush crackling beneath the shoes and bare feet of the approaching Confederates. "Within five minutes," noted John R. Tisdale of the 29th Missouri, "the storm was upon us, coming down the line from our right like a cyclone." Despite the sudden onrush, the surprised Yankees held their fire until the Louisianans had charged into the clearing less than fifty yards from the Missouri line. The first volley fired by the Missourians dropped more than sixty opponents at nearly point-blank range. A Union soldier observed, "Our men, resting their pieces on the top of the barricade, sent forth a continuous sheet of lead which cut down and shattered their front line."[25]

The bullets did not discriminate between officers and foot soldiers. Colonel Richard W. Turner of the 19th Louisiana went down with a bullet wound, likely in that opening volley. His lieutenant colonel was also struck down, as was the adjutant and the ensign. Major Duncan Buie was likewise injured while commanding the nearby 4th Louisiana Battalion. Unprepared captains were forced to take over these two units, while several other company commanders went down with their men.[26]

As the Louisianans prepared a second attempt at the Missouri breastworks, Union rifles mowed them down with unrelenting fury. The Southerners did succeed in forcing back Missouri reserves on the right of the brigade line. These men had no fortified works to protect them. As they retreated a short distance behind the main line, a gap developed and the flank was exposed. Major Philip H. Murphy of the 29th Missouri saw the opening and quickly attempted to close it before Gibson's men could take advantage. He notified his colonel of the problem, but before he could finish his verbal report, a minié ball struck him in the breast, passed through his lung, and exited his body between his shoulder blades. Stretcher bearers gathered up the fallen commander and swiftly rushed him rearward. Murphy survived his severe wound, but his Civil War career ended within view of Ezra Church at 1:00 P.M.[27]

General Gibson anticipated his inability to rout the Federals in front of him. As the right side of his brigade clashed with the bottom of the U-shaped defense, General Clayton rode up to inspect Gibson's progress, only to see that the left of the brigade was already gone. Gibson pleaded for support on his right, and Clayton responded that he would provide it. As the time passed 1:00 P.M., Gibson's Louisiana brigade was nearly wrecked. The 19th Louisiana lost all of its regimental officers and several company officers, along with more than one hundred gun-carrying soldiers. Only the consolidated 16th/25th Louisiana, likely marching in a second line, was spared from crippling losses.[28]

Recognizing that support would be slow to reach him because of the vast underbrush and woods behind him, General Gibson called off the attack. He pulled his men southward nearly 400 yards from the XV Corps defense line to where a ravine would assure his men shelter from small-arms fire. Left upon the battlefield were hundreds of Louisiana soldiers who fell dead or mortally wounded between 12:45 and 1:15 P.M. in the woods and fields south and southwest of Ezra Church. They died literally in heaps, still in their formed attack lines—a testament to the ferocious battle they waged within fifty yards of the Union line. Most of Gibson's wounded were carried, escorted, or dragged rearward. Only 763 unscathed soldiers stood in the protective ravine, an average of eleven men per company. Healthy Louisiana officers (lieutenants, captains, and regimental officers) numbered fewer than forty in all of Gibson's regiments and battalions. More than 500 members of Gibson's Louisiana brigade were gunned down in their most horrendous half hour of the entire war, with upwards of 100 more members missing from their commands. Such was the stunning result of a vicious thirty minutes that wrecked the brigade and forever weakened its identity as a fighting unit for the remainder of the war. An opposing soldier's tribute to the Louisianans was as noteworthy for its respect as for its verb tense: "No braver men ever lived than they."[29]

None of the four brigades of Brown's division lost even half as many men as did the Louisiana brigade. Gibson's total casualties and rate of loss (45 percent) exceeded any other brigade at this point of the battle. This destruction appeared preordained from the moment the brigade marched northward without Gibson at its helm. Although the original intent was for the Louisianans to fight in unison with the rest of Clayton's division—a goal that would have required perhaps just fifteen more minutes of preparation—their best opportunity for success would actually have been to initiate their attack half an hour earlier as the right-flank extension of Brown's division assault against Smith's and Harrow's divisions of Logan's corps. Gibson's approach—whether deliberately or by happenstance—was oblique to Brown's line of assault and could have at least temporarily overwhelmed Oliver's brigade flank with an east–west front simultaneously attacking with a southwest–northeast line. An earlier assault would also have exploited a yet-to-be-filled gap between the 70th Ohio and Wangelin's Missourians posted closer to the chapel.

Had Gibson's brigade isolated the two XV Corps divisions from the third division and from the other corps of Howard's army, a repeat of the rout achieved against the same troops by the same attackers six days earlier would have been possible, albeit remotely. The presence of Black Jack Logan, however, had already changed the character of the Union defenses, compared to the afternoon of July 22 when the same Union soldiers with much better protection and impressive artillery support were uprooted while Logan was away from this part of the battlefield as temporary commander of the army. Logan's inspirational leadership, displayed thrice in the first ninety minutes of battle at Ezra Church, as well as his experience and skill at feeding timely reinforcements into weakened segments of his battle line had produced a casualty disparity in two hours of battle that defied the expected ratio of casualties between an attacking force and a defending force.

At the two-hour mark of the battle, including skirmishing time, the XV Corps had suffered nearly three hundred battle losses on the defense. All of these casualties had been isolated to five brigades in Morgan Smith's and Harrow's divisions plus three Missouri regiments in Charles Woods's division, plus one regiment from the XVII Corps. Although by the standards of the 1864 campaign these losses were not considered severe, they were significant and can be attributed to a combination of tenacious Confederate assaults, weak and primitive barricades of defense, and lack of artillery support. Since Colonel Walcutt had deployed most of his reserve brigade to plug holes in the XV Corps line and extend its flanks, Logan could hardly count on these two divisions to withstand a new series of assaults without support from other brigades from the Army of the Tennessee.

Those assaults could not easily be generated from renewed action by Brown's division or Gibson's brigade. While Logan was losing three hundred prized soldiers defending against these assaults, five out of seven available brigades from Stephen D. Lee's corps as well as his cavalry skirmishers had lost 1,500 officers and men. The five-to-one ratio of casualties easily defied military doctrine that suggested a ratio closer to three-to-one in attackers versus defenders in action where the former dislodges the latter—a calculation assuming strong earthworks and artillery support, neither of which existed for the Union at Ezra Church. And in this case, the defenders were not dislodged, for a combination of several reasons: (1) the skill, experience, and leadership of the Union infantry of the XV Corps; (2) the absence of coordination of the Confederate attacks, which were not conducted in unison; and (3) the blinding woods that proved more disadvantageous to the assaulting force than to the entrenched defense.

In a mere ninety minutes the butcher's bill for the battle approached 1,800 men and boys. No one in the vicinity of Ezra Church at 1:15 P.M. on July 28, 1864, could possibly have appreciated the fact that neither the span of the contest nor its total casualties had yet to reach its halfway point.

7

Change of Plans

Notwithstanding the mauling of four Confederate brigades of General Lee's corps west and southwest of Ezra Church, Hood's newest corps commander had to this point attempted to comply exactly to the mission outlined prior to General Lee's departing for the battlefield at 10:30 A.M. that morning. The problem was the late start, for Lee was forced to act quickly and decisively, but also to act aggressively to seize the high ground above Lick Skillet Road that Hood defined as a necessity to "check" the enemy. The Confederates had sacrificed 1,500 killed and wounded soldiers in their ninety-minute failing effort to drive blue-clad soldiers off the Ezra Church line. Had Hood ordered Lee forward two hours earlier, 7,000 Confederate soldiers and perhaps a battery or two would be on those heights, facing north, and suffering more manageable losses even if subjected to constant attack by Howard's army. Even if Lee had departed one hour earlier than he did, at 9:30 A.M., he would have had a much better chance to seize the high ground and plant his troops atop it.

Despite the atrocious losses and Lee's inability to take the height, Hood's plan was still viable, for Lick Skillet Road and the first parallel height above it belonged to Lee, who could hold his position if no counter attack drove him away for the rest of the lit hours of the day. According to General Hood's battle plan from the previous afternoon, Stewart's corps, with an additional division attached to it, was the designated attacking force that would strike the right flank of the Union force threatening Lee and the road. The attack was scheduled for Friday, July 29, leaving the entire afternoon, evening, and early morning hours for Stewart to march 16,000 soldiers a total of four miles and organize them for the attack.

Stewart collected the three divisions of his corps at his designated post for July 28. They aggregated at the junction of Lick Skillet Road at the point where the Confederate earthworks that ringed the southwestern side of Atlanta crossed the roadbed. At this junction they stood one and a half miles southeast of Clayton's division on Lee's right, and one mile west of Hood's headquarters at the Thrasher house. Missing from Stewart's three-division force was the unnamed fourth division that Hood had intended to at least temporarily attach to Stewart for additional manpower to employ in the July 29 assault. The missing mystery division did not indicate dereliction on Hood's part; it may simply have indicated that Hood had yet to hand-pick the division that he would eventually hand off to Stewart sometime later that day.[1]

General Hood knew that Stewart had arrived at the spot designated by the previous day's instructions, but he was not completely aware of the magnitude of General Lee's battle with Sherman's advance troops near Ezra Church. Hood's imperative was to keep possession of Lick Skillet Road (he spelled that out again and again in dispatches to subordinates that afternoon). Hood was now under the impression that Lee could not meet that objective with the seven brigades under his control. In other words, Hood's battle plan had required Lee to hold Sherman in check throughout July 28; shortly after 12:30 P.M. it had become apparent to Hood that that part of the plan was no longer tenable.[2]

What happened next changed the course of the battle. Hood sent orders to General Stewart to reinforce General Lee with his corps to secure Lick Skillet Road. In so doing, he obliterated his two-day plan in the revised effort to keep the road. "The enemy was already in possession of a portion of the ground Lee desired to occupy," Hood later explained, "and the struggle grew to such dimensions that I sent General Stewart to his support." Hood later notified Lee by courier that "General Stewart has directions to support you fully."[3]

Hood swiftly and drastically changed his initial plan for this second battle in less than a week; in both instances the situation on the field required it. Six days earlier, during the Battle of

Atlanta, he worried about the lack of success by Hardee's flank attack against the Army of the Tennessee and grew increasingly concerned that Sherman would reinforce the resistance and turn the tables on the attackers. That day Hood's grand plan to roll up the enemy army from south to north and fuel the rout with his old corps (commanded by General Cheatham on July 22) no longer was viable. Hood issued a new order to Cheatham to attack the enemy in front to create a diversion to block the reinforcements he feared would arrive. What began as a grand, aggressive, and ambitious plan for David to defeat Goliath by surprising, uprooting, and panicking Sherman's entire department on July 22 swiftly transformed into a battle of one army against an equal-sized opponent. At 1:00 P.M. on July 28, Hood again demonstrated his ability and willingness to swiftly abandon a dying plan and replace it with one more immediately necessary and viable.

General Hood left no specifics about how the two undersized corps would operate against the Union threat west of Atlanta. No known evidence exists to indicate that Hood assigned Lee or Stewart as the nominal field commander once their troops united. Both lieutenant generals shared the same date of commission. Although Lee was more knowledgeable about the battlefield than Stewart (by two hours), Stewart was a practicing corps commander for a month and a half while Lee had commanded his corps for a mere day and a half. Hood's failure to designate an overall commander meant that he would have to arbitrate any serious conflicts between the two during the battle, but he did not venture from headquarters and left no impression that he would ride out to the battlefield at the time Stewart's troops reinforced Lee's.

Although Hood never divulged it, a growing concern independent of what Lee was facing kept Hood in Atlanta. An imminent threat to Atlanta's outer works had begun to materialize, which concerned Hood enough that he warned Hardee about it at 12:30 P.M. General Sherman would later admit that he was attempting exactly what Hood was worried about. Sherman sensed a thinning of the defensive line, although he was not specifically aware that Lee's two divisions left the works on July 27, followed by two divisions with General Stewart the following morning.

Hardee's subsequent shift late in the morning and early afternoon to stretch out five divisions where nine had existed twenty-four hours before apparently caught Sherman's eye, or someone else's who reported the observation to him. "I thought that Hood had greatly weakened his main lines inside of Atlanta, and accordingly sent repeated orders to Schofield and Thomas to make an attempt to break in," Sherman disclosed; "but both reported that they found the parapets very strong and full manned." (Stevenson's division suffered scores of casualties while manning those defenses.) Although Sherman would not press this issue, the attempts against the northeast and northwest sectors of Atlanta are likely the reason Hood remained in the city, rather than venture westward to oversee the battle.[4]

Sherman's newly applied pressure on these other two sectors threatening Atlanta likely forced Hood to alter his battle plan above and beyond the originally intended timetable at Ezra Church. Initially planning to send Stewart out with four divisions, Hood sensed that he could not spare the additional 4,000 troops, for that would leave Hardee with only three divisions to cover 180 degrees of works as a counter to Sherman's threat. Not only would the never-named fourth division not serve with Stewart, Sherman also determined to withhold French's division from Stewart's corps and keep it in the southwest sector where it had been positioned all along. This left only two divisions for Stewart. Hood gambled that the fight Lee had been waging would be decided by doubling the Confederate presence to the size of a large corps, unaware that Lee's attempt to take those heights away from the XV Corps defenders had already reduced Southern strength by the equivalent of two brigades.

Stewart's corps had united at Lick Skillet Road and the Confederate earthworks when Stewart received Hood's revised instructions. According to one of his division commanders, Stewart "parted from me to ride out on the Lick Skillet road." The reason for Stewart's departure, which coincided with the Louisianans' assault two miles northwest of his corps, was likely to confer with Lee, measure the progress of the battle, and determine the best use of his men.[5]

As Gibson's brigade was being mauled southwest of Ezra Church at 1:00 P.M., General Stephen D. Lee must have realized that his corps alone was not sufficient to remove the Union threat west of Atlanta. With five of his seven available brigades having been or currently committed to the fight, General Lee needed more than the two brigades remaining from Clayton's division to entertain any hopes of winning the battle.

Lee's attention to the battle in front of him was temporarily diverted by a galloping courier from General Hood who reined up and delivered a message written at noon. The hour-long delay in transferring Hood's orders to Lee was incomprehensible. General Hood's headquarters was less than three miles from the Poor House; therefore, any message between Hood and Lee should have reached its destination in under thirty minutes. In fact, a *walking* courier would have been able to leave Hood's headquarters and reach Lee in less time than it took this particular dispatch to transfer between the two generals. Hood enclosed a dispatch from Red Jackson, one that ostensibly warned of the presence of Union troops who could potentially threaten Hood's left. "If the enemy should make an assault upon our left," read the dispatch from Lee's adjutant, "the general directs you to strike him in flank." Despite being woefully outdated, the dispatch must have indicated to Lee that at the time Hood wrote the missive (noon), Lee was facing the front, not the flank, of the enemy force Hood wished him to attack.[6]

Lee first learned that Stewart would support him, not from Hood's headquarters courier, but directly from General Stewart, who rode up Lick Skillet Road into Lee's view, surrounded by his staff. Stewart conferred briefly with Lee, who described the situation in front of them and the consequences of the status quo. Lee finalized his arrangement with Stewart shortly after 1:00 P.M., with Stewart sending an aide back to his corps to order up the advanced division. Those troops from the new corps would not arrive near the Poor House and align for nearly another hour. When Lee learned of the fate of Gibson's Louisianans, he sought available troops within his two engaged divisions to commit or recommit to the fight. With General Clayton expected to deploy his other two brigades to the right or rear of where Gibson had deployed, Lee looked to Brown's nearly spent division.

All four of Brown's brigades had attacked the position held by Harrow's and Smith's divisions of the XV Corps for nearly an hour to open the battle. Throughout the half-hour span of

Gibson's attack, Brown's men had settled in their retreated positions to exchange fire with the Union troops on the ridge but dared not attack again. Lee sought to change that between 1:15 and 1:30 P.M. as Gibson's men receded from the ridge, brutalized, bloodied, and utterly beaten. Lee instructed General Brown to send a brigade up to attack again. The corps commander specified Manigault's brigade for the attack—the third attempt for the Alabamans and South Carolinians.

Manigault received the decision through one of General Brown's aides. "I could scarcely credit my senses," complained Manigault, who remembered it as a "repetition of the old order, again to attack and carry the height, alone, unsupported, after two failures, and with the command reduced to seven hundred men." Inwardly convinced of the futility and fatality of the order, Manigault dutifully set his troops in motion to form lines of battle. With the deployment under way, Manigault galloped over to General Brown for an explanation. Brown assured Manigault that the order was specifically General Lee's and not his. According to Manigault, Brown disapproved of the order and felt that Manigault's men could not accomplish any more this day. Manigault remembered Brown as appearing "much annoyed and excited as I turned to leave him."[7]

Trotting back to his brigade and assured of the pending doom that awaited it, Manigault was taken by surprise to hear his name called from behind by General Brown. He informed Manigault that he was withdrawing the orders. Manigault maintained that Brown intended to "abide by the consequences" of reversing General Lee's orders. The brigade was instead moved back along an old farm road safely tucked away from opposing fire. General Brown's stature was raised in Manigault's eyes for the decision, which wiped out any hard feelings that naturally would have existed because Brown had taken over the division reducing Manigault to his subordinate, despite the fact that Manigault outranked his division commander by date of commission.[8]

Manigault's faith was woefully misplaced. General Brown's battle report never hinted at the incident. Instead, Brown went out of his way to laud the other three brigades and singled out each of their commanders for their bravery under trying circumstances.

Not only did Brown pointedly omit Manigault's name from the officers to be praised for their performance, he also raised many eyebrows by dedicating one four-word sentence to their performance at Ezra Church: "Manigault's men behaved badly."[9]

General Lee later complained, "I found it difficult to rally Brown's division and move it against the enemy a second time." In fact, Manigault's and Toulmin's brigades had already conducted two charges. General Sharp claimed that his Mississippians attempted a second assault as well, admitting that he was unable to proceed as far as he did at noon when he struck the main Union line of defense. On the Confederate left, General Brantly revealed that he also received orders "to move forward and engage the enemy, which I did, but was unable to drive him." By this time Colonel Wells S. Jones's defensive alignment on Battle Hill was too formidable for General Brantly to do much more than tentatively approach it. All of these second efforts had been weakly attempted and aborted before Manigault's was called off.[10]

The Confederates' only advantage at this stage of the battle was artillery dominance, which they would have had with just one deployed cannon. Because no specific number or location has come to light, General Lee may have had only one or two batteries deployed behind the lines of Brown's division on the left and rear of Clayton's division. He also had enfilade cannon fire belched from the redoubt southwest of Atlanta. From these hillocks, Confederate gunners rained iron upon the XV Corps lines in an effort to soften the position. The Southerners generally fired unopposed, for General Howard in his first battle as an army commander had been unsuccessful at deploying any Army of the Tennessee cannons to return fire. Since Major Clemens Landgraeber's section of twelve-pounder Napoleons was withdrawn from the opening of the contest, no Union artillery could be accounted for over the next several hours of the contest. A Confederate general claimed Union guns were "feebly" engaged before 2:00 P.M., "either because their guns had not arrived, or they found much difficulty getting them in position." One injured Union artillerist was the only evidence of any participation by Northern batteries thus far in this contest. General Logan succinctly stated why in two curt sentences in his report; only the first one could be refuted: "The enemy used one battery of artillery. We used none whatever."[11]

Despite its huge advantage, the Southern artillery barrage was clearly not going to drive the Union infantry from the heights adjacent to Ezra Church. Lee needed to deploy troops to win the battle, but he made no overt effort to bring the rest of his corps out to the battlefield. This included one brigade (Abda Johnson's) from Clayton's division, but more significantly, one full division remained out of the contest. Brigadier General Carter Stevenson and the four brigades that comprised his division had begun the morning six miles from Ezra Church north of Atlanta near the Peachtree Creek battlefield. Although the largest of Lee's three divisions with more than 4,500 officers and men present for duty, it had underperformed throughout the Atlanta Campaign, particularly at Resaca, Kolb's Farm, and most recently at the Battle of Atlanta on July 22. Hood's decision to leave Stevenson's entire division behind when the rest of his corps moved out on Thursday morning appears to have been a deliberate one to simultaneously show strength in numbers in northern Atlanta while preventing weakness of performance west of Atlanta.[12]

Until Stewart's corps arrived, Lee had but two unengaged brigades remaining from Clayton's division to count on to attack a new part of the Union line and, if unable to rout the troops from their defense, to apply constant, withering pressure upon the Army of the Tennessee. Clayton's deployment had been inexplicably slow. His troops had been in position since 12:15 P.M., but only Gibson's brigade had been ready to do battle during the next hour, which it did with fearful results. Now with Gibson repulsed, General Clayton's other two brigades were ready to enter the fray, but their piecemeal deployment guaranteed failure. Clayton may have understood this and decided not to throw all of his available troops into the fight, but to comply with his orders he extended the battle line eastward. However, he would only commit one of his brigades and held the other in reserve.

General Clayton chose the Alabama troops of Brigadier General Alpheus Baker to fight. He held Colonel Bushrod Jones's brigade—also Alabamans—in reserve. Both brigades had been heavily engaged at the Battle of Atlanta the previous Friday, and both had suffered horrific losses east of the city in that great battle. Jones's brigade was reduced to fewer than 700 men from its fight at the Battle of Atlanta, while Baker's brigade carried at least 250 to 300 more soldiers. The disparity in brigade strength was the likely determinant as to which would advance and which would support. The decision at Ezra Church to commit one brigade and hold back the other proved to be a life-and-death matter. It is also apparent that the decision was changed after 1:00 P.M. At that time Jones's brigade was deployed in front and on the right of Gibson, with Baker nestled in reserve behind this intended attack line. General Clayton had actually ordered Jones's brigade forward at the commencement of the Louisiana assault against the southward-facing Union line; however, as soon as Clayton received Gibson's plea for support, he changed his mind. "I immediately ordered up Baker's brigade," he reported.[13]

Baker was thirty-six years old at the Battle of Ezra Church. A South Carolina native who moved to Alabama and served in that state's constitutional convention in 1861, Baker entered the war as a private; three years later he had risen by promotions to brigadier general, surviving capture at Island Number 10 (he was exchanged soon afterward) as well as a serious foot wound during the Vicksburg Campaign that took him out of action for thirty days. He was not in command at the Battle of Atlanta on July 22, a battle in which his Alabama troops put up an anemic fight, apparently reinforcing the brigade's maligned reputation. Rumors eventually circulated that Baker's brigade would be broken up and the regiments dispersed to the other brigades of Clayton's division. A member of this unit dared write what others were at least thinking: "The Brigade has a poor reputation and of course it reflects on the Brigade commander."[14]

Baker's regiments consisted of the 37th, 40th, 42nd, and 54th Alabama, an infantry force of nearly 1,000 officers and men. They rushed in on the right of Gibson's Louisianans as that brigade had fallen back toward the big bend in Lick Skillet Road at 1:30 P.M. For the first and only time in the battle, Confederate troops would attack directly toward and north of Ezra Church. With the exception of three regiments that exchanged fire with Gibson's Louisianans at this time, Union troops from Brigadier General Charles Woods's division of the XV Corps would engage in this contest for the first time to repel the Alabamans.

Woods's division was the most lightly engaged division at the Battle of Atlanta and was never considered numerically strong. One regiment, the 31st Iowa, was detached as train guards at Roswell. Two regimental commanders of Missouri regiments had taken sick in the middle of the month and had been replaced by their respective seconds in command. Making life more aggravating for the soldiers in this division was an incompetent ordnance officer whose failure to detect flawed shells had led to several division infantry suffering unexpected wounds from the premature explosions of these rounds.[15]

No Union artillery had been deployed to support Woods's division, matching the missing arm of war on the opposite side of the battlefield. Like all the Confederates who had attacked before him, General Baker would only face infantry as his Alabamans surged from southeast to northwest toward the untested line. Although the Union works in this region were likely more developed, Woods's brigades defended much flatter ground compared to the heights on which Harrow's and Morgan Smith's men deployed west of the chapel. A thicker body of woods somewhat shielded Baker's approach, although Union skirmishers provided ample warning to the Iowans, Missourians, and Ohioans in Woods's division. The Southerners spooked the fauna as they negotiated through the flora; animals scampered for cover with their habitats disrupted for the only time this day.

Baker's men struck north of the church where the left flank of Wangelin's brigade, Colonel Milo Smith's brigade, and Colonel James A. Williamson's brigade defended. Joining the primarily Iowa force was Theodore Davis, the sketch artist of the Atlanta Campaign working for *Harper's Weekly Illustrated Newspaper,* a very popular pictorial periodical in the North. Davis sketch of the eastern side of the field during the fight includes the only depiction of Ezra Church known to exist. His etching from behind the Iowans

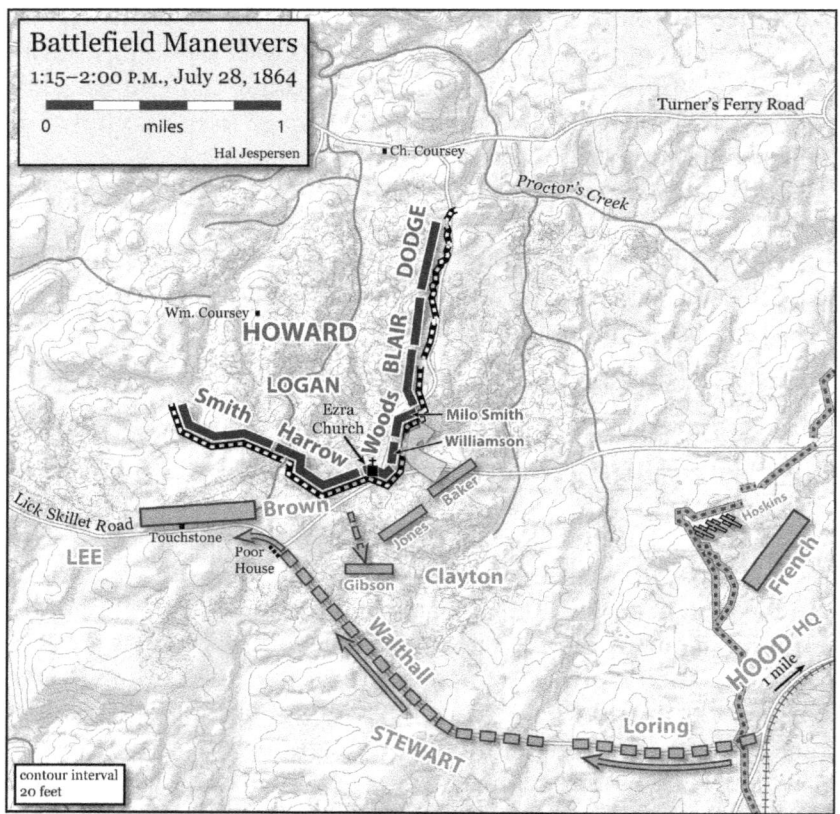

Copyright © 2016 University of Oklahoma Press

captured their volleys into the woods where a smoky line of Alabamans appeared within a hundred yards of the Union defense of log breastworks.[16]

Davis captured a couple of casualties on the Union side in his on-the-spot image. There would be many, many more. Baker's men struck hard, and Williamson and Milo Smith countervolleyed even harder. In about fifteen minutes, at least fifty Union soldiers went down with bullet wounds delivered by the skilled shooters in Baker's brigade. Eight members of the 9th Iowa Infantry were struck in the shoulder or above it, including their luckless colonel David Carskaddon, who survived a serious head wound and became the highest-ranking Union officer to succumb to enemy bullets in this battle. Three members of the neighboring 25th Iowa also went down with head wounds. These regiments occupied the right flank of their brigade; their commander, Colonel James A. Williamson, determined that the left flank of Baker's attack "did not extend farther than to a point opposite my right flank." Yet despite Williamson's claim, the rest of his brigade to the left of the 9th Iowa and Colonel Milo Smith's brigade that was deployed north of Williamson still somehow suffered two dozen casualties in those fifteen minutes.[17]

Baker's command suffered far worse under the withering fire of the westerners in the same quarter-hour interval. Baker received an undisclosed wound, one serious enough to pull him from the battle and the rest of the campaign. The wound was described as slight, but must have been severe. (At Champion Hill on May 16, 1863, Baker had suffered a broken bone on the instep of his foot and refused to leave his command for five more days.)[18] After Baker went down at Ezra Church, Colonel John Higley of the 40th Alabama slid into Baker's position as the ranking subordinate while Ezekiah S. Gulley resumed command of Higley's regiment as he had done in battle six days earlier.

Captains commanded half of Higley's regiments before this fight, and more would be called to ascend to regimental command during the battle. Captain Robert K. Wells of the 42nd Alabama died on the spot, replaced by Captain William B. Kendrick. As the Louisianans to his left had experienced, Higley's command was peppered by a hailstorm of Yankee lead. Missouri and Ohio bullets tore into the Alabamans mercilessly. Higley's command disintegrated, shredded by the loss of hundreds of men. Company B of the 40th Alabama lost both its lieutenants and more than ten privates to opposing small-arms fire. The 54th Alabama was hit particularly hard by the XV Corps troops surrounding Ezra Church. More than half of the members of this regiment were pierced by whizzing bullets. The flag attracted considerable Union fire, with forty bullets ripping into the silken standard.[19]

No exact casualty figures for the entire brigade have emerged; however, General Clayton claimed that the brigade lost half of its numbers in the failed assault. This would equate to a range of 450 to 500 officers and men killed, wounded, or missing in a fight that lasted no more than twenty minutes. Indeed, Clayton would later write that Baker was repulsed "in much less time" than Gibson, while surviving Alabamans characterized the assault as transpiring in mere minutes from start to finish. This rate of loss rivals or perhaps even exceeds the devastation suffered by Gibson's Louisianans on Baker's left half an hour before. One Alabaman summarized what he and his comrades experienced in those horrid minutes: "It was a terrible charge."[20]

Higley's defeated troops streamed rearward—many of them carrying and dragging the wounded of their ranks—between 1:30 and 1:45 P.M. The Alabamans were forced to leave more than seventy killed and mortally wounded comrades in front of Woods's division. No counterassault threatened them, but in this sector of the field, a Union battle cry was raised in tribute to the African American soldiers massacred by Confederate Major General Nathan Bedford Forrest near the Mississippi River the previous April. According to an Ohioan in the XVII Corps, he could hear the front-line troops "hallowing at the Rebels as they retreated 'Fort Pillow Fort Pillow.'"[21]

General Clayton worried that the huge void his repulsed brigades created would induce an immediate Union counterattack. He ordered his remaining brigade, the undermanned troops commanded by Colonel Bush Jones, to cover the area where Gibson's and Baker's brigades had just been forced to vacate the field. These Alabama regiments hustled into position behind the lip of the ridge line to stay out of view of Woods's and Harrow's XV Corps troops but within a quarter mile of them. While Jones's brigade covered their withdrawal, Higley's Alabamans fell back nearly to Lick Skillet Road. There they took stock of the atrocious losses they had endured. A member of the 40th Alabama remarked, "I can truthfully say that I never saw so many wounded men in the same length of time before."[22]

No counterassault commenced from the XV Corps as a distinct lull enveloped the field at 1:45 P.M. The respite would be short lived, for a fresh Confederate corps closed in upon the field from Atlanta. General Lee needed Stewart now more than ever. Six out of seven brigades from his two divisions had shed blood from more than 1,800 killed and wounded soldiers from his corps. Thus far, one out of every three of Lee's soldiers engaged in this battle had been struck by a bullet. Lee refused to acknowledge the sacrifice, remarking, rather, that if all his troops "had displayed equal spirit" to the XV Corps troops they faced, his corps would have been victorious. Lee believed that because "the enemy's works were slight," his force should have been able to prevail, adding, "besides they had scarcely gotten into position when we made the attack."[23]

Lee had spent six out of seven brigades in slightly under two hours by attacking the misshapen "U"-shaped Union line, striking the entire 2,500 yards of the XV Corps defense. Lee held Lick Skillet Road, but he must have appreciated now more than ever why Hood desired the heights currently owned by Logan's men. Unless the Union troops could be dislodged from those heights within a half mile of the road, Lee's defense of the road would be short lived, particularly if Union artillery could eventually be emplaced and sweep them away. "The enemy was still within easy range of the Lick Skillet road," assessed Lee regarding this point of the battle, "and I believed that he would yield before a vigorous attack."[24]

The pending attack from Stewart's corps would indeed be a vigorous one. The strength of the assault and the resolve of the Union defense would determine whether Lee's belief would be realized.

8

Walthall's Assault

After riding away from the battlefield during the morning's final hour, General Sherman passed the first two hours of the Battle of Ezra Church at headquarters. Elated to learn of the successful repulse of Hood's assaults, Sherman also took in the reports of the tenacity of the Confederates as they were seemingly unrelenting in their attack. Sherman exhibited more respect for Hood's infantry during July's closing week than he ever had before. "We have Atlanta close aboard as the Sailors say but it is a hard nut to handle," he admitted to his wife two days earlier, adding the chief reason why: "These fellows fight like Devils and Indians combined, and it calls for all my cunning & Strength." Sherman wished to add timely reinforcements to assure that Hood would not prevent his grand sweep to East Point. He also hoped to destroy a significant portion of Hood's infantry with a surprise flank attack.[1]

The closest and potentially most impactful troops at Sherman's disposal marched in unison as General Jefferson C. Davis's division, currently conducting a flank movement toward Turner's Ferry, about six miles northwest of Ezra Church. Sherman had sent the order for Davis's movement during the 9:00 A.M. hour, at least two hours before the battle began. Sherman galloped back to division headquarters, ostensibly to send one of Davis's staff officers out to order Davis to abort the Turner's Ferry mission and immediately come in on Howard's right flank by a more direct route. He was unpleasantly surprised to see Major General John Palmer, head of the XIV Corps, sitting on the front porch of General Davis's headquarters. Palmer informed Sherman that Davis was inside the house, too sick to lead his division's flank march that morning. Sherman learned then and there that the senior brigadier, James Morgan, had taken over the division at Davis's request and was completing the march to the ferry to comply with Sherman's midmorning directive.[2]

Sherman was incredulous that Davis was not with his division. Not accepting his illness as a legitimate excuse, Sherman paced the porch, chomping on a cigar and berating General Palmer. Learning from Palmer that Morgan had set out "some five hours ago," Sherman lamented, "I wish to God Davis was in charge of his division today." As Sherman later explained, "I attached great importance to the movement." Sherman was not only looking to Davis's men as reinforcements; he also saw them as the potential decisive force to roll up Hood's army with a surprise counterassault upon the Confederate left and rear.[3]

Sherman's rant began and ended on the front porch of headquarters, but the window to Davis's room was open; he heard it all. Shamed to respond, Davis rose from his sickbed, called for his servant to aid him in getting dressed, and stepped outside where his staff and his horse awaited him. Sherman witnessed the effect his mix of denunciation and plea had upon the Union-loyal Jefferson Davis: the ill general mounted his horse and rode away to overtake and hurry forward the movement.[4]

General Sherman had lost perception of time and distance, for even if Davis reached his division near Turner's Ferry as swiftly as possible, the time would be no earlier than 5:00 P.M. before the new movement could commence. The trip to the Union right at Ezra Church was six miles from the ferry, with would require at least two hours and force the attack to occur at dusk on July 28, provided no impediments obstructed Davis's new mission.[5]

Davis's ill health killed Sherman's plan. As Davis and his staff rode out on Turner's Ferry Road, Davis collapsed in his saddle, too sick and weak to go on. Aides escorted the ill commander back to his headquarters and placed him in his bed. An orderly carried orders out to Turner's Ferry for General Morgan to act upon. Before this incident occurred, Sherman returned to headquarters shortly after 2:00 P.M., oblivious to the futility of his effort to restore General Davis to his division by strength of will.[6]

By 2:00 P.M. General Lee's corps was virtually used up at Ezra Church, but the Confederate effort to win the battle was not. The vanguard of General Stewart's corps was up and aligning westward from the Poor House, the same staging ground where Brown's division of infantry had prepared and performed over the previous three hours. The leading division of this corps was the Alabama, Arkansas, Louisiana, and Mississippi infantrymen of Edward C. Walthall's division. The thirty-three-year-old Walthall, Virginia born but Mississippi bred, was a young star in Hood's army. He began the war as a lieutenant and escalated his rank and responsibility in three years to major general in charge of three brigades.[7]

Walthall's promotion transpired at the expense of one of his brigade commanders, Brigadier General James Cantey, who had led the division for months but was demoted in July as Walthall ascended to take his place. Cantey's frequent health problems likely influenced the decision to reduce his field responsibilities. He was sick again in the summer of 1864 and could not take the helm of his brigade at Ezra Church.[8] Colonel Edward A. O'Neal, the senior brigade officer, took over Cantey's brigade of Alabama and Mississippi regiments at the end of June and continued to lead them one month later on July 28, in O'Neal's third battle as a brigade commander.

O'Neal had led Walthall's advance westward from Atlanta, his men marching four abreast on Lick Skillet Road. When they reached the Poor House, the Southerners filed off into the fields west of the facility, nearly repeating the alignment of Brown's division three hours earlier. They formed the left of Walthall's division and aligned with the left flank on Lick Skillet Road at a point west of the big bend, near the Touchstone home. From left to right, O'Neal's alignment began on the left with the sharpshooter battalion, followed by the 29th, 26th, and 17th Alabama, with the 37th Mississippi taking up the right flank. Their line of march would carry them over the same path trod by the left side of Sharp's brigade of Brown's division.[9]

To O'Neal's right formed the rank and file commanded by Brigadier General Daniel H. Reynolds. Reynolds's command consisted of more than his five Arkansas regiments (two of them former mounted regiments), reduced by tough campaigning to four hundred gun-toting soldiers on the morning of July 28. He had two other commands attached to his command to bring his strength up to 1,000. A cavalry militia brigade of 450 dismounted Mississippi horsemen joined him, commanded by Colonel John McGuirk, in the absence of newly minted Brigadier General Samuel J. Gholson. In addition, a battalion of dismounted cavalry militia recruited from among mechanics of nearby Columbus, Georgia, swelled Reynolds's ranks by another 150. This battalion was commanded by Major E. H. Youngblood.[10]

With the additional reinforcements added to Reynolds's brigade, Walthall's strength exceeded 3,000 officers and men, two-thirds in a battle line that bisected the arc of Lick Skillet Road. General Walthall had Reynolds's troops thrown forward of O'Neal's men. In reserve behind O'Neal's brigade stood the Alabama and Tennessee regiments of Brigadier William A. Quarles's brigade. The troops did not stand very long. "The heat was almost intolerable," recalled Captain W. W. McMillan of the 17th Alabama; "the firing in our front was very heavy. We were ordered to lie down as the bullets were coming very thick, but as the line was in an open field with nothing to shield us from the burning rays of the sun, we suffered intensely from the heat, especially as we were fatigued by our previous rapid marching."[11]

As the time passed 2:00 P.M., Walthall received his orders from General Stewart to attack the enemy and "drive him to Ezra Church."[12] With two brigades of infantry in his front line stretched out for two-thirds of a mile in a double line of battle, Walthall's men advanced against the western side of the XV Corps line. Although they trod over the same footprints left by Brown's division, Walthall's front-line attackers faced a more formidable opponent. Ten new regiments occupied the line laid out by the original four brigades from Smith's and Harrow's divisions, all of them from XVI and XVII Corps brigades replacing worn-out regiments from the XV Corps. The infusion had occurred between 1:30 and 2:00 P.M., just before the new storm of Southern attackers from Stewart's corps rained upon them.

Three regiments from Harrow's harried division, the 97th and 99th Indiana and the 48th Illinois, were excused from the front line during the lull in action. The 13th Iowa from Giles Smith's division of the XVII Corps filled in the gap left by the two regiments of departing Hoosiers. Many in the 99th Indiana could no longer load their weapons—the barrels became so hot that the powder flashed the instant it was poured into them. According to a Hoosier diarist, "Just then the reserves came up, and if there was anyone pleased it was us. . . . Our men, almost exhausted, laid down and cooled and cleaned their guns." The rest of the 12th Indiana moved out from its reserve role in Williams's brigade, splitting up to occupy spare ground on each side of the 26th Illinois, ground made more open by the leftward shift of the 90th Illinois.[13]

Harrow's remaining six regiments welcomed the fresh infusion. Farther north and to their right, Morgan L. Smith's division had been worn down by seemingly relentless and vicious Southern assaults that began before noon. Regiments within Smith's ranks were spent. As the entire corps was deployed and most of it engaged, Logan had called for reinforcements from the XVII Corps of the Army of the Tennessee. The connection between the two corps was isolated to the fourth division of the XVII Corps—more specifically to its commander, Brigadier General Giles A. Smith.

Throughout the spring and early summer months of the Atlanta Campaign, Giles Smith had commanded a brigade within the XV Corps division commanded by his brother, Morgan L. Smith. He transferred to the XVII Corps exactly one week before the Battle of Ezra Church to replace a wounded division commander. He fought well with his new promotion the very next day at the Battle of Atlanta, but his division took more casualties than any other Union division on the field that day. Six days later Giles Smith had aligned his depleted ranks to the left of the first division of the XV Corps, north of Ezra Church. Ordered to send help to his brother before noon, he detached two regiments—the 15th Iowa Infantry, commanded by Colonel William Belknap; and the 32nd Ohio Infantry, led this day by Major Abraham M. Crumbecker—to reinforce Morgan L. Smith's division line. Belknap, three days from receiving a brigadier's star, commanded both XVII corps regiments on July 28, as Giles Smith and each of the brigades from which the two regiments originated remained in their line several hundred yards east of Morgan L. Smith's line.[14]

Colonel Belknap's two regiments had rested in reserve in woods behind Morgan Smith's division throughout the assault of Lee's corps against Smith's and Harrow's lines. Shortly before the renewal of the attack by Stewart's corps, Belknap sent the 32nd Ohio to the right (northwest) to lend support to Lightburn's brigade up on Battle Hill. Called upon for his regiment, Belknap led the 15th Iowa forward, nearly due west into the line occupied by both Martin's brigade and the left flank of Lightburn's brigade. Rather than add their numbers to the line, the 15th Iowa replaced a used-up regiment, the 6th Missouri. "Their faces were literally begrimed with powder and covered with perspiration," observed an Iowa soldier about the Missouri men; "and their muskets so hot from repeated firing they could scarcely handle them."[15]

Giles Smith also sent the three companies of the 3rd Iowa over to infuse Martin's brigade. Three more XVI Corps regiments also wedged into the line, relieving Ohio and Illinois regiments that had used up their energy and their gunpowder repelling three assaults from Brown's division. The 12th Illinois replaced the tiny but effective 30th Ohio. The 64th Illinois Infantry, another reinforcement from the XVI Corps, was armed with more than one type of weapon, but unique to the regiment was the fact that more than one hundred members carried a sixteen-shot Henry repeating rifle, able to fire its full chamber of rounds in the same time that two shots could be fired from a traditional single-shot rifle that the remainder of the regiment and most of the army carried. The special weapon was the brainchild of Governor Richard Yates of Illinois, and the unit was tagged with the name "Yates Sharpshooters." The 35th New Jersey, also from the XVI Corps, squeezed into the reinforced line, relieving the 111th Illinois, to complete the formation of a small hodgepodge brigade of reinforcements.[16]

Lightburn's brigade farther north and west on the ridge was desperate for support and reinforcements. The 12th Wisconsin remained with it on Battle Hill after its timely arrival from the XVII Corps to help repulse Brantly's Mississippians shortly after noon. However, the other XVII Corps regiment sent with the Badgers, the 31st Illinois (General Logan's original 1861 command), remained in reserve and never fired its guns on July 28.[17]

The greatest surprise of the ten reinforcing regiments to the XV Corps was the regiment not sent. This was the 66th Illinois Infantry, a XVI Corps regiment from Colonel Robert Adams's brigade of the Second Division. Nearly two hundred soldiers of the 66th Illinois carried sixteen-shot Henry repeating rifles and had fired these repeaters with great effectiveness in the great battle east of Atlanta on July 22. Curiously, while two other regiments from Adams's brigade, the 81st Ohio and the 12th Illinois, crossed over to the western side of the Ezra Church battlefield, the 66th remained idle several hundred yards northeast of the action. "We rested on the 28th," reported Captain William S. Boyd, commanding the 66th Illinois. The omission of this unit among the reinforcements indicates a lack of appreciation of the power of the repeating rifle by Generals Howard and Logan.[18]

To this point on July 28, Morgan L. Smith was nothing less than solid as a division chief, holding his line of defense against swarms of Southern soldiers. At 2:00 P.M., with tired men in line and fewer reinforcements than he felt comfortable with, Smith used the power of deception by shuffling his finite force to magnify its true numerical strength. Ordering all flags to remain protruding from the works, Smith countermarched the 15th Iowa and other new arrivals in an effort to deceive the Confederates into thinking that more reinforcements were strengthening the Union defense.[19]

If Walthall's attackers even observed Smith's ruse, no one in the Southern ranks ever commented upon it. O'Neal's and Reynolds's men cleared the woods several hundred yards from the Union line and attacked in unison, in the sixth and largest coordinated assault of the day. The totality of Confederate blows against the suboptimal defense was as impressive as it was brutal. The defense did not waver. The line of Union troops ahead of them was not optimally protected by earthworks, but the hasty entrenchments were stronger than they were when Brown's division attacked them earlier in the battle. Moreover, the line was stronger with the added firepower of upwards of 1,000 more soldiers than were in place there at noon, with at least one hundred of them armed with repeating rifles.

The XV Corps defenders from Morgan Smith's division welcomed the additional regiments as well as the replacement units.

The timing of their arrival could not have been more propitious for the Union. The guns of the 47th and 54th Ohio were so fouled with powder as to be totally ineffective and unsafe; at least one Buckeye was rendered hors de combat when his reload ignited and exploded in the barrel while he was ramming it. Unable to fire the choked-up weapons and unwilling to waste precious drinking water from their canteens to clean out the barrels, both Ohio regiments welcomed the relief force composed of the 81st Ohio from the XVI Corps. Then the XV Corps Buckeyes went to the rear and cleared their rifles of the excess powder by urinating down the barrels.[20]

The troops from Lightburn's and Martin's brigades were spent from repelling charge after Confederate charge in stifling heat, their guns were less reliable from all the gunpowder choking the barrels, and they still were not buttressed by artillery. They were, however, more confident than they had been two hours earlier, and they certainly were more prepared. The result was more men firing than before with a much higher percentage of their shots striking Southern targets than ever before.

O'Neal's troops on the Confederate left withered from the intensity of Union volleys. The Alabamans and Mississippians descended the declivity between their hill and the Union-held ridge ahead of them. A fusillade of small-arms fire prevented these Southerners from ascending Battle Hill. Martin's brigade blocked O'Neal's advance directly in front while the XVI and XVII Corps troops on the hill enjoyed a position to enfilade O'Neal on his right. Compared to Brantly's assault earlier in the afternoon, O'Neal's line of advance was three hundred yards south, more in line with the left flank of Sharp's (and Manigault's) attack against Martin's men. A blue-clad soldier was awestruck at the bravery and tenacity of the Southerners. Twenty years later he marveled at the "display as they took up their line of march down the hill, marching as coolly and deliberately as if they were going out on battalion or grand review, till they were fully half way up to the fence, when, from our fire, they commenced falling, being killed or wounded, but they never wavered, but closed up and came steadily on toward our works." An Ohioan concurred. "The slaughter was terrible," he wrote; "they seemed to melt like wax figures in the flame."[21]

Colonel O'Neal reported the resisting fire to his advance as "hot and galling." Most impressive—at least to soldiers outside the regiment—was the 35th New Jersey, the regiment that replaced the 111th Illinois in the middle of Martin's line. Distinctive in their colorful Zouave uniforms, the Jersey men stood out for something beyond their appearance: they were excellent combat soldiers. "They fought like Bull dogs," lauded a XV Corps soldier regarding these XVII Corps troops and their fighting ability at Ezra Church. The 111th Illinois could not see how stellar the 35th New Jersey was because they rested behind their Garden State replacements during O'Neal's assault, but they were experienced enough to use the sound of battle to gauge their effectiveness. One of the Illinois soldiers raved, "I do think they did the prettiest firing by volley that I ever heard."[22]

Bullets ripped men from O'Neal's ranks. Union soldiers spared no Confederate regiment, but they absolutely pummeled the luckless 17th Alabama positioned just inside O'Neal's left flank. Major Thomas J. Burnett was the acting colonel and took three hundred Alabamans into this fight. He was the only line officer in the regiment that necessitated two company commanders to assume the role of acting lieutenant colonel and major. Yankee volleys made quick work of Burnett, his acting regimental commanders, and several company commanders. Burnett survived the slaughter but was out of the fight with a bullet in his shoulder. A sergeant wrote three days later, "There were too many for us and they having breastworks on us too. We lost a great many men.... All our Officers was wounded." Noncommissioned officers and privates suffered severely as well. Bullets thudded into 115 officers and men of the 17th Alabama, with more than threescore more captured or missing. The regiment could claim only 120 healthy rank and file at the close of the action—aptly described as "a shocking affair" by one of its wounded captains.[23]

Colonel O'Neal believed the right wing of the 17th Alabama became detached from his brigade line, but what he was likely viewing was the remnant of the regiment. To the right of the Alabamans, the 37th Mississippi did lose contact as it marched into heavier brush than the other brigade regiments on the left. Cohesion evaporated and with his command thinned considerably, O'Neal and his regiments took shelter behind a fence lining one of the country paths. There they traded volleys with Martin's brigade soldiers in front of them and Lightburn's men on Battle Hill.[24]

O'Neal's ranks had dwindled from the slaughter they faced prior to their realignment at the fence line. The new position offered O'Neal's troops rudimentary protection—certainly improved from the open-field maelstrom they faced in the initial advance—but the colonel still watched officers and men fire and fall behind the mere strips of wood covering them.[25]

An instant target—at least an intended one—was General Walthall. Atop his dappled gray horse perhaps 250 yards from the Federal line of defense, the Confederate commander was conspicuous to the Union troops, particularly in front of the 15th Iowa. Walthall urged his men forward by waving his sword, grabbing as much attention from foe as from friend. "It seemed as if half the army were firing at the General," claimed an Iowan; "I took several shots at him myself, as fast as a musket could be loaded for me." Walthall somehow escaped unscathed. "It is not strange that I did not hit him," surmised the same soldier, "but I have often wondered how he escaped, as I learned, and his horse also did, unhurt, with all those sharpshooters after his scalp."[26]

Brigadier General Daniel H. Reynolds advanced nearly simultaneously with O'Neal, marching well to O'Neal's right. Reynolds began his advance with slightly more than 1,000 officers and men. Colonel McGuirk's dismounted cavalry brigade marched on Reynolds's left and closest to O'Neal's right flank. In Reynolds's center marched Major Youngblood's dismounted cavalry battalion, while the five Arkansas regiments of Reynolds's original brigade kept pace on the right by guiding leftward. Reynolds led his men over the same ground previously traversed by Johnston's (and subsequently Coltart's and Toulmin's) Alabama brigade to start the battle. They headed directly into the position manned by the brigades of Harrow's division.[27]

According to Captain John W. Lavender of the 4th Arkansas Infantry of Reynolds's brigade, "When our lines Entered the open Field some three Hundred yards from their works they opened a terrific Fire of Shells & Small arms on our line." The Union volleys tormented the Confederate rank and file mercilessly. Colonel Henry G. Bunn of the 4th Arkansas (Captain Lavender's commander) reeled from a minié ball that broke his arm. Bullets also penetrated both thighs of the very unfortunate colonel. Ordered to hold their fire, Reynolds's troops drove in Union skirmishers as they hustled into the open field at the double-quick. His Arkansas regiments on the right were characteristically reliable; McGuirk's Mississippians were surprisingly steady as they faced down hundreds of belching rifles when they entered the open field. The same was not true for Youngblood's battalion of 150 Georgians in the center of Reynolds's brigade line. This was their first battle experience, and most of them could not handle it. They fled upon the first fire. Reynolds acknowledged that, as a whole, Youngblood's men "did not behave with the coolness and courage of veterans," although several in his ranks "acted very gallantly."[28]

The Union troops in this sector of the line had not been opposed by Confederate soldiers for more than an hour, well after they effectively repulsed the right flank of Brown's division. Rested and reinforced, the bluecoats confidently steeled themselves for the renewed onslaught of butternuts. Still lacking in their defense were two prime ingredients universally deemed necessary in 1864 battles: full protective earthworks and artillery support. Two brigades of Harrow's division, Oliver's and Williams's, had fought for more than two hours in a cramped line of four hundred yards that must have reduced the frontage of the seven regiments to a battalion apiece. The necessity of terrain protection prevented the brigades from lengthening their lines. No more than five hundred soldiers squeezed into the front line. Behind them the rest of the two brigades stood ready either to pass them loaded guns and ammunition or to offer to replace them if a front-line soldier weakened or held a gunpowder-choked weapon.

The repeater-carrying soldiers were not alone in discharging an impressive number of rounds in this fight. Most of the other engaged Union regiments carried the standard issue Enfields or Springfields, which could fire up to three rounds per minute. By the time this battle ended, the 26th Illinois claimed to have expended 70,000 rounds—more than two hundred rounds per man engaged. A reasonable estimation puts the total of minié balls fired on July 28 by all of the engaged troops in Harrow's and Morgan Smith's divisions at more than one million, all from within a line barely one mile long. Walthall's new wave of attackers had been tasked with conquering a region where the air was teeming with incessant, whizzing bullets.[29]

The incredible rate of small-arms fire on the Union side created an unanticipated problem for the defenders. "What worried me most and caused the greatest fear on my part, was ammunition," recalled Colonel Reuben Williams concerning his brigade at Ezra Church. "Being a purely infantry fight," he continued, "the troops were using up ammunition at a rate that alarmed me." Intensifying his concern was the source of small arms ammunition. The last six boxes (each carrying 1,000 rounds and weighing one hundred pounds) were on their way to the front line, each box hauled by an unlucky detached soldier, one of whom fell prostrate from the effects of the weight of his load and the heat. No XV Corps ordnance wagons could be found to continue the supply. Williams spied a XVI Corps ordnance wagon train passing a half mile in his rear. The brigade commander was able to bypass corps protocol, procure two wagonloads of ammunition, and unload them amidst shrubbery right behind his brigade line to guarantee at least two more uninterrupted hours of small-arms fire.[30]

The adjustment behind Union lines meant the attackers were at a disadvantage. One would never have known this, however, from the intensity of their assault. Reynolds had wisely put Youngblood's men in the center of his brigade. This kept several skittish soldiers in the ranks and allowed files to swiftly close when most of the battalion bolted to the back. Reynolds commanded a charge and the rest pressed forward, nearly nine hundred strong, moving simultaneously with O'Neal's brigade north of them.

The Arkansans and Mississippians beelined across the field, charging right at Harrow's division, the most tired portion of the Union line, reinforced by only one regiment and one battalion. Reynolds struck with unabated fury, closing to within forty yards of the Union defense line. Reynolds worried that his flanks were unprotected, but fortunately for his assaulting lines, his left flank was also free from harassing enfilade fire. He also faced no companies armed with repeating weapons.

Reynolds's men failed to penetrate the defense, getting as close as thirty yards but no closer. Their strength in numbers at the launch of their assault dwindled by nearly a third in less than half an hour. The defenders' aim was accurate, but the Arkansans and Mississippians were firing too high, failing to exploit the skimpy protection in front of Harrow's soldiers that exposed most of their bodies to bullets. The disparity was telling. McGuirk's Mississippians forced two distinct charges, which melted his 450-man command down toward three hundred; conversely, the 13th Iowa opposing them lost fewer than ten men. The Arkansans on the right of the brigade lost 167 killed and wounded, including four out of five regimental commanders, while Oliver's command lost no officers and fewer than thirty men during Reynolds's assault. Reynolds claimed that his angle of assault exposed his right flank to enfilade fire, but no Union troops existed in this sector to support that claim. Regardless, Reynolds could do no more than drop back forty yards to a safer position. Starting with 1,000 men at 2:00 P.M., in forty-five minutes Reynolds's brigade had shrunk below six hundred officers and men—the equivalent of two normal-sized regiments.[31]

Like his division commander, General Daniel H. Reynolds escaped the battle unscathed, but his prized horse—Reynolds named him "Robert"—took his first battle wound. A bullet penetrated the horse's head a few inches above the left nostril. Reynolds successfully had the ball "cut out" of the horse's head, and the animal recovered quickly to carry the general through the rest of the campaign. Three weeks after the battle, Reynolds proved he was not the only one to consider "Robert" valuable. The horse was appraised for $3,800.[32]

As the time passed 2:45 P.M., Brigadier General William A. Quarles's brigade of Tennesseans and Alabamans entered the contest by filling the gap between O'Neal's and Reynolds's brigades. Stripped of two regiments, the 42nd and 49th Tennessee, to comply with General Walthall's order to support Captain Putnam Darden's Mississippi battery rolling into the advancing Confederate line, Quarles directed his remaining four regiments to rush upon General Reuben Williams's defense. Now all three of Williams's regiments were deployed—the 90th Illinois shifted to the left to replace the 48th Illinois, which had anchored the right flank of Oliver's brigade; the 12th Indiana moved from its reserve role to occupy the original space of the 90th Illinois, with four companies; and four other companies anchored the right flank of the 26th Illinois. The numerical strength of Williams's three regiments likely totaled no more than five hundred officers and men present for duty, partly due to the retirement of a portion of the 26th Illinois to clean out their guns in the rear.[33]

Quarles's four regiments did not outnumber the portion of the Union line he attacked. The long odds did nothing to deter the Southerners; they rushed forward with reckless ferocity. Having witnessed three separate assaults by Brown's division two hours earlier, Williams's men were amazed and appalled at the same time by the overwhelming presence of Quarles's Confederates. Lieutenant Colonel Robert Gillmore, perched atop a hillock with his 26th Illinois, called this attack "the most desperate assault of the day." It certainly impressed him more than the earlier failed attempts by brigades from Brown's division during the forenoon and noon hour, including Toulmin's attack that had penetrated the line to the right and left of him.

The lone consolidated regiment of Quarles's brigade exemplified the élan of the Confederate infantrymen at Ezra Church. The 46th/55th Tennessee, Quarles's old regiment, joined as a single fighting unit after the Port Hudson Campaign of 1863. Despite campaigning so heavily as to force consolidation, the regiment received the special thanks of the Confederate Congress for unanimously reenlisting for the duration of the war. They entered the Atlanta Campaign three weeks after it began and had escaped any more severe thinning of its ranks until this very day. Led by Lieutenant Colonel Joseph Dillard Wilson, the 46th/55th Tennessee carried 250 officers and men toward the right flank of Quarles's attack force and charged directly at the 26th Illinois and the 12th Indiana companies protecting each flank of the Prairie State regiment.[34]

Renting the air with a rebel yell, Lieutenant Colonel Wilson spurred his men toward the muzzles of several hundred Yankee rifles leveled and firing at them. The danger seemed to matter not at all to the Tennesseans. Those that carried guns fired them; those that had affixed their bayonets followed their metal spears

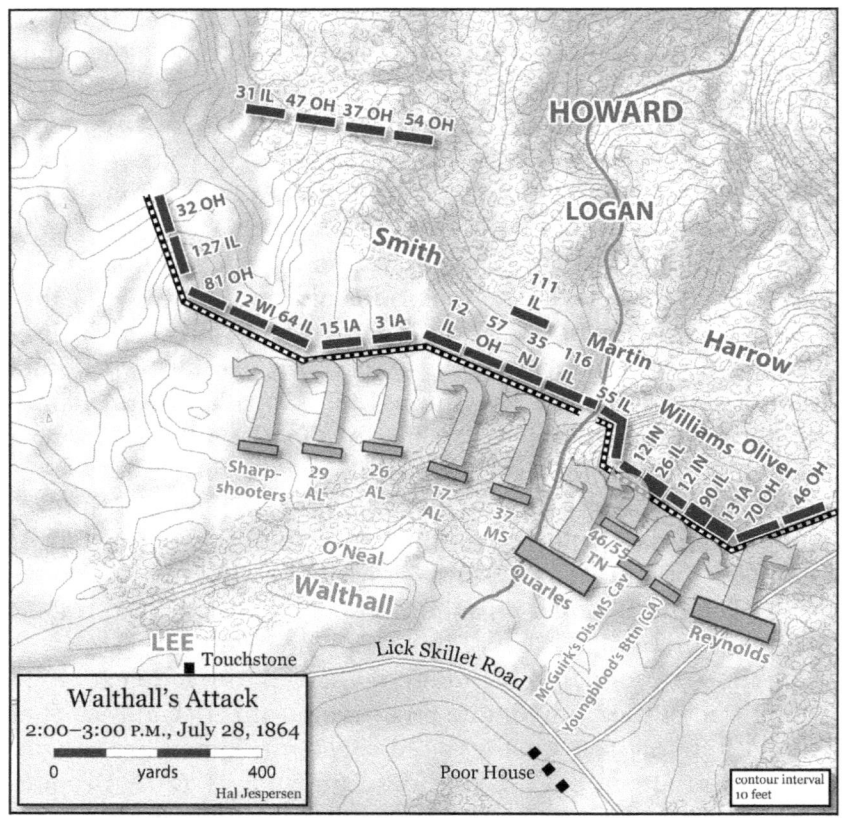

to the works. Much of the regiment charged to within ten paces of Williams's brigade, while several outpaced their mates and reached the short barricade, gunned down as they attempted to jump across.

The 46th/55th Tennessee flag bearers sacrificed life and limb in front of the works. Ensign Paul A. Sullivan was the first to fall with flag in hand. He survived—his successor did not. Captain W. S. Adams took the colors, and Illinois defenders took his life by sending at least twenty rounds into his body. Lieutenant James A. Hemphill, seized the flag from Adams and went down soon afterward with a bullet to the head. Sergeant William D. Wilson took the threatened flag and then took a bullet through his arm, which dropped him to the ground. "I saw their flag fall four times as they advanced in front of our line," confirmed a front-line soldier in the 26th Illinois; "but we . . . kept shooting them down so fast that they had to run back what few of them could get back."[35]

Union defenders crossed over to the west side of the works, prepared to meet the assailants in hand-to-hand combat. The next flag bearer of the 46th Tennessee (whose name is lost to history) turned the standard into a weapon—more precisely, the sharpened ornament adorning the top. He stabbed the top of his flagpole through one of the Illinois men, killing the soldier by impalement. Almost immediately a 26th Illinois comrade of the dead soldier sent a bullet into the brain of the flag bearer and felled him. The same Prairie State soldier jumped the barricade, retrieved the 46th Tennessee's flag, and vaulted back to his side of the wall with the prized colors.[36]

Scores of Tennesseans from Wilson's regiment buckled from the barrage. Lieutenant Colonel Wilson still refused to yield to the impossibility of the task before him, even after a minié ball found its mark in his body. Wounded enough to disrupt his momentum but not enough to maim him, the Tennessee officer remained at the head of his command, where he continued to urge on his rapidly depleting regiment. He stepped within arm's distance of the works of Company F of the 12th Indiana, one of four Hoosier companies protecting the right flank of the 26th Illinois. Wilson likely never perceived just how close he was. "There was perfect Clouds of smoke in the Air," observed a soldier in this sector.

Captain Sam Boughter of the 12th Indiana took advantage of the chaos. The Company F commander collared Wilson and yanked him over the knee-high works to complete the brigade's second prize capture from the 46th/55th Tennessee. Boughter pulled him in so strongly that the gold stars on each lapel of the lieutenant colonel's collar were yanked off; the captain kept the trophies as evidence of his work at Ezra Church. "He was the sulkiest prisoner that I have ever seen," maintained an observer to the aftermath of Wilson's capture, "and for more than half an hour he showered the most vindictive curses upon us, one and all."

General Quarles erroneously reported Wilson as killed in action. He was indeed out of the war, destined to spend the final year of the conflict at Johnson's Island prison on Lake Erie.[37]

The capture of Lieutenant Wilson and the unit's flag took away the leader and the rally point of the 46th/55th Tennessee, but their total casualties were enough to end their further effectiveness. By 3:00 P.M. those not killed or wounded fell back to escape the annihilating barrage of small-arms fire. "The field was as if hogs had been killed," remarked one of the Tennessee survivors to his parents. Six of ten regimental personnel were hit by bullets; only one hundred company officers and men escaped the slaughter pen physically unscathed. Colonel Gillmore reported that the 26th Illinois hauled in thirty-three wounded Southerners and twenty healthy prisoners. In addition to the captured flag, Gillmore remarked that his men successfully shot down the bearers of another standard in front of their position, but Confederates pulled away the fallen flag before the Illinois men had a chance to snare their third prize of the day.[38]

The regiments to the left of the 46th/55th Tennessee fared little better. They essentially retraced the steps of Sharp's Mississippians against the Union line manned by Martin's brigade, but their approach was on an angle more unfortunate for them. Whereas Sharp's Mississippians attacked in parallel line to their opponent, Quarles's assault was more perpendicular, as it angled in almost due east versus northeast by the Mississippians before them. This exposed the left flank of Quarles's advance to an enfilading fire by Union defenders. According to General Walthall, Quarles "made a bold and bloody assault, but his command was checked by the strong force in his front and the unopposed troops which lapped his left and poured into it a damaging flank fire." The 53rd Tennessee was wrecked in this battle. All three line officers were killed or wounded, leaving a captain in charge. The privates took a much greater toll of casualties both by numbers and by percentage. "We went in with 97 guns and came out with 27," tallied a Tennessee private, who was equally devastated that they were not able to carry their casualties back with them. "We was all very much grieved to leave them," he lamented.[39]

The lone regiment in Quarles's brigade not hailing from Tennessee was not spared any of the Union wrath. Captain Richard Williams took over the 1st Alabama after its lone line officer, Major Samuel L. Knox, was gunned down at the opening of Quarles's assault. The Alabamans lost scores of valuable gun-toting privates who found it impossible to press on. According to a surviving witness in the regiment, the Alabamans moved forward "with heads bent down as though breasting the cyclone, pressed onward, till Gen. Quarles, seeing that none could survive to reach the enemy's lines, gave the order to halt and fall back."[40] Another member of the regiment vividly recalled the harrowing experience of attempting to assault that Union line on July 28, 1864:

> We were ordered forward. Reaching the top of the hill on [Reynolds's] left, and now ourselves under heavy fire, we were ordered to double-quick. We charged over the level space, down the descent and steep hill into the slough. A few in their zeal started up the hill beyond the slough, but were ordered back. All were ordered to lie down; Many of our comrades were left dead or wounded behind us. [Reynolds's] brigade was not on our right as expected, nor did we again see anything of it during the battle. Two double lines of the enemy stood behind their breastworks in front. We waited half an hour for reinforcements and orders to advance. In the meanwhile the enemy were enfilading our position in the slough, and rapidly killing and wounding our men. While in this position lying on the ground John Reeves was on my left and between me and Lieut. A. Haley. The latter called my attention, and asked: "Isn't John killed?" I looked at Reeves. He had not changed his position on the ground or even, uttered a groan. Still, he was lying motionless and made no reply. A moment later I noticed the blood gushing from a wound in his head. He was dead.[41]

After barely thirty minutes of action, Quarles watched in horror as his command teetered on the verge of disintegration. More than five hundred soldiers, including twenty-nine regimental and company officers, were killed or wounded in front of the XV Corps. Lieutenant Ashton Johnson, Quarles's aide de camp, was killed as he attempted to direct one of the infantry regiments into the fight. Another aide, Polk G. Johnson, survived but was wounded and also lost his horse to enemy fire. Caught up in the furor of battle, Polk Johnson sought and received permission from Quarles to aide Yates's battery as it was wheeling close to Quarles's line.[42]

The batteries needed the volunteer help. The two regiments detached to support Darden's guns were not spared the devastation wrought upon Quarles's infantry; in fact, they lost more in the commissioned ranks than any other regiment in Quarles's attack line. The 49th Tennessee in particular suffered the loss of officers at Ezra Church in greater proportion than any other regiment in a battle throughout the Atlanta Campaign. It began when Colonel William F. Young went down from a bullet that shattered his right arm (the limb was subsequently amputated). Bullets wiped out Young's successor as well as the subsequent officer. Captains tried to ascend to the command of the 49th Tennessee only to be violently shot down one by one. The final unscathed captain who kept command of the regiment was Thomas H. Smith. This officer became the *seventh* man to lead the 49th Tennessee in thirty minutes of action.[43]

Quarles lost two horses shot out from under him during the short-lived assault. The general reeled from a wound but never disclosed the specifics. Seeking relief for his brigade, Quarles requested reinforcements from General Walthall, only to learn that every man in the division was already engaged. Neither advancing nor retiring without confirming orders, Quarles and the survivors of his brigade pulled back to take cover behind the crest of the adjacent ridge behind them to escape further depletion in numbers.[44] A survivor of this experience revealed how dangerous retreating was in front of such a devastating defense:

> The retreat, as usual, was more disastrous than the advance, because the fire of the enemy was more deliberate, and in consequence more accurate; and our men, now having to move up hill instead of down, and being hot and fatigued, required a longer time to recross the same space. The regi-

ment was re-formed on the same ground where it had been first formed for the battle, and again charged into the slough, being ordered as before to halt and lie down. The enemy was now sweeping the slough with a leaden tempest. Men were being killed and wounded faster than on the charge. After another half hour we were ordered to fall back, and were again exposed to a fearful fire. Forming again at the same place we charged the third time into the same slough, and the third time were ordered to halt and lie down in this ravine of destruction. Again, after half an hour we were ordered back. Almost completely exhausted by heat and exertion, we could scarcely walk. Many did not attempt it; but, resigned to their fate, awaited death or capture. Others, mastering all their strength and courage, began the retrograde movement in a slow walk back across the open space. The ravine and field were thickly strewn with the dead and wounded of the regiment.[45]

Without knowing the specifics of how Brown's division failed to seize and hold the high ground over the same line of advance, Walthall had grasped that his division-sized assault was meeting the same fate, despite conducting a more cohesive, and oftentimes more spirited, attack. "If it had not been for the daring of officers and the desperate fighting of the men to have overcome such odds in numbers and strength of position as we encountered . . . all along my whole line, the enemy must have been beaten," Walthall surmised, "but double the force could not have accomplished what my division was ordered to undertake." The cost for Walthall was atrocious: 1,152 total casualties, with one out of every eight of them a commissioned officer. His force reduced by more than a third of its effectives to fewer than 2,000 rank and file, Walthall's fleeting opportunity disappeared.[46]

9

Final Scene

Lieutenant General Alexander P. Stewart's first major decision on the Ezra Church battlefield was a disastrous one. By sending General Walthall's division on the same course of destruction that General Lee chose for Brown's division, Stewart assured little for the Confederates except a swollen casualty list. Walthall's division suffered the most of the three engaged divisions, raising Hood's losses on July 28 to 3,000 killed, wounded, or missing. Except for the briefest breach of the reinforced Army of the Tennessee line, the assault accomplished nothing.

Of the three division assaults, Walthall's was the most tactically puzzling, particularly since there was no consideration for any of three reasonable alternatives: to overwhelm the Union flank, to strike in a region not yet attempted, or to not attack at all. Stewart should have highly considered the latter option in particular, given what had happened to Lee over the previous two and a half hours over the same ground. Lee was certainly persuasive in directing Stewart to attack the same position where he had failed, but Lee did not outrank Stewart. Furthermore, no indication whatsoever points to Lee as the field commander when Stewart came to his aid. This leaves Stewart as the one responsible for Walthall attacking where he did.

Major General William Wing Loring's three brigades and Bush Jones's brigade from Clayton's division were the only fresh troops remaining from a severely strained Confederate force at Ezra Church. With Clayton's division pulled back to a reserve role, no attempt was made to call upon Jones's brigade to support Loring. More ominous for the Confederates was that Stewart had ordered up Loring to align on Lick Skillet Road directly behind Walthall's division at the waning moments of his spirited, but ultimately failed assault. Unless he designed to shift Loring's division eastward or westward, Stewart appeared to be preparing Loring's men to attack on the same path where two divisions had lost 2,000 soldiers.

Loring was a survivor, a trait that eventually would raise him to the senior Confederate major general on active field duty by the close of the war. His life almost ended seventeen years earlier during the Mexican-American War. At the Battle of Chapultepec, Loring's arm took so severe a wound as to require amputation. Loring survived the grievous injury, and he ordered that his severed limb be buried where he nearly died, with the hand pointing toward Mexico City. In the Civil War, the one-armed Loring's wintertime service with Major General Thomas J. "Stonewall" Jackson in 1862 required unique survival skills for a brigadier general—to escape court-martial charges by a superior officer. Not only did Loring endure Jackson's wrath, he was reassigned out of Jackson's district and promoted to major general. Serving in the Army of Mississippi in 1863, Loring avoided capture at Vicksburg and took control of the division that he led from that point onward.[1]

Loring had organized his three brigades and marched them behind Walthall's division prior to participating in Stewart's attack. Once Walthall's men aligned and charged toward the Federal defense line, Loring continued to shift his force to the left in an attempt to align on Lick Skillet Road west of the big bend where Lee and Walthall had launched their assaults. Loring's men remained in the roadbed when their general and his staff dismounted and walked down their line.

Major James Binford of the 15th Mississippi, a regiment in Brigadier General John Adams's brigade, did not waste time during the respite. He halted several Alabama stragglers from Brown's division who had attempted to flee the battlefield altogether rather than risk being sent back in to buttress the reinforcements. Binford collected enough information from the shirkers to determine they belonged to Lieutenant Colonel Toulmin's brigade, which had started the day under General Johnston before that commander was wounded in the first half hour of the battle.

(Earlier in the fight, before they reached the battlefield, Loring's men watched Johnston removed to Atlanta on a stretcher.) Binford and his Mississippians identified the soldiers by their brigade's official name—Dea's Brigade—and their reputation for retreating. Although the devastation they suffered in the opening volleys traded at Ezra Church, which took out two brigade officers and several regimental commanders, had justified their disorder, the stragglers simply reinforced their previous bad reputation.

As Loring and his staff walked past the 15th Mississippi, Major Binford reported to his general that he had several of "General Deas's racehorses" and asked what he should do with them. The disparaging name tickled Loring so much that he could not help but laugh aloud at what he considered the perfect epithet for these stragglers. According to Binford, "General Loring was much amused at the name I gave them and laughed quite heartily and was just in the act of giving me the instructions asked for, when he was shot in the breast." Loring dropped into the arms of Major Binford and Major Henry Robinson, the assistant adjutant general of the division. As they gently laid him down, Binford called for a litter bearer, then he opened the general's shirt to examine the wound.

The bullet that struck Loring was more likely a stray shot than an aimed one; regardless, its path was stopped by a Confederate division commander, the highest-ranking Southern officer injured in the Battle of Ezra Church and the second division commander to fall in eight days. Unlike General William H. T. Walker, who was killed on July 22, Loring was not fatally wounded. It penetrated the fleshy part of his breast, glanced to the left, and left his body from under the arm. "I was much gratified," confessed Binford after he examined the entrance and exit wound, discerning that the path rendered the injury "not being very serious." The wound was serious enough to remove Loring from the field for the rest of the Atlanta Campaign.[2]

As the ambulance corps carried General Loring safely to a rearward field hospital, chain of command immediately dictated an entire change for a division that had lost its commander. Brigadier General Winfield Scott Featherston, the ranking brigadier under Loring, ascended to division command. Featherston was experienced in this role, having commanded three brigades for a previous month of the campaign. His Mississippi brigade had no colonels still standing; most of them were rendered hors de combat at Peachtree Creek on July 20. Likely because of this, Featherston was forced to turn his brigade over to Colonel Robert Lowry of the 6th Mississippi in Brigadier General John Adams's brigade.[3]

Lieutenant General Stewart had been forced to hold Walthall's spent division in its advanced and still-exposed position until General Featherston completed the alignment that Loring began. Satisfied that Featherston had completed his first role as a division commander at Ezra Church, Stewart sent an aide to deliver withdrawal orders to Walthall at 3:30 P.M. After the messenger galloped away from him, the corps commander trotted into an open field, ostensibly to catch a glimpse of the Union line. The exposed position proved detrimental for Stewart. As he faced Logan's formation, a minié ball struck him in the forehead and knocked him from his saddle. Aides immediately carried him to the Fulton County Almshouse buildings to assess the severity of his injury.

Rarely is one considered lucky when shot in the head, but this characterization fit General Stewart in the waning afternoon hours of July 28, 1864. The bullet must have hit him a glancing blow rather than straight on. The result was a wound that etched a V-shaped mark below his hairline and above the bridge of his nose, but his skull was not penetrated. He was initially knocked senseless and subsequently blinded by his own blood. Stewart could not lead troops in combat for three more weeks afterward.[4]

Stewart took his wound less than half an hour after Loring was knocked out of the fight. As the corps commander followed his division commander's route to the field hospital, General Walthall learned the fate of his superior and understood he now led Stewart's corps. Walthall notified General Quarles to take over his division and to withdraw it from the field. Rather than complete Stewart's orders to pull the division behind Featherston's aligned men, Walthall modified the orders and directed Quarles to reform on the left of Featherston's division. The time passed 3:45 P.M.

General Hood never left headquarters on July 28, a command decision so unlike what transpired during the July 22 battle east of Atlanta when he changed headquarters several times to place

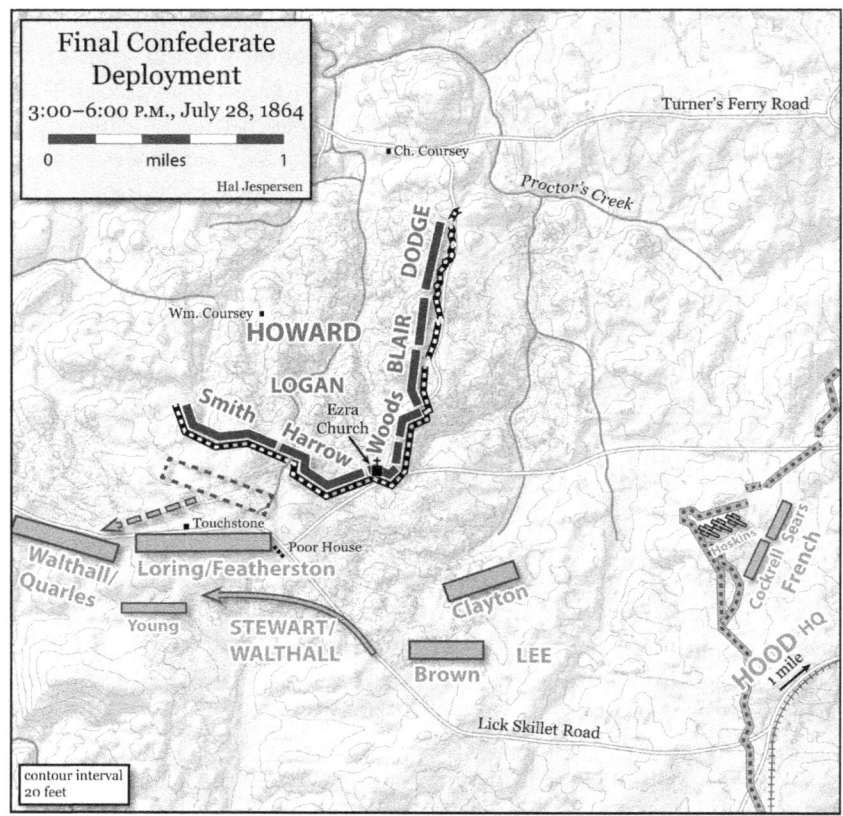

himself closer to the action. The passivity west of Atlanta six days later appears to have been deliberate as Hood called personnel in to meet with him at the Thrasher house throughout the afternoon. He trusted the reports he received, sending summaries out to primary commanders to keep them informed about the progress of action near Ezra Church.

Lieutenant General William J. Hardee was Hood's ranking subordinate commander, whose infantry corps was the only one without troops committed to the battlefield. Hardee represented the right of Hood's deployment with troops spread out to cover the threat posed by General Thomas and General Schofield north and northwest of Atlanta, cooperating with Stevenson's division (from Lee's corps) on the north and French's division (from Stewart's corps) to the northwest, all inside the ring of Confederate works surrounding Atlanta.

Sometime in the middle of the afternoon, Hardee received a message from Hood summoning him to headquarters "without delay." As Hardee and a knot of staff officers rode toward Whitehall Street, another message came from that direction, reinforcing the urgency for Hardee to ride in. Fifteen years after the fact, Thomas Benton Roy, Hardee's adjutant general, recalled, "I myself remember the successive couriers and the urgency manifested, and accompanied General Hardee to army headquarters."[5]

Hardee reached headquarters before 3:45 P.M. At 3:25 P.M. Hood had notified General Stewart that he could pull "a brigade or so" from Bate's division of Hardee's corps. Ten minutes later Hood's aide scribbled another message for Stewart to suggest that if he needed more men he could order them from General French's division. Since French was already subordinate to Stewart, the permission granted to Stewart to call upon his division commander stood as solid proof that Hood was responsible for withholding French's division from Stewart when Stewart left to reinforce Lee earlier that afternoon. A plan that initially had provided Stewart with four divisions was changed to cut that number by half.[6]

Hood sensed the urgency of the action at Ezra Church and was growing uneasy about the progress of the battle and the ability of his two corps commanders to complete their separate and joint objectives. Shortly after 4:00 P.M., Hood and Hardee learned that the situation had turned dire. "While I was with him," Hardee said of Hood, "news came that Stewart and Loring were wounded." Hood had no choice but to call upon the person he loathed more than any other in his army to save the day. Hardee reported that no sanguine news was coming in from Ezra Church. Apprehending "a serious disaster," Hardee reported that "General Hood there directed me to proceed to the field, and, if necessary, to assume command of the troops engaged."[7]

Merely one day before this battle, Lieutenant General Braxton Bragg had confided to President Davis, on Hood's behalf, that

Hood and Hardee could no longer work together: "There does not exist that cordiality and mutual confidence and support necessary." Now Hood needed Hardee to salvage something positive out of this battle, or at the least prevent any further catastrophe falling upon Hood's rapidly dwindling infantry. Hardee took no troops with him—only his staff. He departed toward the Poor House at approximately 4:30 P.M. A new flurry of dispatches left headquarters soon after. Hood reiterated his permission to draw from French's and Bate's divisions, seeming to identify General Walthall as the overall field commander and bypassing any known direct instructions to General Lee. He also reiterated that the army objective was "to hold the enemy in check." To General Cheatham, Hood announced that Stewart was wounded and he needed to "ride to headquarters," obviously to assume control of Stewart's corps as soon as possible. And to General Cleburne (Hardee's ranking subordinate after Cheatham), Hood advised him to be ready to move the division overnight and face the new and rising threat to Atlanta from the west.[8]

Before Hardee had even departed Hood's headquarters, General Walthall received Hood's permission to get a brigade from French and immediately acted on it. General French sent out General Ector's brigade, although Ector was out of action from a hideous leg wound received from the shelling on Wednesday, July 27. Colonel William H. Young led out the North Carolina and Texas regiments between 4:00 and 4:30, nearly the same time that Hardee trotted his horse out to the scene of action.[9]

Featherston's entire 4,000-man division deployed at 4:00 P.M., supported by Walthall's defeated troops (a division directly commanded by General Quarles on his left). Behind them (to the south) were the five used-up brigades of General Stephen D. Lee's corps. Young's men from French's division were still forty-five minutes away from adding 1,000 more fresh infantry to the Confederate line at Lick Skillet Road. General Cheatham was within an hour of being named Walthall's replacement as corps commander at Hood's headquarters, and General Hardee was riding toward the battlefield with orders to take over the entire force as the first designated field commander of the day.

The numerous changes in Confederate army, corps, and division command over the previous hour all but eliminated another mass assault against the Union defense. Featherston sent skirmishers into the area of his front. Departing the open areas of Lick Skillet Road, they penetrated the woods between the road and the Union line. Fortunately for the Confederate troops—both fresh and battle weary—the real estate they held was mainly out of range of small-arms fire from blue-clad Yankees, and surprisingly it was an area not raked by Union artillery fire throughout the entire day of battle.

Near Ezra Church, General Howard toiled to correct a major shortcoming for his army in this battle. The Battle of Ezra Church had been waged over four hours without Union artillery. Under normal circumstances artillery was essential to an army in battle, particularly on the defensive, but Howard's failure to deploy cannon after the only four guns in place to start the action were quickly forced off the field had not cost him any ground. It did, however, affect his ability to throw an effective long-range counterpunch to potentially force the Confederates entirely from the contested region. Never yet in the Civil War had an hours-long battle of 20,000 opposing troops been waged with so little artillery, and with all of it from one side.

As a second lull enveloped the battlefield at 4:00 P.M., General Howard reported having succeeded in placing twenty-six pieces of artillery on the army's right "to sweep the approaches in that direction." His claim is unsupported, however. The artillery did not hail from the XV Corps, the primary corps engaged, and no evidence exists from XVI and XVII corps batteries to confirm Howard's report. Unless cannon from the Army of the Cumberland was used (and no evidence supports this either), the artillery emplacement does not appear to have existed. If it had, it would have been quite a formidable position with more than two dozen cannon ensconced on an open height. It is a position mentioned by no one other than General Howard.[10]

General Howard sought help beyond artillery support. Constantly concerned that a renewed Confederate thrust would pierce his defensive lines, Howard had requested that Sherman send him reinforcements from Army of the Cumberland infantry. Sherman had put off the requests throughout the early afternoon, insisting that General Morgan's division would arrive from Turner's Ferry to smash into the unsuspecting Confederate right and simultaneously satisfy Howard's request for reinforcements. But by 4:00 P.M. Howard was certain those troops would not arrive (he was correct). He sent an aide to Sherman with a request to reinforce him with troops.

Morgan's troops from Turner's Ferry frustrated Sherman by their inability to reach the battlefield. Theirs was an ill-starred mission. General Morgan reached Turner's Ferry with his division shortly after noon, when the battle at Ezra Church had opened five miles east of him. After an hour's rest to feed them, Morgan sent his men marching again, following Sherman's orders to the letter except that he had no decent map to use. During the break, Morgan culled whatever directions he could from locals along the Chattahoochee River. Their directions proved reliable: one mile from the ferry the troops turned right at Mason's Church and accessed the road to East Point specified by General Sherman.

Before all of the mile-long column had gained the north–south road, the vanguard of Morgan's column met stiff resistance in the form of Brigadier General Lawrence "Sul" Ross's Texas brigade of cavalry. This was the second half of Red Jackson's division, sent out in the morning to picket the roads near the Chattahoochee. Ross had sent the 3rd Texas Cavalry to the Mason Church intersection. Lieutenant Colonel Jiles S. Boggess caught sight of Morgan's troops approaching and sent word back to General Ross, then Boggess pulled the 3rd Texas southward on the same road that Morgan's command turned onto. Ross sent the 9th Texas Legion to support the 3rd Texas. Together the two cavalry regiments exchanged fire with Morgan's advance less than eight hundred yards south of the church. Whether this was happenstance or by design, the point of contact between the two forces was ideal for the Confederates, for it impaired Morgan's ability to deploy with half of his men still on Turner's Ferry Road.

General Ross stood close to the village of Lick Skillet with the remaining two regiments of his brigade, less than three miles south of Morgan's division. At 3:00 P.M. Ross sent Red Jackson news of Morgan's approach and also relayed intelligence obtained from a recently captured XV Corps soldier (who must have fled westward from the battlefield and run into Ross's outpost). The news General Ross revealed confirmed exactly what Hood must have realized when he determined that Sherman was attempting to place a flank on Utoy Creek: "I have a prisoner who . . . says that three corps marched from their left last night and are now flanking around to strike the railroad this side of Atlanta."[11]

Morgan admitted that the Confederate cavalry were present in strong numbers and sound postings. Forced to deploy an entire regiment to sweep them away, Morgan marched southward. By 3:30 P.M. his entire division was on the same road and moving in the same direction, resisted by Ross's Texans the entire way. Morgan personally advanced with the head of the column when a courier overtook him—the same aide sent from Davis's headquarters right after Sherman's visit at 2:00 P.M. The message informed Morgan that Howard's army was under attack and ordered him to return to Turner's Ferry Road.

Morgan stood merely half a mile from Lick Skillet Road near its namesake village and three miles west of the unsuspecting Confederate left flank. He could have had his entire division exactly where Sherman wished it to be by 5:00 P.M. However, the orders specified that Morgan return northward to Turner's Ferry Road. As the time closed in on 5:00 P.M., Morgan and his division had turned eastward and then northward—completely away from the battlefield. By the time night fell upon the region, Morgan's division labored to close ranks in a suitable camp. Well aware they had wasted a day and accomplished nothing, the fatigued and furious troops hurled profanity-laden oaths throughout the night. Ironically, a message intended to shorten their route to aid Howard's flank actually suspended a mission that was destined to accomplish that very feat.[12]

Meanwhile, the Union defense line was not stagnant. Aware of the lull but unaware of the large body of skirmishers from Featherston's division advancing to end it, Captain Henry L. Phillips of the 70th Ohio, the acting assistant adjutant general of Oliver's brigade, rode up to his former regiment and declared, "Boys, it is our time to make a charge. You must cross over the works and go for them." Whoever heard the sentences interpreted them as orders from Colonel Oliver, the brigade commander, but Oliver never sent these orders through his assistant adjutant general or anyone else. Captain Phillips appears to have acted on his own volition—caught up in the excitement of the action.

An undetermined number of the 70th Ohio (anywhere between fifty and one hundred soldiers) followed the captain over the works and scurried into the woods south of them. They kept their formation but were moving alone; no other body from any other regiment latched on to these Ohioans. Less than half a mile later, the wayward Buckeyes could hear a booming, Southern-accented voice order unseen troops in front of them to "guide center" and "march." Captain Phillips instantly attempted to correct his error and ordered the Union advance to return to the works. They reversed steps and headed back northward to the protection of their defensive line.[13]

The only troops charging up to the reinforced Union lines were friendly ones. Captain Phillips and the 70th Ohio advance poured out of the woods below the works and raced to get back to their original places. The Buckeyes failed to outrun a volley of bullets delivered by Confederate skirmishers. Adams's Mississippi brigade wounded several Ohioans and killed Lieutenant John W. Krepp of Company I. Captain Phillips escaped any punishment or even criticism for his impetuous and fatal mistake.[14]

More skirmishing parties pushed forward from Harrow's division beginning at 5:00 P.M. The battle that had started with a roar was closing with a whimper as Walthall and Featherston declined to press the engagement with 4,000 soldiers against an opponent that had beaten back similar-sized assaults throughout the afternoon. Fortunately for Walthall, Hood's dispatches teemed with phrases favoring defense over offense—"hold the enemy, but not to do more fighting than necessary" and "hold the enemy in check" were contained in two of the most recent ones he received. Featherston's skirmishing from 4:00 P.M. was costly in itself, with 150 to 200 more casualties suffered by the Confederates after the wounding of Loring and Stewart, most of them in Featherston's brigades. One of Featherston's men expressed alarm at how harrowing their reserve role turned out to be: "subjected to a heavy fire, losing several of our men." There was no rhyme or reason to the losses. The 35th Alabama in Brigadier General Thomas M. Scott's brigade on Featherston's left tallied twenty-seven killed or wounded soldiers, while the 6th Mississippi acting as skirmishers for Brigadier General John Adams's brigade suffered considerably fewer losses (perhaps half as many).[15]

Young's brigade arrived on the Confederate side of the battlefield and eventually moved into a reserve position constructing breastworks behind Quarles's and Featherston's divisions. Young reported no casualty totals; he likely suffered several losses even though no regiment in his brigade fired its weapons on this battlefield. The rearward position proved unsafe, as evidenced by the torment endured by members of Guibor's Missouri battery, commanded by Lieutenant Aaron W. Harris and sent by General French to accompany Young's brigade into the battle. At least four Missourians were struck while moving into a rearward position. One minié ball severed the windpipe of an artillerist, sending the poor man into a frenzy. Several comrades held him down and helplessly watched him suffocate. "He died hard," lamented one of them.[16]

As a part of French's division, Young's brigade represented a portion of the fifth division to be involved in the Battle of Ezra Church; however, these troops never fired a weapon or suffered a casualty on July 28. Still, of the two Confederate corps intended to fight in this battle, only three of the five intended divisions arrived as a complete force (Brown's, Walthall's, and Loring's), one other (Clayton's) had two active brigades, and another (French's) had one. One complete division (Stevenson's) was deliberately kept from the field to man defenses with the remaining two brigades of French's division) and Hardee's entire corps.

Although Hardee's thirteen brigades were held in reserve, the lieutenant general arrived at the Poor House with instructions to command the remainder of the battle. Hardee confided to his wife that although Hood instructed him to "go out there and look after matters," once he arrived he "did not assume command." There was no longer any necessity to do so. "I found that Brown's, Walthall's and Clayton's divisions had been severely handled, and that Lee was acting strictly on the defensive."[17]

At 6:00 P.M. the Battle of Ezra Church had waned toward a quiet conclusion. Skirmish fire resonated as the only battle sounds. The last infantry assault had petered out two hours before, and artillery fire, particularly on the Union side, was eerily absent. On the Confederate side, French's division remained stationed at the outer works of Atlanta with Brigadier General Francis M. Cockrell's Missouri brigade and Brigadier General Claudius W. Sears's Mississippi brigade. They buttressed the six Napoleons and two three-inch ordnance rifles of Major George S. Storrs's Battalion, which consisted of the Alabama battery formerly commanded by the injured Captain Ward and a Mississippi battery commanded by Captain James A. Hoskins (the Missouri battery directed by Lieutenant Aaron W. Harris was detached to accompany Young's brigade to the battlefield). Since early afternoon, those guns had been firing toward the Union position near Ezra Church. As the evening hours settled in, French ordered Hoskins to continue to lay enfilading salvos upon the Union position.[18]

Sensing that the Confederates had punched themselves out and that it was too late to attempt a counterstrike, General Howard walked and rode all along the lines of his army; each regiment greeted him with three cheers as he passed by. The brand-new army commander and his tough army both acknowledged with the display that they had won a terrific and terrible battle. With relief and perhaps a little surprise, the Army of the Tennessee could instantly sense as the contest closed with the day that they had inflicted extraordinary casualties upon Hood's army and had done so without suffering grievous losses in a weaker defensive posture than they had enjoyed on the opposite side of Atlanta six days earlier.[19]

No additional troops would add to the numbers on either side before pitch darkness shadowed the region. "Our division remained all night on the battlefield and my company was placed near where most of the dead and wounded lay," remarked an Alabaman in Adams's brigade of Loring's division. These healthy Confederates spent an awful night listening to the groans of wounded and dying Southerners all around them.[20]

Major Thomas D. Maurice, the chief of artillery of the XV Corps, ordered hasty rifle pits constructed in front of Harrow's division where he emplaced two Napoleons of Battery F, 1st Illinois Light Artillery, under Captain Josiah H. Burton and four ten-pounder Parrotts of the 1st Iowa Light Artillery, commanded by Captain William H. Gay. As the guns were rolled into position to protect Harrow's division, the troops of Oliver's and Williams's brigades processed their wounded and then recorded the first tallies of the grim numbers of battle. Jesse Dozier of the 26th Illinois closed his diary entry for July 28 with an eye opener: "437 dead Rebels were gathered up in front of our Brigade." All the front-line troops garnered a good glimpse of the carnage of all those relentless Confederate assaults before darkness curtained the battlefield. "It beats all the sights I have ever seen," revealed one of Wangelin's Missourians near Ezra Church, claiming it exceeded the carnage of the larger, and recent Battle of Atlanta. A nearby Ohioan agreed wholeheartedly: "It is the most horrible sight I ever witnessed."[21]

Those Union troops who did not glimpse the macabre landscape before nightfall—a scene they created through nearly six hours of intense infantry fire—would take it all in the following morning. Nearly a third of the troops spent the night in the works, the rest in reserve—all ordered to lay upon their arms in order to fend off a potential night attack. Because campfires were disallowed, the victors dined on raw meat and hardtack for their late dinners. Regardless, the night served as a relief to the sweat-drenched soldiers from the swelter of a hot Georgia day and the incredible heat of a hotter Georgia battle. "Laid down and slept on the ground with wet clothes," an Ohio soldier scrawled in his diary the following day: "We were tired and hungry and sleep was sweet."[22]

10

Aftermath and Analysis

As night dropped its black curtain on Atlanta and on Ezra Church three miles west, General Hood sent his daily summary telegram to the Confederate War Department. "The enemy commenced extending his right about 8 this morning," began Hood, explaining that he ordered Stewart and Lee to hold Lick Skillet Road and that they had each departed with "a portion" of their respective corps. Hood mistakenly reported that the battle—he called it "a sharp engagement"—began at 1:30 P.M., about two hours later than its actual commencement. Hood informed the War Department that "no decided advantage to either side" resulted from the fight. "We still occupy the Lick Skillet road," Hood maintained, before revealing in his final statement on the battle that night that Stewart and Loring were both wounded.[1]

Except for the starting time of the battle, Hood's dispatch was factually accurate for the conditions on the night of July 28, at least based on what was presented to him at the time. Since Hood had not yet learned of the horrifying cost of the battle to his side, his claim that "no decided advantage" had been gained by either side applied more to the position of the opposing forces at the end of the fight compared to the start of it. The loss of a corps and division commander did not necessarily indicate a battle loss, particularly since Sherman claimed victory on the opposite side of Atlanta a week earlier, notwithstanding the death of a Union army commander. General Shoup, Hood's chief of staff, reinforced the view from headquarters in his journal entries for July 28. Shoup also believed the action had begun later than in fact it had—"at 1 P.M." when Sherman "massed a heavy force near Ezra Church," from which he "advanced with the purpose of driving us from Lick Skillet road." The "hot contest" that ensued lasted until nightfall and was favorable to the Confederates, he wrote, because "the enemy [was] repulsed and [our] position retained." Shoup's brief narrative left the impression that the battle occurred half a mile south of its actual site when a large body of Union troops, rather than one regiment, struck Lick Skillet Road and Lee counterassaulted, driving the enemy away and retaining the road.[2]

Hood, it seems, was not going to let darkness close this fight. That night, he fielded a message from General Hardee and responded to it ten minutes before midnight. "[Hood] also directs me to acknowledge the receipt of your communication of 10:45 P.M.," relayed Shoup from headquarters, "referring to the proposed night attack." Nothing more was ever reported about the night assault that never happened, leaving all details about it shrouded in mystery. Assuming the "proposed night attack" was a recommended Confederate offensive (and not a Union one about which Hardee was warning Hood), then the communication concerning an effort to coordinate an assault for the benefit of the Southern cause reveals a temporary détente in the animus brewing between Hardee and Hood.[3]

Both headquarters understood within hours of the final gunshot of the Battle of Ezra Church that the Confederates had sustained heavy losses. Red Jackson's cavalry returns would never materialize; if he had tallied his losses from the morning action, they would probably have ranged between fifty and one hundred dismounted horse soldiers. Fourteen infantry brigades from five Confederate divisions—upwards of 15,000 Confederate soldiers—were sent out on Lick Skillet Road on July 28. Two divisions sustained little or no loss at all. Loring's division, positioned in a reserve role at the road from 3:00 P.M. to the close of the fight, absorbed slightly more than the cavalry skirmishers, likely 150 to 200 officers and men (including Loring). Colonel Young's brigade suffered its only known official casualty the previous day when General Ector was struck by artillery. The last Confederate force to enter the battlefield on July 28, Young's brigade, was never engaged and reported no casualties for the day, but likely suffered some loss as evidenced by the casualties inflicted upon the artillerists moving with this brigade. All of the casualties from Loring's division were likely recovered and removed from the field overnight.

Except for the few hundred losses suffered by the cavalry and from Loring's division, the other three divisions—two from Lee's corps and one from Stewart's corps—took the brunt of the Confederate casualties at Ezra Church. Walthall's command absorbed the most of any division, with nearly 1,150 (152 officers and "nearly 1,000 men"). General Clayton engaged two of his three brigades in assaults; together, Gibson and Higley (after Baker was wounded) sustained between 900 and 1,000 casualties, with the reserve brigade under Bush Jones adding perhaps up to 100 more since it was within rifle range of the Union line. Brown's division from Lee's corps tallied 807 aggregate losses. Without exacting numbers, Hood's total sacrifice at Ezra Church ranged between 3,100 and 3,300 officers and men.

In sum, approximately 3,000 Confederate infantry losses hailed from nine brigades of 9,000 soldiers that launched attacks against the Union right, center, and left. The remaining 300 (maximum) casualties came from among either the cavalry or the 5,000 to 6,000 Confederates in 5 infantry brigades in reserve roles. Thus, 1 out of every 3 Confederate attackers became a casualty—and nearly all the killed and wounded were struck by bullets. And several hundred of them were necessarily left behind by their comrades who were forced to fall back to Lick Skillet Road without them.

Hood's army suffered appreciable losses on July 28 away from Ezra Church, resulting from Sherman's probes to ascertain the strength of Confederate defenses in Atlanta's northern sector. Not only was this cannonade likely responsible for holding Hood within Atlanta and preventing him from inspecting the Ezra Church battlefield, it also placed scores of Confederates on the casualty list. The 30th Alabama, for example, lost four killed and eight wounded (two mortally) on July 28, all victims of artillery fire from Thomas's and Schofield's batteries. If all the other regiments in Stevenson's division suffered nearly equally to the Alabamans, then upwards of 220 Confederates from that division were added to the casualty list that day. A more reasonable estimate lowers that total to half, but this does not include the still unaccounted losses suffered by Hardee's three divisions on July 28.[4]

Casualties from the Army of the Tennessee are more specific than for Hood's army for this battle. The three-corps army numbered little more than 20,000 rank and file on the morning of July 28; the XV Corps comprising almost half of the army, but fielding approximately 8,000 for the battle due to straggling and the limited space on the heights. Logan reported a loss of 562 from the XV Corps; however, the official list from the corps shows 50 killed, 445 wounded, and 45 missing soldiers for a total loss of 540 soldiers, all but one of them infantry. Dodge's XVI Corps regiments that helped repulse Walthall's attack suffered an additional 40 losses; and Blair's XVII Corps added anywhere from 20 to 40 more. Total Union losses did not exceed 620 officers and men and were likely closer to 600. Compared to the losses from the Battle of Atlanta, the Battle of Ezra Church was only one-sixth as costly to the Army of the Tennessee.[5]

The disparity of losses between the two armies and between the two battles failed to prevent the soldiers of Howard's army from considering Ezra Church one of their toughest battles of the entire war. Remarkable in the aftermath of this battle is the high regard in which the Union defenders held their beaten foe. An Ohio soldier lauded the victory to his hometown paper while describing the Southerners as "bold." Major Tom Taylor went further when he told his wife, "I never saw more stubborn assaults and more bloody repulses." His men were stationed on Battle Hill; however, his assessment matched other Union defenders at the other end of the Confederate attack line. "It was the toughest fight of the campaign," a member of the 103rd Illinois entered into his diary. No Union soldier derided the Confederate attack at Ezra Church (whereas, a negative characterization would become commonplace regarding the Battle of Jonesboro one month later). On the contrary, years of hindsight enhanced the respect and admiration of Army of Tennessee attackers by Army of the Tennessee defenders. "These Confederate charges never received due recognition and credit," argued John C. Arbuckle, a former private in the 4th Iowa Infantry regarding what he remembered about Ezra Church. "In every respect, they are worthy of being placed alongside of Pickett's deadly charge at Gettysburg. For the Confederate army, this was distinctly a day of reckless and unavailing sacrifice."[6]

Friday morning's light unveiled the result of that "reckless and unavailing sacrifice." "I never saw so many Rebels dead," remarked a member of the 103rd Illinois. "I never saw at Shiloh or any battle such slaughter of the enemy," observed Lieutenant Lyman U. Humphrey of the 76th Ohio. Major A. J. Seay of the 32nd Missouri concurred with his division mate upon walking the field early on July 29. "The most fearful slaughter I ever witnessed," entered the veteran in his diary; "The [enemy] lay dead in solid lines, many in shooting posture." An Ohioan admitted to his wife that he considered the Southern losses "truly sorrowful," due to the incredible number strewn upon the field. "I was over the battlefield this morning," relayed an Iowa soldier to his wife; "the dead rebels lie there all over the ground, a horribly sickening sight." Some made note of the number of bullets that had struck the bodies they observed. "On some of the dead was counted as many as forty bullet holes," claimed an Ohio colonel, while an Iowan came across what he thought was a wounded Confederate leaning against a tree—only to discover that the man was dead with five bullet holes in his chest.[7]

The infantrymen of the 70th Ohio were unofficially honored for the toughness of their struggle by the number of bodies in front of their position—probably all of them Louisianans from Gibson's brigade. Several witnesses came across the position of Lieutenant Colonel Thomas Shields of the 30th Louisiana Battalion. One of the earliest visitors to the field pinned an identifying note to the breast of Shields's uniform, claiming he was from Ohio, when in fact he was born and bred in Mississippi. Many of the early-morning battlefield visitors took note of the small pines cut down by rifle fire between the two lines. Captain Charles Dana Miller of the 76th Ohio made a most unusual observation of the impact of the rifle fire upon the flora and the horrid side effect of postbattle heat. "The growth of sassafras in this country was very luxuriant," he noted, "and here the bullets had so barked the trees and brush that it gave an odor to the surrounding atmosphere which, with the smell of the dead rapidly decomposing in the hot sun, produced a sickening sensation that I shall never forget." William Royal Oake of the 26th Iowa apparently forgot about the smell, but not the sight of what the bullets did to the vegetation. Nearly fifty years later Oake wrote, "During my three years of Service I don't think I ever saw a field where the timber and underbrush were cut down by bullets as it was at the battle of Ezra's Church."[8]

"Our men have been burying the dead all day," wrote Captain F. H. Magdeburg, the Wisconsin commander of Worden's Battalion, to his wife on July 29. Burial details of soldiers and African American pioneers found bodies already bloated and blackening, the decomposition accelerated by the intense heat. Using hooked poles, they dragged corpses by the clothes to a mass grave. "Their dead had to be buried in heaps and piles of a dozen, twenty, thirty, and forty, thrown promiscuously together," observed an Indiana soldier, who added that grave sites for the mass dead varied: "some in pits or holes, and some with mother earth thrown over them just as they were lying." Estimates of the number of buried Confederates varied wildly, although there was a serious attempt to get an accurate count. Higley's Alabamans lay dead in front of Woods's division; seventy-two were buried there (including a colonel, major, three lieutenants, ten sergeants, and sixty-two privates). Brigadier General William Harrow reported 273 bodies buried in front of his division late on July 29 and estimated 150 more still not interred. An Ohioan claimed the total official count was 879 bodies, but a member of the 55th Illinois scoffed at that figure. "Oh, you ought to [have] seen the long graves where our fellows deposited the bodies of the rebel dead," he wrote to a former company mate; "the boys said they buried 800 in front of our corps. I could have buried as many more."[9]

Although they did not always bury their vanquished opponents with the same dignity they expressed in their verbal tributes to the Confederates, the Federals showed more respect for their adversaries by marking the high tide of their advance. This honor was made possible because the Confederates were unable to pull their dead from the field at the point of contact with XV corpsmen. The Union soldiers buried their most respected CSA adversaries where they fell. This included Captain Sharp of the 44th Mississippi, and the unidentified intrepid color bearer of the 19th Alabama who was buried where he fell with the following inscription: "Here lies a rebel color bearer who planted his colors here."[10] The somewhat impromptu attempt to preserve the valor on a Civil War battlefield did not catch on with subsequent occupiers of the Ezra Church battlefield; the markers disappeared, ostensibly when the bodies were reinterred.

The XV Corps soldiers remained entrenched near the rebel bodies they had buried. The adjutant of the 99th Indiana wrote his mother, revealing the unpleasantness of a battlefield to the victors. "They are not all buried up," he admitted regarding the hastily dug Confederate graves, "but the arms of some, the heads and legs of others protrude from the ground, presenting a very disagreeable spectacle to one unaccustomed to it." The Hoosier could live with it for a very important reason: "It suits me, however, to know that they will not be again in our front." Another Indiana regiment, the 100th, missed the Battle of Ezra Church while on detached service in Marietta, but returned to the front to be greeted by the gruesome scene. The Hoosiers' first duty was to cover the bodies more thoroughly because—according to the regimental historian—the dead "had been so hastily buried that they had become very offensive." Colonel Reub Williams noted how relieved his brigade was to move southward from the Ezra Church battlefield to defend new ground: "The stench was more than a man with even the strongest constitution could stand." Captain Jacob Ritner of the 25th Iowa did not feel so fortunate when the brigade he was in also left the battlefield two days after the fight. "Our division [Woods's] moved back a short distance and are now lying in reserve," he informed his wife three days after the Battle of Ezra Church. "There are plenty of good springs near by. But we are so close to the battlefield of the 28th inst. that the smell is very disagreeable."[11]

Rampant rumors raced through the corps regarding an exchange that transpired between a captured Confederate major and one of his Union captors. Unkindly shown the carnage of his decomposing Southern brethren, one of the captors asked the captive how many men were left to defend Atlanta. "Enough for one or two more killings," came the drawled response. The rejoinder could be taken two antithetical ways. On the one hand, it demonstrated pure Confederate defiance. Knowing they had been smacked at Ezra Church in a casualty disparity reversing that at Kennesaw Mountain one month earlier but rarely ever before that for either side, Confederates trumpeted their demolition as a warning that they were willing to repeat Ezra Church—twice if necessary—to demonstrate their resolve to repel Northern invaders from Southern soil. That a version of this response had been uttered earlier in the war lends credence to this interpretation. On the other hand, the more accepted interpretation, from a Northern standpoint, was that the Confederates were admitting that the campaign as well as the war was coming to a close; there were not enough soldiers to protract it. Regardless of which interpretation was accepted, the anecdote quickly became an oft-told story associated with the immediate aftermath of Ezra Church.[12]

General Hood did not have much more than what the prisoner claimed the army had left. The loss of more than 3,000 officers and men in the fighting at Ezra Church was the culmination of eight days of heavy battles that bled out and removed by capture 12,000 Southern soldiers, more than 90 percent of them serving as infantry. Complete army returns were reported three days after Ezra Church, listing a present-for-duty strength of 51,793 rank and file—a far cry from a numerically strong army that topped off close to 77,000 seven weeks earlier. Misleading in this total was the heavy cavalry representation as present for duty within the Army of Tennessee. Hood's three infantry corps had suffered severely from those July battles as well as the eleven weeks of heavy campaigning that preceded. On July 31, 1864, a total of 38,722 infantry officers and men were listed as present for duty within the three corps of the army.[13] If militia forces were removed from that total, it dipped below 35,000 experienced soldiers—closer to 30,000 of them shouldering rifles. Not too many "killings" remained within those numbers.

Confederate brigade, division, and corps commanders assumed new roles almost immediately after Ezra Church. Major General Benjamin Franklin Cheatham ran Stewart's corps while that general convalesced, restoring General Walthall back to his division. General Brown transferred from Lee's corps to Cheatham's new corps in command of Loring's division, which put General Featherston back to his brigade. Hood bolstered his army the day after Ezra Church when Major General James Patton Anderson trained into Atlanta from Florida to resume division command in the Army of Tennessee. Hood sent him out the next day to take over

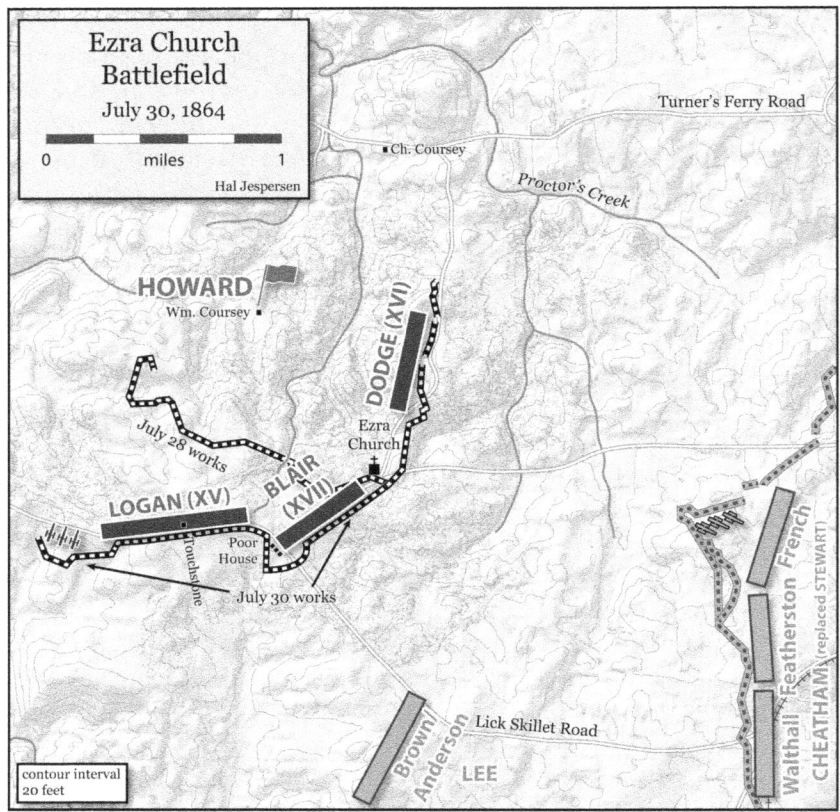

Brown's division of Lee's corps. "My division was on the right of Lee's Corps," Anderson reported, "my right resting on the Lick Skillet road, my left on Utoy Creek." Anderson's four brigades numbered only "about 2,800 bayonets." The new commander put his men to work night and day entrenching in their new position, eight hundred yards from Sherman's bluecoats.[14]

Lee's corps essentially occupied the position where Hood feared Sherman was aiming to reach had the Confederates not challenged him on July 28. A similar aftermath to the Battle of Atlanta transpired west of Atlanta. Sherman's rapid counterclockwise movement slowed down considerably at Ezra Church. On July 30 the XV and XVII Corps took up new positions along the bend of Lick Skillet Road. Three days later they were only able to creep an additional four hundred yards toward Atlanta. In the meantime Hood's infantry built a new line of works between the forks of Utoy Creek to thwart Sherman's chances of a quick railroad strike by his infantry.

Hood's July ended on a better note; Sherman's month ended miserably as a result of the Stoneman-McCook cavalry raid. The joint cavalry operation commenced simultaneously with Sherman's advance toward Ezra Church. The success of the raid required coordination between the two Union cavalry forces: the clockwise raiders led by Major General George Stoneman, and the counterclockwise-riding cavalry under Brigadier General Edward McCook. Both forces were expected to rendezvous at Lovejoy Station, a depot twenty-six miles down the Macon & Western line from Atlanta. McCook had crossed the Chattahoochee the day before the Ezra Church fight and swept southeastward, burning five hundred Confederate wagons and tearing up railroad tracks and telegraph lines near Palmetto. McCook reached Lovejoy's Station the morning of July 29, then proceeded to destroy railroad tracks while awaiting Stoneman's arrival from the east.

But Stoneman never came into view. Instead, Major General Joseph Wheeler closed in upon McCook and his division. By 2:00 P.M. McCook's three brigades retreated westward from Lovejoy Station in an effort to recross the Chattahoochee. Three brigades from Wheeler's force, which included the same Texans under Sul Ross that had harassed Morgan's division as it tried to reach the Union right at Ezra Church two days before, rode down McCook's men, surrounded them at Brown's Mill, and attacked them into disorder, successfully breaking up this portion of the raiding party.

McCook at least escaped; Stoneman fared much worse. While McCook was in the process of being routed on July 30, Stoneman and his 5,000 horse soldiers rode down to the outskirts of Macon, where they were turned away by Georgia militia, aided by General Joseph E. Johnston, who had been in the town for nearly two weeks after he was relieved from army command in Atlanta. With his momentum thwarted and his hopes of freeing the Andersonville prison completely dashed, Stoneman rode northward toward

Clinton but was stopped in his tracks by another of Wheeler's divisions, this one commanded by Brigadier General Alfred Iverson. Three days after the Battle of Ezra Church, Iverson reversed Confederate fortunes at Sunshine Church, capturing Stoneman and six hundred cavalrymen while killing, wounding, or dispersing the rest of his raiders. Sherman's great cavalry raid to destroy Hood's remaining railroads turned into a fiasco.[15]

By the first week of August, and within eight days of Ezra Church, no quick Union thrust to the railroad was possible, either by infantry or by cavalry. Sherman began resorting to siege tactics as the civilian populace read about the Battle of Ezra Church for the first time in their local newspapers. The most detailed and widely circulating account was provided by the *Cincinnati Daily Commercial,* which had a reporter traveling with the Army of the Tennessee. Published under the subtitle "The Third Battle before Atlanta, July 28," the front-page report was printed on August 5, with smaller papers reproducing the piece over the next two weeks. The *Chicago Tribune* also heralded Ezra Church under the front-page headline "The Great Victory of General Logan," published two weeks after the battle, which helped keep Ezra Church in the news well into August.[16]

Newspaper reports and soldiers' letters published in newspapers brought word of the fighting at Ezra Church to the public before the opposing war departments did. The Battle of Ezra Church, like every other Civil War battle before it, required official reports by its key participants to help determine the decisions and actions responsible for the Union victory and the Confederate defeat. Since he never set foot on the battlefield or even came closer than two miles from it the entire day of July 28, General Hood's official report relied more on subordinates' reports than any other battle he had ever waged or been involved with. Neither of Hood's primary two subordinates in the battle, General Lee and General Stewart, compiled an immediate report of this one-day battle; instead they, like Hood, were ostensibly permitted to wait to include the battle as part of a five-week report of the campaign.

General Hood must have fielded at least a verbal report from each of his two corps commanders, as well as from General Walthall, who replaced Stewart after the latter's incapacitation on the battlefield. If Lee's verbal report to Hood was consistent with his writing several months later, he painted a misleading picture of the battle to his commanding general. Lee portrayed his corps as lacking spirit in their assaults against the XV Corps. Maintaining that he primarily faced two corps rather than two divisions, Lee acknowledged that his men's first attack against the works was repulsed "with considerable loss." However, Lee's portrayal of the second attack was less charitable. He maintained that the casualties incurred in this attack were primarily due to "the failure in attack" of two brigades of Brown's division and an undetermined portion of Clayton's division. Lee heaped more credit than he should have upon himself for directing the location of Walthall's attack and fabricated a cohesiveness of his two divisions by asserting that Clayton's men attacked "about ten minutes after Brown's advance" when, in reality, Gibson's Louisianans inaugurated Clayton's assault nearly half an hour after Brown initiated his attack.[17]

Lee's analysis was formed largely by personal observation, but he also was influenced by General Brown, who wrote out his report of July 28 and submitted it just three days after the battle—even before he fielded any of his four brigade reports. General Lee clearly followed Brown's assessment that two of his four brigades "acted with great gallantry": Sharp's and Brantly's. (Ironically, Brantly would admit the shortcomings within his attack when he filed his report to Brown's assistant adjutant general.) Brown went on to laud "the major portion" of Johnston's brigade although he misidentified Colonel Hart as succeeding Coltart as the third commander of the brigade; in fact, Hart was wounded before Coltart while in charge of the 22nd Alabama, a fact Colonel Harry Toulmin, the brigade's final commander, delineated in the brigade report he submitted three days after Brown wrote his version.[18]

This left a scapegoat for Brown and for Lee to isolate for the failure to drive away the XV Corps from its threatening position overlooking Lick Skillet Road. General Manigault and his five regiments of Alabama and South Carolina infantry were blamed by General Brown in no uncertain terms: "the greater portion of Manigault's brigade behaved badly." Considering that Manigault had the reserve brigade and still took nearly a quarter of the division's casualties, including one officer for every seven men who went down, he and his men were a most meddlesome mark for Generals Brown and Lee to blame for the failure on July 28. Further rubbing salt in Manigault's wound was the likelihood that, according to Manigault, General Brown rescinded Lee's order for Manigault to make a forlorn third attempt at the impenetrable enemy line in front of him—a contention opposite to Brown's report, in which he faults Manigault for not attacking the line.[19]

The soldiers of Lee's corps were unhappy and unimpressed with their new corps commander. "The soldiers do not like him at all," confessed an Alabaman to his wife. "Very few have any confidence in him as a Commander. . . . He attributes all the blame of defeat to the troops and they to him. We certainly need another Corps commander. The men will never fight with any degree of confidence so long as he is in command." A Louisianan took issue with Lee's criticism of their performance at Ezra Church in a post-battle speech. "This is what he felt . . . ," the soldier explained, "but he was not in the charge on foot with a musket when our men were forced back. . . . He certainly had no more at stake than the rest of us." General Clayton revealed that the troops of his division had never felt as demoralized as they did in the aftermath of participating in the attacks at Ezra Church, but they believed the battle was the culmination of two failed assaults in six days under two different corps commanders. Clayton wrote his wife that the troops were "very much depressed after the battles of the 22d and 28th."[20]

General Hardee echoed those sentiments based on his own observations. Several months after the battle, Hardee bristled at Hood's deception that Ezra Church was not the utter failure that Hardee perceived it to be. Hardee insisted that "it was well known throughout the army that so great was the loss of men, organization, and morale in that engagement that no action of the campaign probably did so much to demoralize and dishearten the troops engaged in it." Although Hardee's animus against Hood steered his blistering commentary, his assessment not only agreed with others in the know; it also was borne out in subsequent weeks of the Atlanta Campaign.[21]

General Hood appeared to escape criticism in the immediate aftermath of the battle, but the outcome of the campaign was less sanguine for the Confederates. "Gen. Hood is fast gaining the confidence of the army & all are satisfied that we are done falling back," claimed the hopeful Newton Davis just three days after Ezra Church. South Carolinian William Elliott concurred with the Alabaman regarding Hood, but disagreed about the Confederates' prospects. "My private opinion is—you must not mention it to any one—that Gen. Hood was put in command too late," confided Elliott to his wife. "In other words that the mischief had already been done and consequently that Atlanta will go up."[22] "This is the third time in eight days we assaulted their works," summarized a Mississippian to his wife the day after the Ezra Church fight. "Hood does not permit the army to be idle, lively times are looked for under his management. This is the 90th day of the campaign, and I hope tho I fear not, that it will be terminated before it reaches its 100th." A South Carolina surgeon was more demonstrative for his desire to close the campaign when he wailed: "When is this horrible drama of blood & carnage to come to an end?"[23]

Ezra Church buoyed the spirits of the Union soldiers fighting for Atlanta. Many had sensed that Hood's numbers fell drastically in the wake of the assaults of the previous eight days. An Ohioan was pleased at what he was witnessing in the immediate wake of Ezra Church. "Hood is the General to our taste," he wrote three days after the battle; "I wish he could be persuaded to assault our stubborn lines every day, and it would take but a week to annihilate the entire rebel army under his command."[24]

Confederate companies never looked as depleted as they did after Ezra Church, as a very rough July for Southern infantry came to an end. "The companies in our regiment are getting very small, many of them having 12 and 15 men only for duty," decried Lieutenant Robert M. Gill of the 41st Mississippi. The lasting effect of this battle was on the psyche of the men. "There is much demoralization in the army," lamented Lieutenant Gill, who confessed to his wife two weeks after the battle that "desertions are numerous; some of the best soldiers are leaving. . . . I am much disheartened and think this cause is a desperate one."[25]

Hood immediately toiled to keep his fighting numbers up. He pulled in all available Georgia militia, which added numbers to the defensive lines for the Southerners, but it was distasteful for the veteran volunteers to see the grizzled men attempting to do the same duties of troops decades younger than them. "I am happy to see these 'play outs' out into the service," a Texan recorded, "but I do hate to see old grey headed men lying in the ditches taking the mud and water as it comes." Hood took additional measures to maximize the firepower of his army. A new cache of rifles left Richmond the day after the battle and arrived in Macon, whence they were subsequently sent to Hood, who armed a new set of troops. "Gen. Hood is putting guns into the hands of every available man in the army," reported a newspaperman. Cooks were armed and entered the lines, their duties taken up by slaves. Any men in the quartermaster and commissary departments who could be spared shouldered arms and entered the ranks. Hood also required artillery teams to bear arms, except for the six men at each gun absolutely necessary to load the cannon. The additional men kept the present-for-duty strength as elevated as possible, but it clearly demonstrated the dire state of the Army of Tennessee in the wake of the Battle of Ezra Church.[26]

By contrast, General Sherman's three armies now enjoyed overwhelming infantry strength. The Military Division of the Mississippi boasted in rank and file 75,650 infantry. This presented a clear two-to-one advantage in the major fighting arm of the Union army group over Hood's army, and a more comfortable margin of dominance on August 1 compared to the nine-to-eight advantage held in May. The strength advantage was not so extreme enough as for Sherman to be comfortable enough to bull-rush the Confederate defense, but it did allow him to engage in siege tactics without fear of Hood launching any further offensives against him as he had on July 20, July 22, and most recently at Ezra Church on July 28.[27]

It was not until late in August, as the Atlanta Campaign neared its inevitable close, that two newspapers brought the stark reality of the Battle of Ezra Church to the populace of the North and South. The influential *Mobile Register* published a gripping piece immediately picked up by the highly respected *Times-Picayune,* the dominant New Orleans daily. The *Times-Picayune* stunned its readers on the one-month anniversary of the battle with its "List of Casualties in Gibson's Louisiana Brigade, in the Fight near Atlanta on July 28," which consumed the entire front page of the newspaper. The list identified 474 Louisianans by name, company and regiment, and severity of injury (for those not listed as killed). Most disheartening for Southern readers was what some of them may have already realized—the list was still incomplete.

The country's most popular illustrated newspaper literally put Ezra Church front and center at the same time the Mobile and New Orleans papers did. On August 27 *Harper's Weekly Illustrated Newspaper* reached out to its 100,000 readers and viewers with a series of Ezra Church battle scenes that highlighted two pages of its center. Theodore Davis, the esteemed wartime artist assigned to Sherman's campaign, authored all the sketches, featuring a full-page depiction of XV Corps soldiers (likely from Woods's division) firing from the meager breastworks toward a line of Confederate soldiers (probably from Higley's Alabama brigade) lurking in the woods in front of their position (figure 7). In figure 8, a view of the latest hoopskirt fashions is oddly juxtaposed with three Ezra Church battle scenes, including wounded from the battle being treated near Sherman's headquarters and the macabre image of the creek running north from the Southern line and through where Martin's brigade stood (called "Dead Brook" in the image), eerily adorned with dead and wounded Confederate soldiers. In the upper-left corner of figure 8, Davis's sketch of the simple structure of Ezra Church peers out of the shadows of the trees. Ironically, this was a postmortem view of the chapel, which had lain in ruins since the middle of August—destroyed by cannon fire three weeks after the battle.[28]

Two weeks later Ezra Church made the cover of *Harper's Weekly* with an image of Harry Davis of the 46th Ohio pulling the tattered flag of the 30th Louisiana Battalion from its severely wounded and prostrate color bearer.[29] For a reading public who encountered faraway Atlanta and its featured battle sites such as Peachtree Creek, Bald Hill, Decatur, Utoy Creek, and Jonesboro, a small chapel known as Ezra Church and the slaughter that took place there had come to the forefront. It epitomized the campaign that turned from stalemate to decisive Union victory.

The Northerners' ultimate success more clearly materialized immediately after their victory fifteen miles south of Atlanta at Jonesboro. Hood evacuated Atlanta the following day, and Sherman's army filled the void and occupied the newly surrendered city. "So Atlanta is ours and fairly won," chimed General Sherman matter-of-factly in the middle of a 324-word telegram to the U.S. War Department on September 3. Those words signaled the only successful culmination of Grant's several simultaneous movements in May. It also immediately buoyed Abraham Lincoln's prospects for reelection a mere eleven days after the president circulated a blind memorandum for his cabinet members to sign acknowledging the inevitability of his defeat at the polls. Atlanta's capture was a political reversal: Lincoln won reelection, and six months later, the Union won the war.

Why did the Confederates lose at Ezra Church—and lose so decisively compared to the Battle of Peachtree Creek and the Battle of Atlanta? The attacking force failed to dislodge and rout the defending force even after launching its assaults before the defenders had adequate time to prepare their line with strong and tall breastworks and buttress their position with any artillery. This battle's lopsided outcome is made more puzzling by precedent. Six days before Ezra Church on the opposite side of Atlanta, basically the same armed attackers routed the same defenders from excellent earthworks, overcoming a defense supported by ten glistening artillery pieces. What was so different on July 28, 1864, compared to July 22 to produce an antithetical outcome?

Time and terrain had an effect, but even together they do not satisfactorily answer the question. The battle commenced shortly before noon and petered out six hours later before dusk and darkness. The heights defended by the Army of the Tennessee were penetrable. No creeks ran parallel to these hills to serve as moats, and the slopes leading to the heights were gentle and primarily wooded, which afforded some protection for the Confederate attackers while simultaneously limiting their view of the Union defenders and hampering their ability to unlimber any batteries to harass their opponent. At the outset, the right flank of the defense was an extremely weak one, vulnerable to collapse. Indeed, that collapse materialized within the first half hour of the contest, which itself complicates an analysis of the outcome.

A disparity in quantity and quality between opposing forces oftentimes determines a battle's outcome—but not at Ezra Church. The accolades heaped upon the Confederates at Ezra

Church by the Union participants speak volumes of the quality of the Southerners as soldiers. The most astounding tribute was generated from the most unlikely source: Major General John A. Logan, a veteran of more than a dozen battles who was loath to praise the Confederacy at all in the final twenty years of his life, offered only praise for the efforts of the Southern foot soldiers at Ezra Church: "Perhaps in the history of the war there was never more persistent and desperate gallantry displayed [on] the part of the rebels."[30]

Scores of Confederates shirked their duty on July 28 just as they had done in every battle before this one and as Union soldiers had across all theaters of the war, but no evidence supports the notion that a substantial percentage of them sapped the strength of the overall assault. Military doctrine dictates a greater than two-to-one ratio of assaulters versus defenders to succeed in carrying a strong defense (one with strong works and artillery support). The requisite ratio for success improved considerably at Ezra Church due to the weaker defense. Although the midafternoon assaults by the three brigades of Walthall's division failed in large part because there were too many fresh blue-clad soldiers awaiting them, the same explanation does not hold for the 4,000-man attack launched by Brown's division two hours earlier against a mile-long portion of a rushed line initially defended by no more than 2,500 troops from Harrow's and Morgan L. Smith's divisions. Although this disparity is considered suboptimal for an expected rout, previous offensive victories throughout the course of the war had been achieved against longer odds and against stronger defenses.

Technology and strength of firepower can also be ruled out as significant contributors to the Union victory and the Confederate defeat on July 28, 1864. Only Union soldiers carried repeating weapons, but less than 4 percent of the Federal soldiers who pulled triggers at Ezra Church could do so without immediately reloading—but once they were forced to reload, the process essentially removed that same 4 percent of the Union firepower for considerably longer than those carrying traditional arms. Furthermore, the companies carrying repeaters stood on two different parts of the field, facing in different directions, and were never active at the same time. The Confederates deployed no more than five batteries during the course of this battle; still, from noon onward, they enjoyed exclusive artillery dominance on this field.

Ruling out all of these factors leaves leadership decisions on both sides of the line as the key drivers of the outcome at Ezra Church. Union battlefield generalship is the most overlooked factor for the Confederate failure. Hood's army unknowingly assaulted what should have been the most vulnerable portion of Sherman's department. The XV Corps of the Army of the Tennessee had demonstrated its prowess at Resaca, Dallas, and Brushy Mountain in the earlier months of the Atlanta Campaign. Although the troops of this corps were instrumental to ultimate battle victory during the late afternoon of July 22, they were also routed en masse from strong defenses, nearly collapsing the entire army. That shaky performance during the Battle of Atlanta could easily have carried over to July 28, primarily due to the corps' upper command. Major General Morgan Smith had not excelled as a corps commander, and Brigadier General Joseph A. J. Lightburn had utterly failed as a division commander. The corps artillery was decimated at the Battle of Atlanta, while the corps infantry was reduced by 1,000 from losses during that battle.

Ironically, what salvaged the XV Corps before the Battle of Ezra Church even began was General Logan's demotion from army command the morning before the battle. Once Logan returned to the helm of the XV Corps the day before the battle, Morgan Smith resumed division duties and Lightburn went back to brigade command. Notwithstanding the decimation of the corps by the bloodbath east of Atlanta, only one regimental commander was new to his command on July 28, while every brigade and division commander led the same troops for the start of the second consecutive battle in six days. Such stability was essential for success, particularly during the assault of 4,000 Confederates against a line that had no time to dig in. The experience of the men, their regimental officers, and their brigade and division commanders enabled General Howard to post his first victory as an army commander against a force with dozens upon dozens of officers in new roles.

Logan's presence was instrumental for the victory. The ultimate inspirational commander, Logan instilled competence and confidence riding up and down his lines throughout the course of the battle. His ability to keep his wits, while his men showed signs of another inglorious rout during the opening assault of Brown's division, salvaged his corps by restoring his line in three vulnerable places. Logan also displayed a keen sense of timing by leading reinforcements to Battle Hill and feeding them to the height to drive out Brantly's Mississippians before they had the opportunity to nestle into their newly won position.

Moreover, the nonbureaucratic, unselfish style of the Army of the Tennessee preserved victory later in the afternoon against a most vicious assault by Walthall's division. In an unprecedented move, ten regiments from the XVI and XVII Corps replaced and reinforced the XV Corps line—without one of their original brigade commanders accompanying them. This force—equivalent to a division—answered to the commanders they were sent to reinforce without any animus displayed by their "native" brigadiers or their division and corps commanders. This unique characteristic of the Army of the Tennessee was displayed to a lesser degree during the battle of July 22, but at Ezra Church the teamwork within this army was as effective as it was admirable. The Battle of Ezra Church put on display a near perfect performance by a force sharpened by three years of brutal war.

In addition to the incredible efficiency of Howard's army, Confederate leadership ultimately spelled Southern doom at Ezra Church. The primary culprit is the overall Confederate commander, General John Bell Hood, who never stepped upon that battlefield. Hood committed an unrecoverable error by sending a two-division corps westward from Atlanta at least two hours too late. This major mistake robbed his subordinate, Stephen D. Lee, of the preferred objective to engage his opponent on the defensive while occupying the exact ground of Hood's choosing. Those same hills that gave the Union a J- and then a U-shaped defense would have provided Hood's men with a concave line facing an open basin formed by creek beds north of it—a perfect killing field to concentrate converging cannon and rifle fire from three directions against any Union thrust thrown against it.

Lee's late start was indeed Hood's decision, not Lee's. The revelation by Hood's chief of staff of troops "skirmishing feebly" against

Sherman's advance on July 27 strongly indicates that Hood knew the path of the Union army and essentially the point where Lee could intercept Lick Skillet Road. Had Hood sent Lee out no later than 8:30 A.M. with the same two divisions that lost nearly 2,000 soldiers in fruitless assaults that day, Lee could have smoothly deployed all of his 7,000 infantrymen and three batteries of artillery on the dominant zigzagging ridge line half a mile above the bend in the road—the same series of hills so staunchly held by three XV Corps divisions during the actual battle—while allowing his men at least ninety uncontested minutes to entrench. With Lick Skillet Road at the backs of the Confederates, Hood would have enjoyed a safe execution of the first stage of his battle plan by Lee and his subordinates while forcing Sherman to resort to costly offensive tactics to dislodge Lee's corps and open the Union path southward—or, as Hood believed at the time, expose the Union right flank had Sherman decided to turn Howard's army eastward for a thrust at Atlanta's western defenses. The likely scenario for Sherman would have required him to commit upwards of 20,000 infantrymen in an effort to take those heights—nearly the equivalent size of all three corps of Howard's Army of the Tennessee—with expected casualty differences more resembling Kennesaw Mountain.

Had Hood been more prompt and decisive that morning, he still would not have been assured ultimate victory at Ezra Church, for even if Stephen D. Lee had reached and dug in to the high ground, he would eventually have become vulnerable to flank attacks once Sherman and Howard invested enough manpower to attempt the dislodging of his force. Still, Hood's decision to hold his men within Atlanta past 10:00 A.M. certainly did prevent a much more time-consuming and costly effort for Howard's army, and it clearly did cost Lee an atrocious number of casualties. The late start may indeed have been the key that prevented a Confederate victory. It was absolutely inexcusable, particularly since Hood had spelled out a plan with his chief subordinates fifteen hours before that required two Confederate divisions to move out a mere two miles to occupy those heights. Whereas Hood displayed sound judgment throughout the first ten days of his tenure as chief of the Army of Tennessee, his faux pas on the morning of day eleven, July 28, was arguably his biggest mistake of the campaign.

Hood's second major shortcoming regarding Ezra Church was also a product of his indecision. A major battle was waged three miles west of his headquarters for more than four hours before Hood assigned a field commander to oversee the deployment and conduct of his army. Hood was clearly unaware of the magnitude of the contest and consistently appeared about ninety minutes behind the time regarding it. He also was certain Sherman would assault Atlanta from other locales that day and ostensibly refused to personally leave the city because of this threat. In hindsight, Hood did at least swallow his animus against Lieutenant General Hardee, albeit two hours late, when he called Hardee to headquarters and ordered him to take charge of the battle. However, this also smacks of vacillation, particularly since Hood created a scenario where two equally ranked corps commanders, Stewart and Lee—peers down to the same date of commission—operated on the same battlefield without Hood assigning one of them the field command at the time they united.

Hood did not cast aspersions on his corps commanders for their conduct and leadership on the Ezra Church battlefield. (In contrast, he showed no compunctions in assigning blame to corps commanders at the Battle of Peachtree Creek or the Battle of Atlanta.) Ever opinionated, Hood's unwillingness to fault either corps commander at Ezra Church in his official battle report and in his memoirs bears strong evidence that both lieutenant generals acted in accordance with Hood's plans and expectations. Recent historiography has not shown the same restraint as Hood uncharacteristically displayed regarding culpability; as a result, one corps commander has been universally viewed as the chief architect for the Confederate loss while the other has been widely absolved of any serious wrongdoing. The evidence suggests otherwise for both of them.

Hood's best opportunity for success was Lee's initial assault. As the time approached noon, only fifteen battalion-sized Union regiments nestled in position to receive an attack from the southwest—a scantily protected force of no more than 2,500 officers and men. Half a mile southwest of them, General Lee began to unpack his two divisions—seven brigades composed of thirty-seven regiments that numbered close to 7,000 rank and file facing off against a Union corps positioned in a U-shaped defense and numbering more than 7,000 men in position in the forenoon hour with no more than half of them facing south, southwest, and west. Although military doctrine would normally favor the defense even when outnumbered two to one, the fact that Lee opposed a corps that had been routed from a much stauncher defensive position six days earlier and that was not protected by artillery on July 28 vastly improved his odds for success. Those odds weighed even more heavily in his favor were he to gain the flank of his opponent with the possibility of a double envelopment.

Lee sent General John C. Brown on a full-division assault as soon as his brigades had deployed into line of battle, while expecting General Henry D. Clayton's brigades to be ready for battle within minutes. Lee was oblivious to the fact that most of Clayton's division was still pulling off Lick Skillet Road at the start of Brown's attack. Rather than wait the additional twenty to thirty minutes necessary to coordinate a two-division assault, one in which he could have sent five brigades on a two-mile-wide battle line with two brigades in reserve, Lee sent one division forward before the second one was deployed to buttress it. In reality, if Lee had waited up to half an hour longer to send a total 5,000 front-line troops, with 2,000 more behind them, the golden opportunity for success may have actually diminished or disappeared as the Union protection would definitely have been made stronger and more troops would have filled in the gaps of a defense line that could have been twice as difficult to penetrate as it was half an hour earlier. Perhaps the best Lee could have hoped for was to split the difference: wait ten or fifteen minutes longer before sending Brown's attackers into the field so that Clayton's division could have marched off fifteen minutes after them on their right, effectively approaching the Union line *en echelon*.

In hindsight, the greatest shortcoming within Lee's initial attack was its piecemeal approach centered on his three front-line brigades. To Lee's credit, he and General Brown did align and send off those three brigades as a unified 4,000-man assault force (3,000 in front, 1,000 in reserve) so the piecemeal outcome was more a reflection of unanticipated terrain obstacles, uneven Union skirmishing resistance, and a forced halt and realignment of General

William F. Brantly's brigade on the extreme left, which assured it would strike last. Lee personally rallied wayward commands while also attempting to speed up Clayton's deployment off to his right.

The only feasible chance Lee's assault could have had to succeed at the time he launched it would have been to align farther northwest with heavier, two-directional pressure applied to the yet-to-be-deployed right flank of the XV Corps. Lee's postbattle hazing of the effort of his men was unbecoming, but his rapid deployment and huge hit upon the defensive line was impressive: six of his seven brigades attacked, temporarily pierced, and inflicted casualties upon nearly the entire two-mile U-shaped defense confronting them, and did so all within three hours after receiving Lee's orders two miles from the point of deployment from marching column to line of battle. That Lee was able to attempt this in his second day as a commander of men he had never seen before, while coordinating the effort in full compliance with his mission and instructions, is a worthy performance—not perfect, but also not the cause of his corps' defeat.

By the time General Alexander P. Stewart arrived with two divisions of his corps, the odds of Confederate success had waned considerably. Ten fresh regiments from the XVI and XVII Corps had worked their way into the southwestern-facing part of the Union line to provide relief for several hundred spent members of the XV Corps. Regardless, General Edward C. Walthall's division attacked with incredible vigor and verve, but the futile thrust ultimately shed more than 1,100 soldiers from his ranks.[31]

Stewart's wounding and consequent early departure from the battlefield has masked a critical evaluation of his generalship from the point where the vanguard of his leading division (Walthall's) marched into the battle arena on Lick Skillet Road shortly after 1:30 P.M. No evidence exists that Lee was placed in charge over Stewart. In fact, Lee's report never suggests it, and headquarters dispatches to Stewart and his successor, Walthall, regarding potential reinforcements are striking for the fact that they were not sent to Lee. With this in mind, Stewart's decision to send Walthall's attack exactly where Lee had failed is suspect, and to order it forward so quickly upon his arrival to the battlefield magnifies the doubt concerning Stewart's acumen as a sound offensive tactician—Peachtree Creek notwithstanding. Regardless of Lee's urging and influence from the moment Stewart's men arrived, Stewart was not obligated to follow directly in Lee's failed footsteps, nor should he have been compelled to immediately do so. Stewart personally reached the battlefield half an hour or so before his troops did, which suggests he had made up his mind where to send them, rather than reconnoiter farther west beyond Logan's right flank or consider the eastern side of the battlefield, which had only just been tested by Baker's/Higley's brigade. Walthall's thousand-plus casualties were incurred in vain; his 3,000 attackers could have been more successful had they struck just about anywhere else except the freshest and numerically strongest part of the XV Corps line.

Stewart matched his curious decision to direct Walthall's path of assault by ordering Loring to pull his division directly into the rear of Walthall's troops as the latter battled the staunchly reinforced Union line. By not deploying Loring's men off of either flank of Walthall's force, Stewart seemingly assured that they would follow the same path where one division (Brown's) had failed and the another (Walthall's) appeared destined to do the same. Loring's and Stewart's battle-ending injuries also brought an end to the Confederate assaults for the day and subsequently to Stewart's culpability for his tactical shortcomings. Overall, Stewart's uninspired leadership of two divisions on July 28 reveals that had Hood's original plan commenced with Stewart in charge of twice as many troops for a July 29 flank assault, the chances of Confederate success, in hindsight, appear questionable at best.

"The Battle of Ezra Church was a turning point in the Atlanta Campaign."[32] So wrote General Howard thirty years after the final guns of the Civil War fell silent. Those three decades instilled within Howard a perspective of the battle's impact on the outcome of the campaign that he understood better at the close of the century than he did when he fought it. Appreciating how important the Atlanta Campaign was to the political and military outcome of the war, Howard realized that the thirty engagements within this campaign were hardly equal in their impact and that the immediate effect of even the largest battles tended to be so subtle at the time they were fought as to escape the notice of their participants. Howard also came to recognize how decisive the collective battles fought from July 20 to July 28—all Union victories—were to the eventual outcome of this all-important campaign.

Ezra Church was the final of four contests fought eight days apart from first to last. Howard realized that this battle further crippled a reeling opponent while allowing his blue-coated victors to escape devastating losses in both quantity and quality that would have weakened him significantly—as they did General Hood. (Howard may have understood that this outcome would likely have been reversed if Lee had beat him to the heights near Ezra Church and forced him into the attacker's role instead.) Howard seemed to recognize this immediately, and his multitude of writings on the subject bear this out. Impressed as he was (as were Logan, Sherman, and seemingly every Union soldier who raised a rifle that day) with the ferocity and resolve of the assaulting Confederate foot soldier, Howard only realized one month later, during the first day of the two-day Battle of Jonesboro, that Ezra Church must have severely weakened the resolve of the Confederates. For at Jonesboro, as the same Confederate corps of his former West Point classmate, Stephen D. Lee, again attacked the XV Corps line, the assault was weaker and more irresolute than any other battle he had witnessed. By contrast, General Hardee's men had attacked more ferociously at the Battle of Atlanta than they did two days before that at Peachtree Creek, despite suffering a bloody repulse in the earlier battle; and the men who breached the Union defenses under General Cheatham north of Bald Hill on July 22 were the same troops who attacked even more ferociously six days later at Ezra Church while serving under General Lee.

But the Southern slaughter at the chapel throughout the burning hot afternoon of July 28, 1864, broke the resolve of the Confederate infantryman. At the same time, Union resolve was stiffened. Several factors converged at the close of the contest at Ezra Church to produce a growing unease in the mind of the Southern foot soldier: crushed by a lopsided battlefield thumping, the culmination of several consecutive defeats in barely over a week, an increasing awareness that the number of experienced comrades in arms still standing was critically low that proper battlefield leadership was wanting, and that they were risking their lives in a lost cause. Whatever the reason or reasons, General Howard and his army watched the result of it in their next and last major engagement of the campaign at Jonesboro.

Howard probably understood right at the close of the campaign, but most certainly in the postwar years, that the Battle of Ezra Church had a major impact on the outcome of the campaign for Atlanta. It culminated eight days of major clashes of infantry revealing a break in what easily could have been a stalemate around the city. True, the campaign dragged on another five weeks after July 28, 1864, but the outcome appeared much more certain after July 28 than it had on the morning of July 20. Hood's infantry was wrecked for the campaign—devoid of leadership by the loss of so many officers, devoid of strength by the loss of so many men. Unlike any of the preceding battles during Hood's first eleven days as army commander, the defeat at Ezra Church broke the fighting spirit of the Confederate infantrymen at Atlanta. No longer would they fight with the esprit de corps that characterized their attacks at Peachtree Creek, Bald Hill, and at Ezra Church. The latter battle stole their élan; it robbed them of their unified willingness to attack. More than any single action of the campaign, Ezra Church broke the Confederates' resolve and withered their strength.

General Howard indeed was justified in his bold assessment: Ezra Church was a turning point in arguably the most important campaign of the Civil War. Less than a week after the largest and most decisive battle of the campaign east of Atlanta to date, one that went a long way to take the Confederate soldier out of the fight, the Battle of Ezra Church took the fight out of that soldier.

Appendix A

Order of Battle of Forces Present at Ezra Church, July 28, 1864

Abbreviations

p	promoted
k	killed
mw	mortally wounded
w	wounded
ds	on detached service, not engaged
ne	present, not engaged

UNION ARMY
MILITARY DIVISION OF THE MISSISSIPPI
MAJOR GENERAL WILLIAM T. SHERMAN
ARMY OF THE TENNESSEE
MAJOR GENERAL OLIVER O. HOWARD

XV Army Corps: Major General John A. Logan

First Division: Brigadier General Charles R. Woods

First Brigade: Colonel Milo Smith
    26th Iowa Infantry: Lieutenant Colonel Thomas G. Ferreby
    30th Iowa Infantry: Lieutenant Colonel Aurelius Roberts
    27th Missouri Infantry: Major Dennis O'Connor
    76th Ohio Infantry: Colonel William B. Woods
Second Brigade: Colonel James A. Williamson
    4th Iowa Infantry: Major Samuel D. Nichols
    9th Iowa Infantry: Colonel David Carskaddon (w);
        Major George Granger

25th Iowa Infantry: Colonel George A. Stone
31st Iowa Infantry: Colonel William Smyth (ds)
Third Brigade: Colonel Hugo Wangelin
   3rd Missouri Infantry: Colonel Theodore Meumann
   12th Missouri Infantry: Lieutenant Colonel Jacob Kaercher (w); Major Frederick T. Ledergerber
   17th Missouri Infantry: Lieutenant Colonel Francis Romer
   29th Missouri Infantry: Major Frederick Jaensch
   31st Missouri Infantry: Lieutenant Colonel Samuel P. Simpson
   32nd Missouri Infantry: Major Abraham J. Seay
Division Artillery: Major Clemens Landgraeber
   2nd Missouri Light, Battery F: Captain Louis Voelkner
   Ohio Light, 4th Battery: Captain George Froehlich

Second Division: Brigadier General Morgan L. Smith

First Brigade: Colonel James S. Martin
   55th Illinois Infantry: Captain Francis H. Shaw
   111th Illinois Infantry: Captain Reuben W. Joliff
   116th Illinois Infantry: Captain John S. Windsor
   127th Illinois Infantry: Lieutenant Colonel Francis S. Curtiss
   83rd Indiana Infantry: Captain Benjamin North
   6th Missouri Infantry: Lieutenant Colonel Delos Van Deusen
   57th Ohio Infantry: Lieutenant Colonel Samuel R. Mott
Second Brigade: Brigadier General Joseph A. J. Lightburn
   30th Ohio Infantry: Colonel Theodore Jones
   37th Ohio Infantry: Major Charles Hipp (w); Captain Carl Moritz
   47th Ohio Infantry: Major Thomas T. Taylor
   53rd Ohio Infantry: Colonel Wells S. Jones
   54th Ohio Infantry: Major Israel T. Moore
Division Artillery: Captain Francis De Gress
   1st Illinois Light, Battery A: Captain Francis De Gress

Fourth Division: Brigadier General William Harrow

First Brigade: Colonel Reuben Williams
   26th Illinois Infantry: Colonel Robert A. Gillmore

APPENDIX A 211

90th Illinois Infantry: Colonel Owen Stuart
12th Indiana Infantry: Lieutenant Colonel James Goodnow
100th Indiana Infantry: Lieutenant Colonel Albert
  Heath (ds)
Second Brigade: Colonel Charles C. Walcutt
  40th Illinois Infantry: Major Hiram W. Hall (w); Captain
    Michael Galvin
  103rd Illinois Infantry: Captain Franklin C. Post
  97th Indiana Infantry: Lieutenant Colonel Aiden G. Cavins
  6th Iowa Infantry: Major Thomas J. Ennis (mw); Captain William H. Clune
  46th Ohio Infantry: Lieutenant Colonel Isaac N. Alexander
Third Brigade: Colonel John M. Oliver
  48th Illinois Infantry: Major Edward Adams
  99th Indiana Infantry: Lieutenant Colonel John M. Berkey
  15th Michigan Infantry: Lieutenant Colonel Frederick S.
    Hutchinson
  70th Ohio Infantry: Major William B. Brown

XVI Army Corps: Major General Grenville M. Dodge

12th Illinois Infantry: Lieutenant Colonel Henry Van Sellar
  (Second Division, First Brigade)
81st Ohio Infantry: Lieutenant Colonel Robert N. Adams (Second Division, First Brigade)
64th Illinois Infantry: Lieutenant Colonel Michael W. Manning (Fourth Division, First Brigade)
35th New Jersey Infantry: Colonel John J. Cladek (Fourth Division, Second Brigade)

XVII Army Corps: Major General Francis P. Blair

31st Illinois Infantry: Lieutenant Colonel Robert N. Pearson
  (Third Division, First Brigade)
12th Wisconsin Infantry: Lieutenant Colonel James K. Proudfit (Third Division, First Brigade)
Worden's Battalion: Major Asa Worden (Third Division, Third Brigade)

3rd Iowa Infantry (3 companies): Lieutenant Lewis T. Linnell (Fourth Division, First Brigade)
13th Iowa Infantry: Colonel John Shane (Fourth Division, Third Brigade)
15th Iowa Infantry: Colonel William W. Belknap (Fourth Division, Third Brigade)
32nd Ohio Infantry: Major Abraham M. Crumbecker (Fourth Division, First Brigade)

CONFEDERATE ARMY
ARMY OF TENNESSEE
GENERAL JOHN B. HOOD

Hood's Corps: Lieutenant General Stephen D. Lee

Brown's Division: Brigadier General John C. Brown

Johnston's Brigade: Brigadier General George D. Johnston (w); Colonel John G. Coltart (w); Lieutenant Colonel Harry T. Toulmin
    17th Alabama Battalion Sharpshooters: Captain James F. Nabers (w); Lieutenant A. R. Andrews
    19th Alabama Infantry: Lieutenant Colonel Harry T. Toulmin (p); Major Solomon Palmer
    22nd Alabama Infantry: Colonel Benjamin R. Hart (k); Captain Isaac M. Whitney
    25th Alabama Infantry: Captain Napoleon B. Rouse
    39th Alabama Infantry: Captain Thomas J. Brannon
    50th Alabama Infantry: Colonel John G. Coltart (p); Captain George W. Arnold (w); Captain Archibald D. Ray
Sharp's Brigade: Brigadier General Jacob H. Sharp
    9th Mississippi Battalion Sharpshooters: Lieutenant J. B. Downing
    7th Mississippi Infantry: Colonel William H. Bishop
    9th Mississippi Infantry: Lieutenant Colonel Benjamin F. Johns
    10th Mississippi Infantry: Lieutenant Colonel George B. Myers
    41st Mississippi Infantry: Colonel J. Byrd Williams

APPENDIX A   213

44th Mississippi Infantry: Lieutenant Colonel Robert G. Kelsey
Brantly's Brigade: Brigadier General William F. Brantly
   24th/27th Mississippi Infantry: Colonel Robert P. McKelvaine (w); Lieutenant Colonel William L. Lyles
   29th/30th Mississippi Infantry: Lieutenant Colonel James M. Johnson
   34th Mississippi Infantry: Captain T. S. Hubbard
Manigault's Brigade: Brigadier General Arthur M. Manigault
   10th South Carolina Infantry: Lieutenant Colonel C. Irvine Walker (w); Captain Charles C. White
   19th South Carolina Infantry: Captain Thomas. W. Getzen (w); Captain Elijah W. Horne (w); Adjutant James O. Ferrell
   24th Alabama Infantry: Captain Starke H. Oliver
   28th Alabama Infantry: Lieutenant Colonel William L. Butler
   34th Alabama Infantry: Major John N. Slaughter

Clayton's Division: Major General Henry D. Clayton

Gibson's Brigade: Brigadier General Randall L. Gibson
   1st Regiment Louisiana Regulars: Major S. S. Batchelor (w); Captain William H. Sparks (k); Lieutenant Charles L. Huger
   4th Regiment Louisiana Infantry: Colonel Samuel E. Hunter
   13th Louisiana Infantry: Lieutenant Colonel Francis L. Campbell
   20th Louisiana Infantry: Colonel Leon von Zinken (w); Captain Robert L. Keen
   16th/25th Louisiana Infantry: Colonel Joseph C. Lewis
   19th Louisiana Infantry: Colonel Richard W. Turner (w); Lieutenant Colonel Hyder A. Kennedy (w); Captain John W. Jones
   4th Louisiana Battalion (Companies A–F): Major Duncan Buie (w); Captain Thomas A. Bisland
   30th Louisiana Battalion (Companies A–G): Lieutenant Colonel Thomas Shields (k); Major Charles J. Bell (k); Captain Arthur Picolet
   14th Louisiana Battalion Sharpshooters (Companies A–B): Major John E. Austin

5th Company Washington Artillery (four guns): Captain Cuthbert H. Slocumb (ne)
Baker's Brigade: Brigadier General Alpheus Baker (w); Colonel John H. Higley
   37th Alabama: Captain Thomas J. Griffin
   40th Alabama: Colonel John H. Higley (p); Major Ezekiah S. Gulley
   42nd Alabama: Captain Robert K. Wells (k); Captain William B. Kendrick
   54th Alabama: Colonel John A. Minter
Holtzclaw's Brigade: Colonel Bushrod Jones
   18th Alabama: Lieutenant Colonel Peter F. Hunley
   32nd/58th Alabama: Captain John A. Avirett
   36th Alabama: Lieutenant Colonel Thomas H. Herndon
   38th Alabama: Captain Benjamin L. Posey

Stewart's Corps: Lieutenant General Alexander P. Stewart (w); Major General Edward C. Walthall

Loring's Division: Major General William W. Loring (w); Brigadier General Winfield S. Featherston

Featherston's Brigade: Brigadier General Winfield S. Featherston (p); Colonel Robert Lowry
   1st Mississippi Battalion Sharpshooters: Major Milton S. Alcorn
   3rd Mississippi Infantry: Lieutenant Colonel Samuel M. Dyer
   22nd Mississippi Infantry: Major James M. Stigler
   31st Mississippi Infantry: Captain Robert A. Collins
   33rd Mississippi Infantry: Captain Moses Jackson
   40th Mississippi Infantry: Captain W. L. Bassett
Adams's Brigade: Brigadier General John Adams
   6th Mississippi Infantry: Colonel Robert Lowry (p)
   14th Mississippi Infantry: Lieutenant Colonel Washington L. Doss
   15th Mississippi Infantry: Colonel Michael Farrell
   20th Mississippi Infantry: Colonel William N. Brown
   23rd Mississippi Infantry: Colonel Joseph M. Wells

APPENDIX A   215

43rd Mississippi Infantry: Colonel Richard Harrison
Scott's Brigade: Brigadier General Thomas M. Scott
   27th/35th/49th Alabama Infantry: Colonel Samuel S. Ives
   55th Alabama Infantry: Colonel John Snodgrass
   57th Alabama Infantry: Captain Augustus L. Milligan
   12th Louisiana Infantry: Colonel Noel L. Nelson

Walthall's Division: Major General Edward C. Walthall (p); Brigadier General William A. Quarles

Quarles's Brigade: Brigadier General William A. Quarles (p); Colonel Robert A. Owens
   1st Alabama Infantry: Major Samuel L. Knox (w); Captain Richard Williams
   42nd Tennessee Infantry: Colonel Isaac N. Hulme (w); Captain Austin N. Duncan
   46th/55th Tennessee Infantry: Colonel Robert A. Owens (p)
   48th Tennessee Infantry: Lieutenant Colonel Aaron S. Godwin
   49th Tennessee Infantry: Colonel William F. Young (w); [5 more officers (k & w)]; Captain Thomas H. Smith
   53rd Tennessee Infantry: Colonel John R. White (k); Lieutenant Colonel Joseph D. Wilson (w); Major William C. Richardson (mw); Captain J. J. Rittenbury
Cantey's Brigade: Colonel Edward A. O'Neal
   1st Corps (Alabama) Sharpshooters: Captain A. L. O'Brien
   17th Alabama Infantry: Major Thomas J. Burnett (w); Captain Thomas A. McCane
   26th Alabama Infantry: Major David F. Bryan
   29th Alabama Infantry: Captain John A. Foster
   37th Mississippi Infantry: Major Samuel H. Terral
Reynolds's Brigade: Brigadier General Daniel H. Reynolds
   1st Arkansas Mounted Rifles: Lieutenant Colonel Morton G. Galloway (w); Captain John S. Perry
   2nd Arkansas Mounted Rifles: Lieutenant Colonel James T. Smith (k); Captain William E. Johnson
   4th Arkansas Infantry: Colonel Henry G. Bunn (w); Captain Augustus Kile
   9th Arkansas Infantry: Lieutenant Colonel Jefferson W. Rogers

25th Arkansas Infantry: Lieutenant Colonel Eli Hufstedler (k); Captain Edward C. Woodson
Youngblood's Battalion: Major E. H. Youngblood
Gholson's Brigade: Colonel John McGuirk

Cavalry Corps: Major General Joseph Wheeler

Jackson's Division: Brigadier General William H. Jackson

Armstrong's Brigade: Brigadier General Frank C. Armstrong
   1st Mississippi Cavalry: Colonel R. A. Pinson
   2nd Mississippi Cavalry: Major John J. Perry
   28th Mississippi Cavalry: Major Joshua T. McBee
   Ballentine's (Mississippi) Regiment: Lieutenant Colonel William L. Maxwell
Artillery
   Yates's Mississippi Battery: Captain James H. Yates
   Hoskins's Mississippi Battery: Captain James A. Hoskins
Ross's Brigade: Brigadier General Lawrence S. Ross
   1st Texas Legion: Colonel Edward R. Hawkins
   3rd Texas Cavalry: Lieutenant Colonel Jiles S. Boggess
   6th Texas Cavalry: Lieutenant Colonel Peter F. Ross
   9th Texas Cavalry: Colonel Dudley W. Jones

Appendix B

Interpreting the Battle of Ezra Church through the Words of Its Chief Confederate Commanders

To accurately interpret the Battle of Ezra Church, historians depend, as with all other major engagements of the Civil War, on the official reports of the leaders of its troops as a foundation. Complicating an interpretation of this battle is the dearth of vital primary source evidence, particularly from regimental commanders on both sides of the line. Additionally, Union reports for Ezra Church are summarized and truncated within entire campaign reports, thus limiting their potential to reveal the intricacies of the battle.

Confederate division, brigade, and regimental reports for this battle—although all too sparse—do provide the necessary tactical details oftentimes missing from their Union counterparts for this battle. Overlooked and underappreciated about Ezra Church is the vital information provided by General John B. Hood and his corps commanders. The snippets gleaned from their accounts are as enlightening as they are revealing.

Confederate army and corps commanders at Ezra Church delayed making their official reports of the battle. Lieutenant General Alexander P. Stewart's wounding may have been part of the reason he delayed his official report until the following winter. His delay was also caused by that of his subordinate division commander Major General Edward C. Walthall, who did not submit his report until January, despite all of Walthall's brigadiers having filed their reports within a week of the battle. If Major General William W. Loring ever submitted a report, it has never come to light; he likely never wrote one, as he was wounded as soon as his men and he reached the field. None of Loring's brigade underlings shed any light on their participation through official reports.

Lieutenant General Stephen D. Lee's division, brigade, and regimental officers submitted more reports and in a more timely manner than did those in Stewart's corps. Brigadier General John C. Brown uncharacteristically filed his report before all of his brigadiers had turned in their versions of the battle to him, perhaps because he received a new assignment (and promotion to major general), to take Loring's division while that general recovered from his wound. Major General Henry D. Clayton's report of his division's activity did not arrive in Lee's hands until September 16, the same day Clayton fielded Brigadier General Randall Gibson's report of his Louisiana brigade's action on July 28.

Lee himself waited until prodded by General Hood in January 1865 to turn in his report of the Atlanta Campaign—a document that would begin with the Battle of Ezra Church. Hood included a special instruction to Lee that would become an overriding theme of both commanders' reports. "I will be glad," stated Hood, "if you will state as to the morale of the army after the fall of Atlanta as we all regarded a change necessary."[1] Hood's reference to a necessary change referred to a new theater of operation rather than a new commander. Hood had already revealed that his Atlanta Campaign report was going to be crafted as an influential piece beyond a more simple account of the summer in Atlanta, one that attempted to justify taking his army into Tennessee and embarking on a campaign that virtually wrecked his command in the late fall of 1864.

The most important Confederate officer in regard to the Ezra Church battlefield was the commanding general who never stepped upon it. After the bitter defeats at the Battles of Franklin, on November 30, and Nashville, on December 15 and 16, which closed a devastating campaign, General John Bell Hood departed by train to Richmond from Tupelo, Mississippi, as January turned to February; in the Confederate capital he lodged in the Spotswood Hotel, where he fielded his subordinates' reports of the Atlanta Campaign and analyzed them, synthesizing much of his corps commanders' information into his own report to submit to General Samuel Cooper, the adjutant and inspector general of the Confederacy. Of the four major battles waged at the periphery of Atlanta in the summer of 1864, Ezra Church was one of two battles where Hood relied mostly on his subordinates' analyses and observations because he had no personal observations of his own (the other was Jonesboro). Hood's chief sources for the battle were his two corps commanders, Generals Lee and Stewart, with additional input from his chief of staff, General Shoup.

General Lee's official account of what he and his corps did on July 28, 1864, amounted to eleven sentences, about one-fifth of his entire report on the Atlanta Campaign. In his report Lee claimed that he did not receive Hood's orders to march his two available divisions until about 11:00 A.M. (it was actually about forty-five minutes earlier than that). Lee pinpointed neither a council of war nor a face-to-face meeting with Hood regarding his specific mission for July 28; he merely stated, "I received orders to move out on the Lick Skillet road and check the enemy, who was then moving to our left [south], as it was desirable to hold that road, to be used for a contemplated movement." Lee's terminology "check the enemy" did not specify an endpoint of his mission, but his mention of securing the road "for a contemplated movement" suggests that he and his 7,000 soldiers needed to keep Union troops away from that road.

By the time Lee arrived at the Poor House, according to his account, "the enemy had gained the road," leaving no option for him but to drive those Union troops from it. Lee never revealed to Hood how many Union troops were actually on the road (there was only one regiment within two hundred yards), but his rapid deployment of Brown's four-brigade division is consistent with Lee's belief that a much larger body of Union troops was either on the road or advancing directly toward it (a reaction to Red Jackson's report of Union skirmishers who had chased the dismounted cavalry all the way back from Ezra Church). According to Lee's report, the battle did go horribly wrong after Brown's division "handsomely" drove Sherman's troops from Lick Skillet Road for half a mile but were repulsed with "considerable loss" by Union troops behind "temporary breast-works." Lee continued by claiming that Clayton attacked "about ten minutes after Brown's advance" but met with a similar repulse. In his report, Lee spelled out the reason for his inability to seize the Union position, and this explanation must have been what Hood heard and accepted from him in the early aftermath of the battle: that portions of the lines failed to attack, that it was difficult to rally Brown's division for a second assault after the first one failed, and that "if all the troops had displayed equal spirit we would have been successful."[2]

To say the least, Lee's version of the battle suffered from a deficit of accuracy. He likely convinced his direct superior, General Hood, that two divisions assaulted two Union corps (according to Lee) when they really faced and were repulsed by two and a half divisions (about 6,000 men) of the XV Corps. Lee misled Hood into believing that his two available divisions engaged in a coordinated assault when in fact only three brigades attacked in the first thirty minutes, two more in the next hour, and then a final brigade in the subsequent thirty minutes.

Lee's claim that portions of his lines attacked too feebly provides a too-easy explanation for his failure to drive from the battlefield Logan's corps, a body of troops that even Lee acknowledged were protected by slight works and unprepared for the attack the Confederates laid upon them. This flawed "dispirited-Confederate" theory prevailed after the battle with effects beyond Hood's instruction for Lee to highlight the impaired morale of his troops at the close of the campaign.

General Stewart filed a two-month campaign report as corps commander from Tupelo on January 12, 1865. Ten sentences detailed his role in the Battle of Ezra Church. Whereas Lee's report hinted at a meeting to discuss a battle west of Atlanta ("it was desirable to hold that road, to be used for a contemplated movement"), Stewart left no doubt that Hood planned a two-day operation using at least six Confederate divisions, four under Stewart's command, which had been instructed to strike the Union flank on July 29. Stewart cautiously prefaced the plan by opening, "As I understood the instructions" and revealed that "Mount Ezra Church" was the predetermined site of the battle.

Specifying that he and his first two divisions were ordered to rendezvous at the junction of Lick Skillet Road and the outer Atlanta defensive works, Stewart reported, "On reaching the point indicated Lee's corps was found to be engaged [two miles west of them] and in need of assistance." Stewart passively continued, "Accordingly, Walthall's division was moved out, Loring's following as support"—but he left no clue as to whether he was told why he had to rush out to Lee's assistance with two divisions after Hood's initial plan placed four divisions under his command. Stewart did not acknowledge whether he or General Lee was the field commander at the time of his arrival at the Poor House. Surprisingly, with the benefit of nearly six months of hindsight, Stewart committed only two sentences to his ninety-minute battlefield generalship at Ezra Church in which nearly 1,200 of his soldiers were killed, wounded, or captured prior to his own wounding and removal from the field. Those two sentences failed to answer why Walthall attacked where he did rather than exploit a weaker part of the Union line.[3]

The campaign reports from Lee and Stewart together provide a tactical outline of what the Confederates did at Ezra Church, one that is filled in by division, brigade, and regimental reports from two-thirds of Lee's corps commanders. Although more than half of the *what* explains the Battle of Ezra Church from the Confederate perspective, the *how* and *why* regarding the Southern mission to the battlefield, particularly in relation to its initial plan from the evening before, is only teased at by the two corps commanders.

Hood's pending report was all that remained to fill in the gaps left by his subordinates' reports. Not only was the army commander ideally suited to expand upon what his subordinates provided, Hood's reception of both Lee's and Stewart's campaign reports provided him the ripe opportunity to explain his intentions and reasons for an infantry thrust west of Atlanta and its relationship to his overall defense of the Gate City and its remaining viable railroads entering from the south. Writing his report of the Atlanta Campaign half a year after the fact, Hood had the added perspective of how the campaign had played out with the Southern populace, the press as well as his peers and superiors.

The additional time removed from the campaign, and another failed campaign waged in between Atlanta and Hood's official report, proved detrimental to the creation of a revealing recount of his version of the *what, how,* and *why* of Ezra Church. Hood was so consumed by his animosity toward General Joseph E. Johnston and Lieutenant General William Hardee as well as by his need to use his Atlanta Campaign report as a vehicle to justify his decision to embark upon the Tennessee Campaign that he crafted a most unorthodox report, one that a confidant of Hood's advised him came across with "the violence of a party document." Regardless, Hood made only slight revisions before submitting it on February 15, 1865.[4]

Hood's official telling of the Battle of Ezra Church was surprisingly brief, but it did uncover one tremendous nugget not revealed by any of his subordinates. Learning that Sherman was advancing southward and being specifically informed on July 28 that Sherman intended to put a flank of his force on Utoy Creek, Hood reiterated his desire "to hold the Lick Skillet road" and accordingly ordered General Lee "to move his forces so as to prevent the enemy from gaining that road." Hood then repeated the instructions he gave Lee "to hold the enemy in check," just exactly as Lee had reported, but Hood went further than Lee to reveal exactly where he wanted Lee's position to be to accomplish that "check" of the enemy: "on a line nearly parallel with the Lick Skillet road, running through Ezra Church." Hood went on to report that once Lee learned that Union troops had already reached that road, he "engaged him with the intention to recover that line." Not only did Hood not censure Lee for attacking when he would have preferred him to defend, he established and justified the reason for Lee's immediate assault by providing a definition of "hold the Lick Skillet road"—that is, to deploy half a mile north to northeast of the Poor House on the heights running to Ezra Church; and if enemy troops were to occupy that line, to recover the line and then deploy there. Hood's specific identification of the church and the line of hills that ran through it revealed that he had a decent map or had explored the region earlier in the campaign or when he recuperated in the Thrasher house the previous November (1863), from his Chickamauga wound and subsequent amputation.

Hood avoided any description of the battle that ensued and assigned no blame to his corps and division commanders for the outcome. He simply followed his explanation for Lee's attack with a passive acknowledgment that General Stewart "was ordered to support General Lee." Hood disingenuously concluded this portion of his report, stating the battle ran until nightfall with "the road remaining in our possession." True as this literally was, Hood conveniently failed to state that his men were forced from the road the following day. He also shunned mentioning any times, numbers of troops, or casualties. He omitted the wounding of four generals in this battle (including a corps and division commander), and he decided against confessing that he had designed and then was forced to change a plan he had put in place with the same corps commanders prior to Lee's departure from the outer ring of Atlanta's defenses. Hood somehow put the awful outcome in the best possible light—he never acknowledged that Lee's and Stewart's men were repulsed even once, let alone the several failed attempts that actually took place. His report made Ezra Church appear as if it had been a drawn and inconsequential battle.[5]

Hood's report stood as the chronologically final, official, few words about Ezra Church from the Confederate high command. As it turned out, none of his corps or division commanders published any substantial speeches or memoirs about this battle after the war, leaving John Bell Hood's reminiscences as the most read Confederate postwar account for this battle. He began writing his memoirs in the mid-1870s and concluded shortly before his premature death from typhoid in 1879. Hood's postwar writings focused on a defense of his performance in the last half of 1864, first in Georgia and then in Tennessee. Like his official report, his written recollections expanded on the portions of the campaign that related to General Joseph E. Johnston, his main Confederate nemesis, as well as those battles in which William Hardee participated, the latter being the subordinate upon whom Hood would place much of his campaign failures after Johnston left the army. However, aside from Hardee's arrival at the Poor House at dusk on July 28, 1864, neither of Hood's nemeses were involved in the Battle of Ezra Church.

Moreover, Hood's more positive relationship with his two chief corps commanders of this battle, Lee and Stewart, may have influenced his account of a battle gone wrong. Hood corresponded with both men about their service under him, but with General Lee those letters reveal a two-way discussion about the Battle of Franklin and the campaign surrounding it; and with General Stewart the lone known correspondence regarding the Atlanta

Campaign was entirely limited to Stewart's complete recollection of Johnston's removal. Hood did not ask about Ezra Church; Stewart did not offer anything regarding the battle.[6]

During his fourteen-year postwar life, Hood neither sought nor received any significant information regarding the catastrophic loss his army suffered at Ezra Church, a battle fought three miles from his headquarters, completely out of his view and mostly beyond his hearing. By contrast, he was only within viewing distance of the Battle of Atlanta fought on July 22. Still, Hood wrote extensively about his army's loss east of Atlanta six days prior to Ezra Church. He dedicated an entire chapter of his memoirs—seventy-three paragraphs—to the events leading up to and including the Battle of Atlanta, from a detailed discussion of the battle plan provided to his subordinates at headquarters through a description of the battle and a closing analysis. Hood went to great pains to blame General Hardee for the failure of the Army of Tennessee to carry the day.

With Hardee not involved in the Ezra Church battle planning, and having suffered a defeat there that, unlike the Battle of Atlanta, was a loss indisputable in hindsight, Hood evidently saw no reason to expand upon his official report. Given a second opportunity to provide the first definitive Confederate perspective of the battle, Hood produced a memoir passage about July 28 nowhere close to the chapter-length treatment he gave the previous battle:

> On the 28th it was apparent that Sherman was also moving [southwestward toward the Macon railroad] with his main body. Lieutenant General Lee was instructed to move out with his Corps upon the Lick Skillet road, and to take the position most advantageous to prevent or delay the extension of the enemy's right flank. This officer promptly obeyed orders, and came, unexpectedly, in the afternoon, in contact with the Federals in the vicinity of Ezra Church, where a spirited engagement ensued. The enemy was already in possession of a portion of the ground Lee desired to occupy, and the struggle grew to such dimensions that I sent Lieutenant General Stewart to his support. The contest lasted till near sunset without any material advantage having been gained

by either opponent. Our troops failed to dislodge the enemy from their position, and the Federals likewise to capture the position occupied by the Confederates. Although the actual loss was small in proportion to the numbers engaged, Generals Stewart, Brown, Loring, and Johns[t]on were slightly wounded. I desired of Lieutenant General Lee an opinion as to the manner in which our troops had conducted themselves upon the field. In answer to my request, he replied that he could not succeed in bringing about united action; whilst one brigade fought gallantly, another failed to do its duty. I learned afterwards that such indeed was the case, notwithstanding he had led one or more to the attack, and had even offered to lead others. Although this affair occurred subsequent to the improvement of the morale of the Army and the check to desertions, which had resulted from the battles of the 21st and 22d, the lack of spirit manifested in this instance will convey a just idea of the state of the Army at this period.

In reference to the non-capture of the position held by the enemy, [Lee] says in his official report: "I am convinced that if all the troops had displayed equal spirit, we would have been successful, as the enemy's works were slight, and, besides, they had scarcely gotten into position when we made the attack."[7]

This all-too-brief final passage from Hood regarding the Battle of Ezra Church provides very little of the insight expected from a memoir. Hood somehow managed to blame nonparticipant General Joseph E. Johnston for the "lack of spirit" manifested by the army as the chief cause of the defeat. Hood reproduced excerpts from his report and Lee's for much of this battle description. He must have been unaware of how poorly this interpretation presented itself for posterity, particularly Hood's dismissal of his battle casualties as "small in proportion to the numbers engaged," particularly since the erroneous but only publicly available Confederate casualty figures for Ezra Church were from Union estimates, which embellished the losses beyond 5,000—a number that would only be appropriately reduced toward 3,000 Ezra Church casualties more than 110 years later.

Aside from a focus on the perceived morale of his troops, Hood's other alteration to his earlier interpretation of Ezra Church can be found in his opening explanation that he became aware on the day of the battle ("On the 28th it was apparent") that Sherman intended to march his infantry counterclockwise to get to the railroads leading into Atlanta from the south. In reality, Hood was aware of Sherman's shift to the western side of the city two nights before the battle, leading to his council with his corps commanders at his headquarters on July 27, ostensibly when he discussed his two-day plan of battle with General Lee and General Stewart. Hood credited himself with perceiving Sherman's thrust to the railroad, defying his own report and correspondence that firmly confirmed his true belief that Sherman was attempting to attack the city from his new western locale. Not only did Hood conceal a headquarters meeting in which a two-pronged battle plan was discussed, but the reader of his revised Ezra Church history could only conclude the following:

1. No preplanning for battle west of Atlanta was ever discussed.
2. Lee was only sent out in reaction to the late discovery of Sherman's movements.
3. The battle commenced when Lee "unexpectedly" bumped into Union troops near Ezra Church.
4. Hood had no intention for Stewart's corps to be involved in an infantry fight west of Atlanta but felt compelled to send Stewart to aid Lee when the contest grew too large for Lee to fight alone.

All of these points had been refuted by the official reports of Stewart and Lee, both of whom revealed preplanning for the battle. Lee acknowledged he received Hood's orders to mass troops in the western sector of Atlanta's defenses at Lick Skillet Road on July 27, while Stewart left a strong impression that he was made aware that Lee would drive the enemy well away from the road on July 28 to allow Stewart to march four divisions farther out the following morning and attack the Union right flank.

Hood's memoirs also contradict his battle report. Hood stated in his February 1865 version of the battle that in the aftermath of the Battle of Atlanta he became aware "almost immediately" that Sherman would "attempt our left [west]." He did not pinpoint the date of this realization, but the text makes it clear it was before July 28. Indeed, Hood's chief of staff, Brigadier General Francis A. Shoup, wrote "about dark enemy moving toward our left" in his journal entry for July 26 and opened his July 27 entry with: "Enemy still moving toward our left, skirmishing feebly." Adding to this is Hood's correspondences (through the pen of General Shoup) to his corps commanders throughout the afternoon hours of July 27, ordering Lee and Stewart (but not Hardee) to "supply your troops with sixty rounds of ammunition," to be "in readiness to move at a moment's notice," and to move their troops "to the left." Finally, Shoup's headquarters dispatch to Stewart at 4:00 P.M. on July 27 that states, "From present appearances the enemy is preparing to attack our left," with a follow up to "Come to headquarters," absolutely refutes Hood's claim fifteen years later that he first became aware of Sherman's westward threat "on the 28th" and also dovetails neatly with Stewart's report indicating preparation for his corps to be the shock troops of a preplanned battle (hence the headquarters visit), not an afterthought simply to aid Lee.[8]

Why did Hood leave this erroneous impression in his memoirs, particularly when it would be in his best interest for posterity to reveal that he was adept and alert, was not fooled by Sherman's grand counterclockwise shift, and had effectively relayed a plan for two of his corps to disrupt it? It cannot be ruled out that Hood made a conscious decision to leave the impression upon readers of his Ezra Church account that he was completely oblivious to Sherman's movements until the morning of July 28, 1864. Such a misrepresentation automatically prevents the reader from reaching the conclusion that some other general in his stead could have done a better job between the battles east of Atlanta and that at Ezra Church than did he. At the same time, it eliminated one of Hood's worst shortcomings of this battle: the inexplicably late decision to send Lee out onto Lick Skillet Road to thwart the Union advance and keep possession of the thoroughfare.

Hood's two accounts regarding the Battle of Ezra Church appear to have been brief by design, perhaps because he never expected criticism for the battle. Ironically, had he expanded his report and his recollection to describe his battle plan with the same detail dedicated to his more ambitious plan for the Battle of Atlanta on July 22, he would likely have impressed all who studied the account, particularly President Davis, for his heady attempt to make the best use of his forces at hand. Had Hood added just one sentence to reveal his concern for Sherman's threat to Atlanta's defenses at the same time Lee engaged Howard in battle at Ezra Church—a concern for which he had supporting documentation—he would have justified not visiting the battlefield that day as well as provided a feasible explanation for limiting the number of divisions he sent out to block a three-corps Union army near the Poor House.

Not to be overlooked is Lieutenant General William J. Hardee, the general whom Hood sent in the waning hours of the Battle of Atlanta to assume field command. Rather than submit his official report to his superior officer in the campaign, Hardee instead sent his to Adjutant and Inspector General Sam Cooper on April 5, 1865. Hardee's unique theme was a defense against the scathing accusations Hood leveled against him in his official report, which Hardee had read and studied. "This fight of the 28th is mentioned by General Hood in terms to leave an impression of its success," Hardee explained pointedly, going on to claim that no single battle of the Atlanta Campaign did more "to demoralize and dishearten the troops engaged in it" than the fighting at Ezra Church. Although Hardee's statements were certainly affected by his absolute hatred of John B. Hood, his claim that Ezra Church broke the spirit of the Confederate infantryman is strongly supported by the battle of July 28, what its participants said in the early aftermath, and how those troops fought throughout the remainder of the Atlanta Campaign.

Appendix C

The Ezra Church Battlefield after the Battle

Since the day war waged across the wooded, broken, and uneven landscape surrounding Ezra Church and for a hundred years hence, the two square miles of contested ground morphed with each passing decade. The small chapel survived the battle only to disappear three weeks later. "The church is obliterated," revealed a XVI Corps infantryman on August 23—"'wiped out' by army operations." At the same time, the terrain surrounding the church lost trees to the quick work of encamped Union soldiers who expanded their strong latticework of siege defenses. By the close of the war, the battlefield had been sketched by artists and mapped by engineers, but not photographed.[1]

The battle and subsequent siege lines made life difficult for travelers and residents of the farming community surrounding the church in the early postwar years. The Fulton County Almshouse buildings likely disappeared around the same time as the church, and Lick Skillet Road was rendered inoperable as a public thoroughfare. "We find the road heading from Atlanta to Green's Ferry, the most public road in the county, entirely neglected, not having been worked on since the war," came the verdict from a Fulton County grand jury in the fall of 1867, pinpointing the region near the big bend in the road as most damaged. "It is entirely impassable, the traveling public having to wind their way as best they can, thereby lengthening their route and doing much damage to land on that line."[2]

The battlefield changed dramatically in the decades immediately following the war. The roads leading out of Atlanta slightly changed course, and new roads branched from these thoroughfare trunks, while new neighborhoods sprouted from the fields east, south, and west of where the church once stood. In the summer of 1882, merely eighteen years after war raged near Ezra Church, General William Loring rode out of Atlanta with two escorts to view the battlefield and stand at the spot where he was wounded on July 28, 1864. According to the reporter covering the event, "General Loring's memory of the details of the fight was as fresh as if it had occurred only a few weeks ago." Notwithstanding the vividness of his recollections, General Loring was so stung by the rapidly evolved landscape that he could not gain his proper bearings. To him, the battlefield was barely recognizable.[3]

Atlanta's populace expanded beyond the city limits throughout the postwar years of the 1800s. Westview Cemetery was established in the mid-1880s, taking up most of the land within the big bend of Lick Skillet Road, where Stephen D. Lee's brigades from Brown's division initially deployed. In 1895 Ezra Church received a unique tribute from the citizens who incorporated the village of "Battle Hill," which encompassed the entire battlefield on the other side of the road. In 1900 it was populated by 223 locals. The first-known photographs of the battlefield also appeared around this time, indicating a rural and still heavily wooded region. The Battle Hill Sanitarium was built in 1911 to care for infirm patients primarily with the diagnosis of tuberculosis. It stood on the heights where Martin's brigade of Ohioans dug in to repel Sharp's brigade and then O'Neal's brigade. The sanitarium was not, however, a part of the village of Battle Hill for more than two years because Fulton County had swallowed the short-lived incorporated town, which ceased to exist after 1913.[4]

The Ezra Church battlefield continued to fall prey to burgeoning urbanization as the nineteenth century came to a close, as had the Peachtree Creek battlefield in the northern environs of Atlanta and the Atlanta battlefield around Leggett's Hill. In near desperation, preservationists attempted to retain what remained of those three battlefields with a parkway connecting them along with other historic regions of Atlanta's perimeter with the desire to convert the entirety into a national park attraction. The movement attempted to appropriate $250,000 (equivalent to $6.4 million in 2014) for the purchase of 1,202 acres of battlefield property, including Ezra Church lands, and to convert them with improvements "similar to those heretofore made on the fields of Manassas, Shiloh, Gettysburg, Vicksburg, and Chickamauga." Backed by the state's U.S. senators and congressmen and the Georgia chapter of the Grand Army of the Republic, the effort gained momentum.[5] Somewhat surprisingly and extremely lamentably, the movement fell short of raising the funds necessary for land purchases.

Even modest attempts at bringing recognition to the Battle of Ezra Church failed. Shortly after the fiftieth anniversary of the battle in 1914, locals looked to one of the very few open spaces of the region, called Moseley Park, which housed the site of Ezra Church and the rear of the Union lines which defended the area on July 28, 1864. To recognize the historic value of the region (at this time a part of the Seventh Ward of Atlanta) without calling overt attention to its role as a battlefield, discussions took place to simply rename the land "Ezra Park." However, an alderman reminded the Seventh Ward Improvement committee that a verbal agreement existed with the Moseley family, who donated the land for the park, to keep their name associated with the park and the modest movement died. (Today the region has altered the name of the family and the park is called Mozley Park.)[6]

While the battlefield continued to be digested by the city, the battle of Ezra Church sporadically made news seemingly throughout the country due to its relics. The veterans of the 30th Louisiana Battalion negotiated the return of its flag from the state of Ohio which had housed it in Columbus for nearly a quarter of a century. In 1908, an Illinois soldier returned a Bible he took from the haversack of a dead South Carolina soldier, a story which circulated in newspapers in several states. Eleven bullets which killed as many Union soldiers during the battle dropped out of the remains when they were reinterred in national cemeteries. The bullets were carefully lodged in common planking; that wooden board found a home at the General Lander Post in Lynn, Massachusetts, a state which contributed no soldiers to the battle. Nearly eighty years after Ezra Church, the peaceful area where the battle was waged was stunned by an exploded shell from the battlefield. A local caretaker accidently scooped it up in a pile of trash, which he tossed into an outside fire. The jarring "Wham" and scattering trash and grapeshot panicked the yard worker and his neighbors and produced a little story published in newspapers in Florida, Iowa, and Maryland.[7]

The battlefield continued its transformation into a city for fifty more years. In the mid-1920s builders occupied the hill once defended by Reub Williams's brigade to dig and construct the "F. L. Stanton School" (uncovering soldiers' bones and buttons in the process). A train station and track followed as did an extending latticework of asphalt roads. The interstate system of the 1950s and 1960s became the mark of progress for America, but it also marred the interpretation of America's past. The old Ezra Church battlefield became more unrecognizable when Interstate 20 and its entrance and exit destroyed the landscape where Lee and Stewart attacked Logan.

While the battlefield fell prey to modernization, one Atlantan dedicated superlative effort to interpreting the Battle of Ezra Church in the mid-twentieth century landscape. Wilbur G. Kurtz, an artist and historian dedicated to all things Atlanta since he moved there as a twenty-one-year-old in 1903, began visiting the Ezra Church battlefield in the 1930s. This began a thirty-year off-and-on relationship between Kurtz and the battle, interrupted by numerous duties and necessary distractions—such as his stint as historical consultant for the filming of the motion picture *Gone with the Wind,* at the close of the 1930s. Kurtz presented a dedication address on the eighty-third anniversary of the battle at Westview Cemetery, where a new bronze marker to the battle was unveiled. Eleven years later, in 1858, Kurtz's battle interpretation appeared on battlefield markers throughout the neighborhood where the battle was waged.

When Kurtz passed away in February 1867, he left a legacy regarding Ezra Church and an influence that carried on for more than four decades. The battlefield during Kurtz's time and shortly afterward was featured in published driving and walking tours using the existing landscape to deduce where Union troops defended and Southerners attacked. But the neighborhood suffered through hard economic times, with Mozley Park serving as a scene of immense strife—from Ku Klux Klan cross burnings in the 1930s to a father's infanticide of two of his four children in the early 1980s.[8]

Today, a visitor to the Ezra Church battlefield can glimpse the vestige of the landscape from interpretive markers in Mozley Park, placed at the park's southeast corner close to where Ezra Church once stood, sometimes clean and sometimes defaced. The park occupies the inside of the Union lines and is surrounded by sites of Confederate attacks from the west, southwest, south, southeast, and east. The heights are gradual but apparent. In the woods on the high ground an occasional segment of a trench earthwork still exists, as may also be apparent by the raised line of trees running northward from the church site. But the landscape of 1864 is essentially gone; most of the signage that was carefully placed to describe the specific points of battle is admirable for its dedication to detail, but modern technology refutes some of the locations. An overlay of the 1864 engineer map upon the modern landscape reveals a larger battlefield than what the signs appear to interpret.

Although the opportunity for the peak preservation of the Ezra Church battlefield was essentially lost a century ago, it cannot be overlooked that the field was already converted to a neighborhood within fifteen years of the fight. The fact that the field no longer exists in a readily recognizable landscape presents challenges (not unlike the sites of the Battles of Peachtree Creek and Atlanta on the east side of the city), but should not dampen any future attempts to find hidden answers to the questions that still surround the great battle of July 28, 1864.

Notes

Abbreviations

AHC	Atlanta Historical Center
KMNBP	"The Civil War Letters of Elbridge Littlejohn," ed. Vicki Betts, Kennesaw Mountain National Battlefield Park
LOC	Library of Congress, Washington, D.C.
OR	U.S. War Department, *War of the Rebellion: A Compilation of the Official Records of the Union and Confederate Armies* (Washington, D.C.: 1880–1901)
OR Atlas	George B. Davis, Leslie J. Perry, and Joseph W. Kirkley, *The Official Military Atlas of the Civil War* (New York: Gramercy Books, 1983)
USAHEC	U.S. Army Heritage and Education Center, Carlisle Barracks, Pa.

Chapter 1

1. U.S. War Department, *War of the Rebellion: A Compilation of the Official Records of the Union and Confederate Armies* (Washington, D.C.: 1880–1901; hereafter cited as *OR*) 38 (1): 116–17. The 94,000 soldier count is derived from a July 31 effective-strength report with known casualties during the final week of July added in.

2. Union casualties between May 1 and July 24, 1864, obtained from Darroch Greer, "Counting Civil War Casualties, Week-by-Week, for the Abraham Lincoln Presidential Library and Museum," www.brcweb.com/alplm/BRC_Counting_Casualties.pdf.

3. *OR* 38 (2): 904–909; *OR* 38 (5): 235, 237.

4. Robert D. Jenkins, *The Battle of Peach Tree Creek: Hood's First Sortie, 20 July 1864* (Macon, Ga: Mercer University Press, 2013), 395.

5. *OR* 38 (1): 116–17, 120. The number of troops and cannons is determined from comparing the June 30 and July 31 monthly reports with battle losses for the month of July accounted as well.

6. *OR* 38 (5): 240, 243.

7. *OR* 38 (5): 241. Nathaniel Lyon, who commanded a division-sized army when he became the first Union general and first army commander to be killed in battle at Wilson's Creek on August 10, 1861, was commissioned a brigadier general.

8. Grant to Lincoln, February 9, 1863, Abraham Lincoln Papers, Manuscript Division, Library of Congress, Washington, D.C. (hereafter cited as LOC).

9. Grant quote from recollection of William M. Beach (78th Ohio), in Robert Underwood Johnson and Clarence Clough Buel, eds., *Battles and Leaders of the Civil War* (New York: Century Co., 1887), 3:511.

10. *Harpers Weekly Illustrated,* July, 2, 1864; J. W. Long, "Flanking Johnston: The Army of the Tennessee on the Move," *National Tribune,* September 13, 1888.

11. Mark E. Kellogg, comp., *Army Life of an Illinois Soldier, Including a Day-to-Day Record of Sherman's March to the Sea: Letters and Diary of Charles W. Wills* (Carbondale: Southern Illinois University Press, 1996), 239, 241.

12. Mortimer D. Leggett quote in *Report of the Proceedings of the Society of the Army of the Tennessee, at the Twentieth Meeting* (Cincinnati: Published by the Society, 1893), 541.

13. *OR* 38 (5): 242–43.

14. Ibid.; 240.

15. Both of these reasons were first highlighted and convincingly dismissed by the analysis of historian Albert Castel in his landmark Atlanta Campaign study. See *Decision in the West: The Atlanta Campaign of 1864* (Lawrence: University Press of Kansas, 1992), 611n88.

16. William Tecumseh Sherman, *Memoirs of General W. T. Sherman* (New York: Literary Classics of the United States, 1990), 558–59; "From Georgia," *Burlington (Iowa) Weekly Hawkeye,* July 23, 1864; Samuel W. Fordyce IV, ed., *An American General: The Memoirs of David Sloan Stanley* (Santa Barbara, Calif.: Narrative Press, 2003), 180.

17. "Address of W. T. Sherman," *Report of the Proceedings of the Society of the Army of the Tennessee, at the Twentieth Meeting* (Cincinnati: Published by the Society, 1893), 471–72.

18. Sherman interview with "Gath," *Cincinnati Daily Enquirer,* December 31, 1886.

19. *OR* 38 (5): 240.

20. Ibid., 272.

21. For the names of the Union regimental officers who were casualties on July 22, see the Order of Battle in Gary Ecelbarger, *The Day Dixie Died: The Battle of Atlanta* (New York: Thomas Dunne Books, 2010), 233–38.

22. Leslie Anders, "Fisticuffs at Headquarters: Sweeny vs. Dodge," *Civil War Times Illustrated* 15, no. 10 (February 1977): 8–15; *OR* 38 (3): 385–86.

23. A. A. Stuart, *Iowa Colonel and Regiments* (Des Moines, Iowa: Mills & Company, 1865), 237–41; *OR* 38 (3): 596, 598.

24. *OR* 38 (3): 133–34; *OR* 38 (5): 247, 259–60.

25. *OR* 38 (5): 255.

26. Ibid., 260–61.

Chapter 2

1. Stephen Davis, *What the Yankees Did to Us: Sherman's Bombardment and Wrecking of Atlanta* (Macon, Ga.: Mercer University Press, 2012), 174–75; *OR* 38 (3): 906.

2. *OR* 38 (5): 885.

3. Ezra Warner, *Generals in Gray: Lives of Confederate Commanders* (Baton Rouge: Louisiana State University Press, 1959), 203–204; *Atlanta Historical Bulletin* 15

(1970): 94; Castel, *Decision in the West*, 422–23; *OR* 38 (5): 907; Milt Diggins, "Cecil County's Civil War General," Historical Society of Cecil County, www.cecil history.org/mackall.html.

4. *OR* 32 (2): 799.

5. *OR* 38 (5): 885.

6. Norman D. Brown, ed., *One of Cleburne's Command: The Civil War Reminiscences and Diary of Capt. Samuel T. Foster, Granbury's Texas Brigade, C. S. A.* (Austin: University of Texas Press, 1980), 115; Robert Gill to his wife, July 18, 1864, in Bell I. Wiley, "A Story of 3 Southern Officers," *Civil War Times Illustrated* 3, no. 1 (April 1964): 33; Martin Van Buren Oldham diary, July 18, 1864, Civil War Diaries of (Martin) Van Buren Oldham, www.utm.edu/departments/special_ collections/E579.5%20Oldham/text/vboldham_1864.php.

7. Reynolds diary, July 24–25, 1864, in Robert Patrick Bender, ed., *Worthy of the Cause for Which They Fight: The Civil War Diary of Brigadier General Daniel Harris Reynolds, 1861–1865* (Fayetteville: University of Arkansas Press, 2011), 139.

8. *OR* 38 (5): 903, 908.

9. Hiram Williams diary, July 22, 1864, in Lewis N. Wynne and Robert A. Taylor, eds., *This War So Horrible: The Civil War Diary of Hiram Smith Williams* (Tuscaloosa: University of Alabama Press, 1993), 106.

10. June 10 strength revised in Richard M. McMurry, "A Policy So Disastrous: Joseph E. Johnston's Atlanta Campaign," in Theodore P. Savas and David A. Woodbury, eds., *The Campaign for Atlanta and Sherman's March to the Sea*, vol. 2 (Campbell, Calif.: Savas Woodbury Publishers, 1994), 236. July 25 strength derived from July 31 Confederate returns with casualties in the final week of July added into the total, as well as Georgia militia. See *OR* 38 (3): 680.

11. Confederate losses of 15,450 through July 17 calculated in McMurry, "Policy So Disastrous," 237. Losses since July 17 include 2,600 between July 18 and 20, 300 on July 21, and upwards of 6,300 on July 22. See Gary Ecelbarger, "An Ambitious Goal Indeed: An Evaluation of General John B. Hood's Plan and Generalship during the Battle of Atlanta, July 22, 1864," *North & South Magazine* 13, no. 2 (July 2011): 22, 24, 30–31.

12. T. B. Roy, "General Hardee and the Military Operations around Atlanta," *Southern Historical Society Papers* 8 (September 1880): 367; Irving A. Buck, *Cleburne and His Command* (Jackson, Tenn.: McCowat-Mercer Press, 1959), 243.

13. *OR* 38 (5): 907.

14. July 20 losses tallied in Jenkins, *Battle of Peach Tree Creek*, 397.

15. *OR* 38 (5): 892; Warner, *Generals in Gray*, 292–93.

16. *OR* 38 (5): 892.

17. *OR* 38 (3): 631.

18. *OR* 52 (2): 712–13.

19. Herman Hattaway, *General Stephen D. Lee* (Jackson: University Press of Mississippi, 1976), 126; Warner, *Generals in Gray*, 183.

20. Bruce S. Allardice, "'It Was Perfect Murder': Stephen D. Lee at Ezra Church," in Lawrence Lee Hewitt and Arthur W. Bergeron, Jr., eds., *Confederate Generals, in the Western Theater* (Knoxville: University of Tennessee Press, 2011), 3:222–24; Nathaniel C. Hughes, ed., *The Civil War Memoirs of Philip Daingerfield Stephenson* (Conway, Ariz.: UCA Press, 1995), 212.

21. Hattaway, *General Stephen D. Lee*, 165.

22. Warner, *Generals in Gray*, 275–76; *OR* 38 (5): 910, 912.

23. *OR* 38 (5): 910, 912.
24. Ibid., 898, 904, 938, 940.
25. *OR* 38 (3): 688.

Chapter 3

1. *OR* 38 (3): 40.
2. Sherman to Halleck, July 27, 1864, in Brooks D. Simpson and Jean V. Berlin, eds., *Sherman's Civil War: Selected Correspondence of William T. Sherman, 1860–1865* (Chapel Hill: University of North Carolina Press, 1999), 673.
3. Grenville M. Dodge, *Personal Recollections of General William T. Sherman* (Des Moines, Iowa: n.p., 1902), 21–22; Sherman to Logan, July 27, 1864, and Logan to his wife, August 6, 1864, Logan Papers, LOC.
4. Sherman to Halleck, July 27, 1864, in Simpson and Berlin, *Sherman's Civil War*, 673; Hooker to Logan, July 27, 1864, Logan Papers, LOC. Hooker had also resigned from the Army of the Potomac over a slight while the Army marched toward Gettysburg in June 1863.
5. *OR* 38 (3): 40; *OR* 38 (5): 274–75; Oliver O. Howard, "Atlanta Campaign . . . Ezra Church," *National Tribune*, March 7, 1895.
6. Sherman to his wife, July 26, 1864, in Simpson and Berlin, *Sherman's Civil War*, 672.
7. Howard, "Atlanta Campaign . . . Ezra Church," March 7, 1895.
8. *OR* 38 (3): 904; Jack D. Welsh, *Medical Histories of Confederate Generals* (Kent, Ohio: Kent State University Press, 1995), 60; William R. Scaife, *The Campaign for Atlanta*, 4th ed. (Cartersville, Ga.: Civil War Publications, 1993), 182–83, 186; Elbridge Littlejohn to his wife, August 6, 1864, letter no. 46, "The Civil War Letters of Elbridge Littlejohn," ed. Vicki Betts, Kennesaw Mountain National Battlefield Park (hereafter cited as KMNBP).
9. *OR* 38 (3): 680, 688, 953; *OR* 38 (5): 912–17.
10. *OR* 38 (5): 315–17.
11. Dispatches from headquarters to Stewart and Lee were written at 6:40 and 6:45 P.M. (see *OR* 38 [5]: 916–17). It cannot be ruled out that Hardee was also invited, but no dispatch or other supporting evidence has come to light. The J. Windsor Smith house has been misidentified as Hood's headquarters this day. See Franklin M. Garrett, *Atlanta and Environs: A Chronicle of Its People and Events* (Athens: University of Georgia Press, 1969), 1:625. The John S. Thrasher home served as the site from July 22 to August 12 (see Davis, *What the Yankees Did*, 174–78).
12. It must be noted that the plan is merely assumed to have been discussed between the three generals at headquarters Wednesday evening, July 27, based solely on the two dispatches summoning each corps commander to headquarters at the same time. The plan may have been briefly discussed here and modified with subsequent instructions either later that night or the following morning.
13. *OR* 38 (3) 631. Notwithstanding the benefit of six months' hindsight when he compiled his official report, Hood acknowledged that the railroads were the objective of Sherman's cavalry only while the infantry and artillery were directed to "the siege of Atlanta." Any and every secondary source that reasons Hood's goal west of Atlanta was to stop Sherman's infantry from advancing to the rail-

roads has disregarded or misread what Hood reveals so clearly in his report. Otherwise, why would Hood not credit himself for prescience and say he knew that Sherman was going counterclockwise to the railroads? This part of his report reveals an honest limit to his knowledge for the days preceding Ezra Church.

14. General Howard insisted that the true Lick Skillet Road was the one that ran due west out of Atlanta, and that the road upon which the Confederates marched out of Atlanta was Bell's Ferry Road or Green's Ferry Road (which joined roadbeds with Lick Skillet Road at the Fulton County Almshouse buildings). See Howard, "Atlanta Campaign . . . Ezra Church," March 7, 1895. Howard's assertion was seconded more recently by Atlanta historian Wilbur Kurtz. See folder 2 ("Ezra Church 1942–1965, undated"), MSS 130, Box 47, Wilbur Kurtz Collection, Atlanta Historical Center (hereafter cited as AHC). Regardless, all references to Lick Skillet Road east of the Fulton County Almshouse will adopt the Confederate name of the thoroughfare out of Atlanta.

15. Ibid., 688 (Shoup's journal), 762 (Lee's report), 872 (Stewart's report).

16. Peachtree Creek casualties provided in Jenkins, *Battle of Peach Tree Creek*, 397. Stevenson's division strength in Peter W. Alexander Papers, Rare Book and Manuscript Library, Columbia University, New York. Subsequent communication from headquarters suggests that William Bate's 3,300 officers and men would have been that fourth division (*OR* 38 [5]: 921).

17. *OR* 38 (5): 632, 762.

18. Ibid., 762.

19. Ibid., 409.

20. Sally Coplen Hogan, ed., *General Reub Williams's Memories of Civil War Times: Personal Reminiscences of Happenings That Took Place from 1861 to the Grand Review* (Westminster, Md.: Heritage Books, 2004), 186; S. Stocker to the editor, August 15, 1864, *New Philadelphia (Ohio) Tuscarawas Advocate*, September 2, 1864.

21. T. W. Connelly, *History of the Seventieth Ohio Regiment: From Its Organization to Its Mustering Out* (Cincinnati: Peak Bros., 1902), 97.

22. Stewart Bennett and Barbara Tillery, eds., *The Struggle for the Life of the Republic: A Civil War Narrative by Brevet Major Charles Dana Miller, 76th Ohio Volunteer Infantry* (Kent, Ohio: Kent State University Press, 2004), 190.

23. *OR* 38 (5): 274–75. A likely embroidered appearance of this house was recreated twenty years later for the famous painting of the Atlanta Cyclorama.

24. *OR* 38 (3): 40, 104.

25. Ibid., 167, 189; Morgan Smith's Ezra Church report, August 1, 1864, Carton 45, Logan Papers, LOC; "Position of the 16th Army Corps from July 26 to August 26, 1864," map 15, plate LXI, in George B. Davis, Leslie J. Perry, and Joseph W. Kirkley, *The Official Military Atlas of the Civil War* (New York: Gramercy Books, 1983; hereafter cited as *OR Atlas*); J. G. B. to the editor, August 5, 1864, *Clinton (Ill.) Weekly Register*, August 22, 1864; Ezra Church file, Deed Book, vol. C., 437–38, folder 2 ("Ezra Church 1942–1965, undated"), MSS 130, Box 47, Wilbur Kurtz Collection, AHC.

26. *OR* 38 (3): 688, 767. Cavalry numbers derived from the July 31, 1864, strength report (see ibid., 680).

27. Ibid., 767; Henry M. Hope, *The Poor Houses* (Camarillo, Calif.: Xulon Press, 2008), 42–44; folder 2 ("Ezra Church 1942–1965, undated"), MSS 130, Box 47,

Wilbur Kurtz Collection, AHC. Traditionally, the location of the three structures stood where the present-day gate to Westview Cemetery is located.

28. J. G. Deupree, "The Noxubee Squadron of the First Mississippi Cavalry, C. S. A., 1861–1865," in *Publications of the Mississippi Historical Society*, ed. Dunbar Rowland (Jackson, Miss., 1918), 2:12–143, esp. 102.

29. Frank C. Montgomery, *Reminiscences of a Mississippian in Peace and War* (Cincinnati: Robert Clark Company Press, 1901), 191–92.

30. Deupree, "Noxubee Squadron," 102; J. A. Biggers diary, July 28, 1864, Mississippi Department of Archives and History.

31. *OR* 38 (3): 122; J. Willard Brown, *The Signal Corps, U.S.A., in the War of the Rebellion* (Boston: U.S. Veteran Signal Corps Association, 1896), 534–35; "The Signal Corps," *National Tribune*, April 5, 1883.

32. *OR* 38 (3): 872; *OR* 38 (5): 918.

33. *OR* 38 (3): 167. Proof that the church stood inside the Union line exists in the contemporary military maps drawn shortly afterward. See *OR Atlas*, plates LVI (no. 7), LXI (no. 5), and LXXXVIII (no. 1), for three separate examples.

34. Connelly, *History of the Seventieth Ohio*, 97. This road was named West Hunter Street, then Mozely Drive, and is now known as Martin Luther King Boulevard. The modern road closely follows this roadbed. From Ezra Church southwestward the Civil War road ran parallel with MLK Blvd. and slightly south of it. This likely was the true Lick Skillet Road, although the traditionally accepted Lick Skillet Road converged with this one near the Fulton County Almshouse. See folder 2 ("Ezra Church 1942–1965, undated"), MSS 130, Box 47, Wilbur Kurtz Collection, AHC.

35. George Hildt to his parents, August 15, 1864, Hildt Papers, Ohio Historical Center, Columbus.

36. Expected numbers present derived from July 31 strength report with Ezra Church casualties added back in (see *OR* 38 [1]: 116). Based on this method the seven infantry brigades of the XV Corps numbered 9,000 officers and men present for duty the morning of the battle. The number deployed was likely closer to 8,000 due to limited space and stragglers who never reached their lines.

37. Ibid., 305, 310; James B. Swan, *Chicago's Irish Legion: The 90th Illinois Volunteers in the Civil War* (Carbondale: Southern Illinois University Press, 2009), 153.

38. *OR* 38 (3): 343.

39. Sherman, *Memoirs*, 562; *OR* 38 (1): 77.

40. Morgan L. Smith to Robert R. Townes, August 1, 1864, Logan Papers, LOC; *OR* 38 (3): 254.

41. Population Schedules of the Eighth Census of the United States, 1860, Campbell and Fulton Counties, Georgia; Ninth Census of the United States, Fulton County, Georgia, 1870—both in RG 29, National Archives.

42. Sherman, *Memoirs*, 562; *OR* 38 (1): 77–78.

43. *OR* 38 (3): 174–75; Thomas D. Maurice to Colonel [Robert] Townes, September 9, 1864, Logan Papers, LOC.

44. Smith to Townes, August 1, 1864, Logan Papers, LOC.

Chapter 4

1. *OR* 38 (3): 631. Hood and the editors of the *Official Records* made the referenced quote more complicated than it should have been. Hood initially wrote the word "right," which meant flank, without saying it. Either Hood or an editor of this report felt an obvious correction was necessary and did so by writing "desired to place his left [right] on Utoy Creek." The edit appears appropriate based on the distance and expected resistance Howard expected this day. Note: Hood's use of "left" or "right" assumes he still expected an attack eastward from that flank.

2. *OR* 38 (5): 918. The 10:30 A.M. departure dovetails well with a brigadier's report (see *OR* 38 [3]: 781), but others claim times suggesting a much earlier or later departure (see Lee's report [ibid., 762] for an 11:00 A.M. claim). Most sources time the start of the battle between 11:30 and noon. Even noon would be an incredibly short timetable for an 11:00 A.M. departure to move 4,000 soldiers four abreast two miles on Lick Skillet Road; pull off the brigades to the left one by one, while crossing one of the tail brigades in the division column a mile behind the rest; have 3,000 front-line troops deployed in line of battle; and then send them all forward to attack. To have done these maneuvers all in forty-five minutes appears unlikely.

3. *OR* 38 (3): 767.

4. Quote from Charles Smith diary, July 28, 1864, in George R. Cryder and Stanley R. Miller, comps., *A View from the Ranks: The Civil War Diaries of Charles E. Smith, 1861–1865* (Delaware, Ohio: Delaware County Historical Society, 1999), 422.

5. *OR* 38 (3): 632. The specific point that Hood wanted Lee to occupy is clearly stated in the former's report (cited here), but somehow has been overlooked for 150 years since Hood mentioned it.

6. *OR* 38 (3): 762–63, 767, 821, 872. Red Jackson's use of the word "small" comes indirectly from General Brown's version of their conversation. Howard's description of Lee is in "Atlanta Campaign . . . Ezra Church," *National Tribune*, March 14, 1895. His Ezra Church piece was published in two consecutive issues of the weekly *National Tribune*, and was a part of his entire Atlanta Campaign history, which was published throughout the winter and early spring of 1895.

7. *OR* 38 (3): 763.

8. Ibid., 767–94. Brown's division strength is estimated partly from strength reports from two of the four brigades on July 28, and also from officers and men present for duty obtained from a division numerical tally three days later (*OR* 38 [3]: 680) with his Ezra Church casualties (*OR* 38 [3]: 768) added to this number to backdate his strength to July 28.

9. Ibid., 777, 780; Paul Branch, "Johnston, George Doherty," http://ncpedia .org/biography/johnston-george-doherty.

10. *OR* 38 (3): 777.

11. Ibid., 789–91.

12. The brigade's performance at the Battle of Atlanta is detailed in Ecelbarger, *Day Dixie Died*, 161–63.

13. *OR* 38 (3): 799.

14. Ibid., 781.

15. Edward Schweitzer diary, July 28, 1864, typescript, U.S. Army Heritage and Education Center, Carlisle Barracks, Pa. (hereafter cited as USAHEC).

16. Maurice to Townes, September 9, 1864, Logan Papers, LOC.

17. To this day the number and locations of the Confederate batteries at Ezra Church remain a mystery.

18. Warner, *Generals in Gray*, 35–36; Welsh, *Medical Histories of Confederate Generals*, 29.

19. *OR* 38 (3): 218, 288, 294.

20. Ibid., 343, 776, 779–80.

21. Welsh, *Medical Histories of Confederate Generals*, 119.

22. Ibid.; M. D. Gage, *From Vicksburg to Raleigh; or, A Complete History of the Twelfth Regiment Indiana Volunteer Infantry* (Chicago: Clarke and Company, 1865), 223; *OR* 38 (3): 776. General Brown inadvertently misled most historians who attempted to document the chain of command within Johnston's brigade at Ezra Church by mistakenly reporting that Colonel Hart was killed in an extremely brief tenure as the brigade commander. This error was made independently by Brown, who wrote his division report before he received his brigadiers' reports. Had he waited three more days, Brown would have learned that Hart was killed while in charge of his regiment during this initial assault. See *OR* 38 (3): 777.

23. *OR* 38 (3): 776–80; Solomon Palmer diary, July 28, 1864, typescript at KMNBP. Captain Isaac M. Whitney replaced Toulmin at the helm of the 22nd Alabama. Whitney confirmed that Hart was killed while in charge of the regiment (and not the brigade) although he mistakenly stated that Hart died in a later, second charge. This would be impossible because Toulmin—Hart's subordinate—*ordered* the second charge in his first act as a brigade commander. Whitney also fails to mention Toulmin at all in his report. This leaves Toulmin's report as the most reliable representation of chronology and the chain of succession within Johnston's brigade. *OR* 38 (3): 777–78.

24. Scaife, *Campaign for Atlanta*, 178; James Binford's Recollection of the Fifteenth Regiment of Mississippi Infantry, C.S.A., 81–82, manuscript at Chickamauga National Military Park (CNMP). I am grateful to Robert Jenkins for calling my attention to this valuable source.

25. *OR* 38 (3): 218; Roger Boedecker, *The Civil War Service of the 127th Illinois Infantry* (n.p., 2007), 80; Stocker to the editor, August 15, 1864, *New Philadelphia (Ohio) Tuscarawas Advocate*, September 2, 1864. The example of sunstroke is in "Casualties in the 70th Ohio Regiment," *West Union (Ohio) Democratic Union*, August 12, 1864.

26. Committee of the Regiment, *The Story of the Fifty-fifth Regiment Illinois Volunteer Infantry in the Civil War* (Clinton, Mass.: W. J. Coulter, 1887), 328, 349.

27. E. Coombe, "The 28th of July before Atlanta," *National Tribune*, February 7, 1884.

28. Committee of the Regiment, *Story of the Fifty-fifth Illinois*, 345. Numbers present for the regiment derived from same source, which states "the effective force . . . was one hundred and eighty" (348–49). This number of "effectives" excludes commissioned officers, which likely numbered an additional fifteen–twenty members of the 55th Illinois.

29. Ibid., 349. A few of the regiment were killed later in the day, including one man who was a victim of friendly fire.

30. *OR* 38 (3): 790.

31. Ibid., 211; David Thom diary, May 30, 1864, USAHEC.

32. *OR* 38 (3): 211; Schweitzer diary, July 28, 1864; Stocker to the editor, August 15, 1864, *New Philadelphia (Ohio) Tuscarawas Advocate*, September 2, 1864; Hildt to his parents, August 15, 1864.

33. Schweitzer diary, July 28, 1864; Hildt to his parents, July 31 and August 15, 1864; *OR* 38 (3): 789–90, 793; 30th Ohio Casualty analysis, American Civil War Research Database, www.civilwardata.com.

34. *OR* 38 (3): 792.

35. Ibid., 86.

36. Captain J. B. Ridenour, "General Logan in Line," *Elyria (Ohio) Democrat*, December 22, 1887.

37. Samuel Fletcher, *History of Company A, Second Illinois Cavalry* (Chicago, 1912), 65, 203.

38. Hogan, *General Reub Williams's Memories*, 189; Newspaper Scrapbook, vol. 8, Logan Papers, LOC; "From a Private's Diary," *New York Times*, January 15, 1893; Ridenour, "General Logan in Line."

39. *OR* 38 (3): 792.

40. Castel, *Decision in the West*, 430–31; Paul A. Angle, ed., *Three Years in the Army of the Cumberland: The Letters and Diary of Major James A. Connelly* (1959; repr., Bloomington: Indiana University Press, 1984), 245–46.

Chapter 5

1. Warner, *Generals in Gray*, 52–53.

2. *OR* 38 (3): 799–800, 802–803, 807–808, 810.

3. Ibid., 222; Wells S. Jones, "How a Great Battle Was Begun," *American Tribune*, January 30, 1891.

4. Ibid.; Albert Castel, *Tom Taylor's Civil War* (Lawrence: University Press of Kansas, 2000), 164.

5. *OR* 38 (3): 222; Jones, "Great Battle."

6. Ibid.; Scaife, *Campaign for Atlanta*, 110; Castel, *Tom Taylor's Civil War*, 154–55; Edward W. Smith, "Battle of Ezra Church: A Coffee-Cooler's Experience," *National Tribune*, July 5, 1888.

7. *OR* 38 (3): 799. Although Brantly's men brushed away the small Union force at Lick Skillet Road and initially kept pace with Sharp's brigade on their right, Brantly's reorientation of the brigade in addition to the expanded distance it needed to cover as the outermost force in the line, delayed its challenge to the Union line by at least ten to fifteen minutes compared to Johnston and Sharp's opening assault.

8. *OR* 38 (3): 204, 238; Jones, "Great Battle."

9. Ibid.; Howard, "Atlanta Campaign . . . Ezra Church," March 14, 1895.

10. *Reunion of the 37th Regiment O. V. V. I* (Toledo, Ohio: Montgomery and Vrooman Printers, 1890), 50–52; Howard, "Atlanta Campaign . . . Ezra Church," March 14, 1895.

11. *OR* 38 (3): 768, 776, 790, 792. Sharp reported 214 total losses for the battle. It is estimated that most, but not all, occurred in this particular assault.

12. *OR* 38 (3): 319, 333.

13. Boedecker, *Civil War Service*, 80–81.

14. *OR* 38 (3), 333, 810; Ronald H. Bailey and the editors of Time-Life Books, *Battles for Atlanta: Sherman Moves East* (Alexandria, Va.: Time-Life Books, 1985), 137.

15. *OR* 38 (3): 803; Henry H. Wright, *A History of the Sixth Iowa Infantry* (Iowa City: State Historical Society of Iowa, 1923), 309.

16. Ibid.; "Casualties in the 6th Iowa Infantry," *Burlington Weekly Hawkeye*, August 6, 1864.

17. *OR* 38 (3): 41, 569; Hosea Whitford Rood, *Story of the Service of Company E, and of the Twelfth Wisconsin Regiment, Veteran Volunteer Infantry in the War of the Rebellion* (Milwaukee, Wis.: Swain & Tate Co., 1893), 323; James H. Clement file, American Civil War Research Database, www.civilwardata.com.

18. *OR* 38 (3): 808. Levings quoted in Robert W. Wells, "Wisconsin in the Civil War," *Milwaukee Journal*, November 3, 1961.

19. *OR* 38 (3): 800.

20. Ibid., 319, 322–24, 569; "List of Casualties 4th Division, 15th Army Corps for July 28, 1864," Logan Papers, LOC.

21. Ezra Warner, *Generals in Blue: Lives of Union Commanders* (Baton Rouge: Louisiana State University Press, 1959), 534–35; Charles C. Walcutt Commission Branch File, M1064, National Archives; Charles Walcutt biographical sketch in Walcutt Family Papers, Ohio Historical Center; Sherman to Thomas Ewing, January 16, 1863, in Simpson and Berlin, *Sherman's Civil War*, 355.

22. *OR* 38 (3): 238, 248, 254, 260; Castel, *Tom Taylor's Civil War*, 156.

23. R. Lockwood Tower, ed., *A Carolinian Goes to War: The Civil War Narrative of Arthur Middleton Manigault, Brigadier General, C. S. A.* (Columbia: University of South Carolina Press, 1983), 232.

24. *OR* 38 (3): 781.

25. Tower, *Carolinian Goes to War*, 232.

26. Ibid.; *OR* 38 (3): 782, 788; "Memories of War," *Columbia (S.C.) State*, September 7, 1895; "Why General Walker Remembers Macon," *Macon (Ga.) Telegram*, March 23, 1905.

27. Committee of the Regiment, *Story of the Fifty-fifth Illinois*, 346.

28. J. G. B. to the editor, August 5, 1864; *OR* 38 (3): 782; Tower, *Carolinian Goes to War*, 232–33.

29. *OR* 38 (3): 776; 779–80; Reub Williams recollections in *American Tribune*, 1887, Newspaper Scrapbook, vol. 9, Logan Papers, LOC; W. W. Odell to his nephew, August 3, 1864, SC 132, Abraham Lincoln Presidential Library, Springfield, Ill. (hereafter cited as ALPL).

30. Odell to his nephew, August 3, 1864, ALPL.

31. *OR* 38 (3): 777; Gillmore's Ezra Church report, July 31, 1864, copy in author's possession.

32. *OR* 38 (3): 288; Reub Williams recollections in *American Tribune*, 1887, LOC.

33. *OR* 38 (3): 781.

34. Hogan, *General Reub Williams's Memories*, 189; Reub Williams recollections in *American Tribune*, 1887, LOC.

35. Gage, *From Vicksburg to Raleigh*, 223; *OR* 38 (3): 776–77; Solomon Palmer diary, July 28, 1864; Gillmore's Ezra Church report, July 31, 1864.

36. *OR* 38 (3): 783–86.

37. Ibid., 782, 788.
38. Ibid., 784; J. G. B. to the editor, August 5, 1864; Tower, *Carolinian Goes to War*, 233.
39. Tower, *Carolinian Goes to War*, 233–34; *OR* 38 (3): 782–85.
40. *OR* 38 (3): 768–69.

Chapter 6

1. *OR* 38 (5): 919.
2. Ibid. All secondary accounts of this battle that attempt to interpret this dispatch have misinterpreted it as Hood's warning to Lee to counterassault if the enemy struck *Lee's* left flank. If so, Hood would have written "your left" to Lee. His use of "our left," as seen in the text, carries an entirely different meaning.
3. Ibid. Separate dispatch found on same page of *Official Records*, at the top of a string of five published messages.
4. Warner, *Generals in Gray*, 104.
5. Arthur Bergeron, Jr., *Guide to Louisiana Confederate Military Units, 1861–1865* (Baton Rouge: Louisiana State University Press, 1989), 71, 81, 102, 105, 116, 121, 158, 167, 169; "List of Casualties in Gibson's Louisiana Brigade, in the Fight near Atlanta on July 28," *New Orleans Times-Picayune*, August 26, 1864; Stuart Salling, *Louisianans in the Western Confederacy* (Jefferson, N.C.: McFarland & Company, 2010), 161, 178; Janet B. Hewitt, Noah Andre Trudeau, and Bryce A. Suderow, eds., *Supplement to the Official Records of the Union and Confederate Armies* (Wilmington, N.C.: Broadfoot Publishing Company, 1994–98), 2 (24): 442. An unattributed source estimates the brigade strength at 1,500. See "Thirtieth Louisiana: The Veterans Come Together to Make Arrangements for the Reception of Their Old Flag," *New Orleans Times-Picayune*, May 15, 1887.
6. Quote obtained from "Reverend James Hugh McNeilly," www.scvcamp260.org/mcneilly.html.
7. *OR* 38 (3): 821, 856.
8. Ibid., 763, 821, 856.
9. Ibid.; 856.
10. Ibid.; 343–44.
11. "Thirtieth's Flag in Memorial Hall," *New Orleans Times-Picayune*, October 10, 1900.
12. *OR* 38 (3): 338.
13. Ibid., 359.
14. After the battle a report was widely circulated that Shields hailed from Ohio, an error that drew derision from a woman who knew Shields well enough to be called a "near relative" of his. "He was never in Ohio in his life," she scoffed. See "Col. Thomas Shields of the 30th Louisiana," *New Orleans Times-Picayune*, September 21, 1864.
15. The strength of the 30th Louisiana is in "Casualties of Louisiana Regiments July 28," *New Orleans Times-Picayune*, August 21, 1864. Quotes are found in "Thirtieth's Flag in Memorial Hall," *New Orleans Times-Picayune*, October 10, 1900.
16. "Thirtieth Louisiana: The Veterans Come Together to Make Arrangements for the Reception of Their Old Flag," *New Orleans Times-Picayune*, May 15,

1887; Connelly, *History of the Seventieth Ohio*, 99; quote in *OR* 38 (3): 359. Connelly's account describes the same charge at the top and bottom of the page and erroneously confuses them as separate assaults.

17. Salling, *Louisianans in the Western Confederacy*, 189–90.

18. "Thirtieth Louisiana," *New Orleans Times-Picayune*, May 15, 1887; quotes are found in "Thirtieth's Flag in Memorial Hall," *New Orleans Times-Picayune*, October 10, 1900.

19. Ibid.; Connelly, *History of the Seventieth Ohio*, 98; *OR* 38 (3): 359; "A Gallant Ohio Private," *Sandusky (Ohio) Register*, August 17, 1864.

20. "Thirtieth Louisiana," *New Orleans Times-Picayune*, May 15, 1887; quotes are found in "Thirtieth's Flag in Memorial Hall," *New Orleans Times-Picayune*, October 10, 1900.

21. This example of the August 22 *Cincinnati Commercial* account was picked up and republished in "Thirtieth Louisiana," *New Orleans Times-Picayune*, May 15, 1887.

22. *OR* 38 (3): 857; SOR 2 (24): 442; Salling, *Louisianans in the Western Confederacy*, 189; "Casualties in Gibson's Brigade," *New Orleans Times-Picayune*, August 26, 1864; Emmett Ross to Mary, July 31, 1864, Emmett Ross Papers, Special Collections, Mississippi State University, Starkville, Miss.

23. SOR 2 (24): 783; "The Battle of July 28, near Atlanta," *New Orleans Times-Picayune*, August 21, 1864.

24. *OR* 38 (3): 167; Ralph Wooster, ed., "Four Years in the Confederate Infantry: The Civil War Letters of Private R. F. Eddins, 19th Louisiana," *Texas Gulf Historical and Biographical Record* 7 (1971): 37.

25. David Allan, Jr., to his mother, July 30, 1864, Missouri Historical Society, St. Louis; J. R. Tisdale, "Ezra Chapel," *National Tribune*, May, 10, 1888; J. S. Gage, "In the Front Line at Ezra Chapel," *National Tribune*, August 1, 1895.

26. "Casualties in Gibson's Brigade," *New Orleans Times-Picayune*, August 26, 1864.

27. Allan to his mother, July 30, 1864; Tisdale, "Ezra Chapel"; Gage, "Front Line at Ezra Chapel."

28. *OR* 38 (3): 821, 857; "Casualties in Gibson's Brigade," *New Orleans Times-Picayune*, August 26, 1864. The presence of the 19th Louisiana in front of the 29th Missouri is confirmed in Tisdale, "Ezra Chapel."

29. *OR* 38 (3): 857; Tisdale, "Ezra Chapel"; "Casualties in Gibson's Brigade," *New Orleans Times-Picayune*, August 26, 1864. The latter source names and tallies a total loss of 474 officers and men in the brigade; however, it lists within that total a loss of 117 in the 30th Louisiana Battalion. This single tally appears to be underreported by at least 45 casualties (see "Casualties in Louisiana Regiments July 28 in the Fight before Atlanta," *Times-Picayune*, August 21, 1864) and may have undershot the true initial loss by this one unit by 90 men (see "Thirtieth's Flag in Memorial Hall," *New Orleans Times-Picayune*, October 10, 1900). Assuming the accuracy of casualty lists for the other regiments and battalions in the brigade, the readjusted brigade losses likely vary between 550 and 575 officers and men. A historian of the brigade mistakenly calculated the difference between the strength report of July 18 (1,115) and July 29 (763) to tally the Ezra Church losses at 352 (Salling, *Louisianans in the Western Confederacy*, 188). This technique omits officers and does not account for two regiments that joined the brigade

on July 19 whose numbers are included in the latter but not the former brigade report used in the calculation.

Chapter 7

1. *OR* 38 (3): 872. This cited page of Stewart's report includes verbiage that has interfered with interpretation of the battle. After Stewart described his order on July 28 to collect his three divisions at the point where Lick Skillet Road met with the ring of earthworks, he wrote, "On reaching the point indicated, Lee's corps was found to be engaged and in need of assistance. Accordingly Walthall's division was moved out." A misreading of these lines would interpret Stewart as claiming he found Lee engaged when he reached the battlefield. This was not Stewart's meaning; his location defined by "on reaching the point indicated" was not the Ezra Church battlefield; it was the junction of the road with earthworks two miles east of the battle. Therefore, Stewart's subsequent passive phrase, "Lee's corps was found to be engaged and in need of assistance," reveals that Stewart was not the one who found Lee engaged but was ordered to him after headquarters learned he needed assistance. Otherwise, following the former interpretation incorrectly suggests that Stewart marched to the battlefield without orders one day before he was intended to move.

2. *OR* 38 (5): 919.

3. Ibid.; John B. Hood, *Advance and Retreat: Personal Experiences in the United States and Confederate States Armies* (New Orleans: G. T. Beauregard, 1880), 194. Hood's report stated passively, "General Stewart was ordered to support General Lee." See *OR* 38 (3): 632. That order must be assumed to have come from Hood.

Most secondary interpretations of the battle have accorded General Lee too much power regarding the Battle of Ezra Church and pay short shrift to these three independent sources from Hood (or his chief of staff) that confirm that Hood ordered Stewart to support Lee, not be subordinate to him. Not even a hint exists in Lee's report that he ordered Stewart to the battlefield; he merely states he influenced where they would be sent upon arrival. It must be noted that due to their having the same date of commission as lieutenant general, Lee did not outrank Stewart, and no evidence exists that Lee was given any discretion from Hood to pull in Stewart's troops to support his attacks. Likewise, Stewart acknowledged in his report that Lee needed assistance; therefore, Stewart's leading divisions were ordered out to attack (*OR* 38 [3]: 872). Stewart leaves no impression that he issued the ultimate order; if he did, he would have come under censure from Hood for acting against the commanding general's orders (Hood never criticized Stewart—or Lee—for their decisions and actions on July 28). This builds more proof that Hood was ultimately responsible for changing his two-day plan into a one-afternoon effort to drive the Union troops from the vicinity of Lick Skillet Road.

Hood instructed Lee "not to allow the enemy to gain upon you any more than possible," adding "that General Stewart has directions to support you fully." In the *Official Records*, the way this message is transcribed and published indicates it was composed at 4:00 P.M. (see *OR* 38 [5]: 919). Like many dispatches throughout the correspondence sections in the 128-volume series, this message may be timed incorrectly. Proof of the mistiming can be seen when comparing this to other published dispatches sent by Hood on July 28, particularly one sent at 3:35 P.M. by Hood's aide-de-camp to General Stewart. The dispatch (which would eventually be delivered to General Walthall) instructed Stewart to order another division commander in the corps to release a brigade to support the engaged troops (see ibid.; 921). This dispatch reveals that Stewart's corps had been fighting on the battlefield—a point clearly not found in the 4:00 P.M. dispatch sent to Lee. Common sense also dictates that Hood was not three hours behind the reality of the ever-growing battle waged three miles from his headquarters.

4. Sherman, *Memoirs*, 564–65. The 30th Alabama in Stevenson's division suffered twelve losses from Sherman's bombardment, suggesting dozens of other losses throughout the division. See Larry D. Stephens, *Bound for Glory: A History of the 30th Alabama Infantry Regiment, Confederate States of America* (Ann Arbor, Mich.: Sheridan Books, 2005), 263–65.

5. *OR* 38 (3): 926.

6. *OR* 38 (5): 219.

7. Tower, *Carolinian Goes to War*, 234.

8. Ibid., 234–35; *OR* 38 (3): 782.

9. *OR* 38 (3): 768.

10. Ibid., 763, 790, 800.

11. Ibid., 104, 174–75; Tower, *Carolinian Goes to War*, 235.

12. The division strength was obtained from the July 31 strength report (see *OR* 38 [3]: 680) and by Stevenson's trimonthly returns from July 1864 (see Peter W. Alexander Papers, Rare Book and Manuscript Library, Columbia University, New York).

13. *OR* 38 (3): 821.

14. Warner, *Generals in Gray*, 14; Welsh, *Medical Histories of Confederate Generals*, 12; quote from Hubert Dent to Nannie Dent, August 11, 1864, S. H. Dent Papers, Special Collections and Archives, Auburn University, Auburn, Ala.

15. Captain A. A. Perkins to Lieutenant Colonel William E. Strong, July 31, 1864, RG 393, National Archives.

16. *Harper's Weekly Illustrated Newspaper*, August 27, 1864. This sketch appears as a full-page image on page 556; the church appears as an upper-corner image on the following page.

17. *OR* 38 (3): 157; "List of Casualties of 1st Division 15th Army Corps . . . July 28, 1864," Logan Papers, LOC; John C. Brown diary, July 28, 1864, Special Collections, University of Iowa Libraries; D. J. Spencer diary, July 28, 1864, typescript at KMNBP.

18. Welsh, *Medical Histories of Confederate Generals*, 12.

19. Elbert D. Willett, Joseph J. Willett, and John H. Curry, *History of Company B (Originally Pickens Planters), 40th Alabama Regiment, Confederate States Army, 1862–1865* (Anniston, Ala.: Norwood Printers, 1902), 76; Willis Brewer, *Alabama, Her History, Resources, War Record, and Public Men: From 1540 to 1872* (Montgomery, Ala.: Barrett & Brown, Steam Printers, 1872), 666.

20. *OR* 38 (3): 821; quote from Earl J. Hess, *The Battle of Ezra Church and the Struggle for Atlanta* (Chapel Hill: University of North Carolina Press, 2015), 103.

21. "Report of Rebel Dead, Buried by and in Front of 1st Division, 15th A.C.," Carton 47, Logan Papers, LOC; Smith diary, July 28, 1864, 422.

22. *OR* 38 (3): 821; Williams diary, July 28, 1864, 107.
23. *OR* 38 (3): 763.
24. Ibid.

Chapter 8

1. Sherman to his wife, July 26, 1864, in Simpson and Berlin, *Sherman's Civil War*, 671.
2. Sherman, *Memoirs*, 562; Nathaniel C. Hughes, Jr., and Gordon D. Whitney, *Jefferson Davis in Blue: The Life of Sherman's Relentless Warrior* (Baton Rouge: Louisiana State University Press, 2002), 268. Jefferson C. Davis's biographers claim that the movement to Turner's Ferry began at 6:00 A.M., citing a lieutenant colonel's regimental report (*OR* 38 [1]: 662). This is refuted by several primary sources that place the movement at 9:00 A.M., which cast great doubt on the 6:00 A.M. claim. See *OR* 38 (1): 650, 671; and Henry J. Aten, *History of the Eighty-fifth Regiment, Illinois Volunteer Infantry* (Hiawatha, Kans., 1901), 211.
3. Hughes and Whitney, *Jefferson Davis in Blue*, 268; Sherman, *Memoirs*, 562.
4. Sherman, *Memoirs*, 562.
5. Ibid.
6. Hughes and Whitney, *Jefferson Davis in Blue*, 268.
7. Warner, *Generals in Gray*, 325–26.
8. Ibid., 43; Welsh, *Medical Histories of Confederate Generals*, 34.
9. *OR* 38 (3): 942.
10. Ibid., 940; Charles Edgeworth Jones, *Georgia in the War, 1861–1865* (Augusta, Ga.: n.p., 1909), 47.
11. *OR* 38 (3): 927. The quote was obtained from Illene D. Thompson and Wilbur E. Thompson, *The Seventeenth Alabama Infantry: A Regimental History and Roster* (Bowie, Md.: Heritage Books, 2001), 90.
12. *OR* 38 (3): 927.
13. D. R. Lucas, *New History of the 99th Indiana Infantry* (Rockford, Ill.: Horner Printing, 1900), 42–43; *OR* 38 (3): 305, 348, 456, 604. The commander of the 48th appears to have misidentified the regiment that replaced his unit as the 10th Illinois. Sources indicate this regiment was inactive this day (ibid., 348, 533).
14. *OR* 38 (3): 607, 927.
15. Ibid.; William W. Belknap, *History of the Fifteenth Regiment, Iowa Veteran Volunteer Infantry* (Keokuk, Iowa: R. B. Ogden and Son, 1889), 379; Smith diary, July 28, 1864, 422. The 11th Iowa may also have been among the reinforcements sent to the western side of the field. See Mifflin Jennings diary, July 28, 1864, in "The Civil War Diaries of Mifflin Jennings, 11th Iowa Infantry," www.rootsweb.ancestry.com/~ialcgs/mifflinj.htm.
16. "Liber" to the editor, August 2, 1864, *Scioto Gazette*, August 16, 1864; *OR* 38 (3): 211, 456, 495, 507, 512, 604, 607; G. W. Shrum, "Atlanta and Ezra Chapel," *National Tribune*, February 16, 1888; Isaiah T. Dillon to wife, January 31, 1864, Isaiah T. and William L. Dillon Papers, ALPL.
17. *OR* 38 (3): 248.
18. Thomas M. Eddy, *The Patriotism of Illinois* (Chicago: Robert Clarke Company, 1865), 2:67–68; *OR* 38 (3): 459.
19. Belknap, *History of the Fifteenth*, 379.

20. *OR* 38 (3): 462; Tom Taylor to his wife, July 30, 1864, and Taylor diary, July 28, 1864, both in Castel, *Tom Taylor's Civil War*, 154–58.

21. "Walthall's Charge," *Janesville (Wis.) Daily Gazette*, December 30, 1887; Smith, "Battle of Ezra Church."

22. Shrum, "Atlanta and Ezra Chapel"; Dillon to his wife, July 31, 1864, ALPL.

23. Thompson and Thompson, *Seventeenth Alabama Infantry*, 91–92.

24. *OR* 38 (3): 942.

25. Ibid., 943.

26. "Walthall's Charge," *Janesville Daily Gazette*, December 30, 1887.

27. Reynolds diary, July 28 and August 16, 1864, in Bender, *Worthy of the Cause*, 139–40, 142.

28. *OR* 38 (3): 939. Lavender's account is reproduced in editors of Time-Life Books, *Atlanta* (Richmond, Va.: Time-Life Books, 1996), 123.

29. The 26th Illinois bullet claim is found in Hogan, *General Reub Williams's Memories*, 188.

30. Ibid.

31. *OR* 38 (3): 604, 941–42.

32. Reynolds diary, July 28 and August 16, 1864, in Bender, *Worthy of the Cause*, 139–40, 142.

33. *OR* 38 (3): 288, 299, 305, 344, 931, 939; James Goodnow to his wife, August 1, 1864, Goodnow Papers, LOC. Brigade strength is estimated from return of one of the three regiments with the 90th Illinois reporting 183 enlisted men present for duty. See Swan, *Chicago's Irish Legion*, 154.

34. *OR* 38 (3): 294; "46th Tennessee Volunteer Infantry," http://46thtn.homestead.com/history46.html.

35. Edward H. Rennolds, *A History of the Henry County Commands* (Kennesaw, Ga.: Continental Book Co., 1961), 190–91; Stephen Lynn King, comp., *History and Biographical Sketches of the 46th Tennessee Infantry, C.S.A.*, (Bowling Green, Ky.: Stephen Lynn King, 1992), 24; Asail Corsen diary, July 28,1864, Corsen Family Papers, USAHEC.

36. Ibid.; Q. P. F., "Sherman's Army: The Third Battle before Atlanta, July 28, Full Particulars," *Cincinnati Daily Commercial*, August 5, 1864. The flag in the newspaper article was not identified as belonging to the 46th Tennessee in the newspaper account; the regimental history of the 46th Tennessee dovetails perfectly with the *Cincinnati Commercial* piece to identify the flag as theirs (see King, comp., *46th Tennessee Infantry*, 24). The privately owned flag was viewed by the author; it is faintly inscribed by the 26th Illinois with the date of the Ezra Church battle.

37. Hogan, *General Reub Williams's Memories*, 188; Wilfred W. Black, ed., "Marching with Sherman through Georgia and the Carolinas: The Civil War Diary of Jesse L. Dozer," *Collections of the Georgia Historical Quarterly* 52, no. 4 (1968): 324–25; *OR* 38 (3): 932; William Dillard Wilson file, American Civil War Research Database, http://civilwardata.com.

38. "46th Tennessee Volunteer Infantry," http://46thtn.homestead.com/history46.html; King, *46th Tennessee Infantry*, 24; Gillmore Report, in author's possession.

39. *OR* 38 (3): 927; Private William John Watson diary, 1864–1865, #3662-z, Southern Historical Collection, Louis Round Wilson Special Collections Library, University of North Carolina at Chapel Hill.

40. Daniel P. Smith, *Company K, First Alabama Regiment* (Prattville, Ala.: privately published, 1885), 102.

41. Edward McMorries, *History of the First Regiment Alabama Volunteer Infantry, C.S.A.* (Montgomery, Ala.: Brown Printer Company, 1904), 77. This soldier had mistaken Reynolds's brigade for Quarles's brigade.

42. *OR* 38 (3): 931–33.

43. Clement A. Evans, ed., *Confederate Military History: A Library of Confederate States History* (Atlanta: Confederate Publishing Co., 1899), 8:139.

44. Welsh, *Medical Histories of Confederate Generals*, 178; Randy Bishop, *Civil War Generals of Tennessee* (Gretna, La.: Pelican Publishing Company, 2013), 169; *OR* 38 (3): 931–32.

45. McMorries, *First Regiment Alabama Volunteer Infantry*, 77–78.

46. *OR* 38 (3): 680, 927.

Chapter 9

1. Editors of Time-Life Books, ed., *Shenandoah 1862* (Alexandria, Va.: Time-Life Books, 1997), 27; Warner, *Generals in Gray*, 193–94.

2. Binford's Recollection, 81–2, CNMP. Loring returned to the field on September 10. See Welsh, *Medical Histories of Confederate Generals*, 144.

3. Winfield S. Featherston to William D. Gale, April 25, 1865, USAHEC. This document is Featherston's official report of the battle.

4. Welsh, *Medical Histories of Confederate Generals*, 206.

5. Roy, "General Hardee and Military Operations," 370.

6. *OR* 38 (5): 920–21.

7. Roy, "General Hardee and Military Operations," 370; *OR* 38 (3): 699.

8. *OR* 38 (5): 920–21; *OR* 52 (2): 713.

9. *OR* 38 (3): 904. Young claims he received the reinforcement orders at 3:00 P.M. (see ibid., 910), but this is more than an hour earlier than possible. The fact that the orders were sent by Walthall is confirmed by Young's division commander (French), making it necessary that the orders were received after Stewart's injury, not before.

10. *OR* 38 (3): 41. A XVI Corps soldier claims that during the afternoon, "the batteries on our front opened, and were vigorously replied to by the enemy's guns." James P. Snell diary, July 28, 1864, typescript copy in Atlanta Historical Center. If accurate, the bombardment was isolated to Union guns one mile north of Ezra Church exchanging artillery fire with Hoskins's battery in southwestern Atlanta. The exchange killed a XVI Corps Ohio artillerist (see George Hurlbut to Angie, August 2, 1864, KMNBP).

11. *OR* 38 (1): 650; *OR* 38 (3): 923, 963. The roads to and from Turner's Ferry, including the southward turn from Mason's Church, are shown in *OR Atlas*, plate LXXXVIII.

12. *OR* 38 (1): 650; Aten, *History of the Eighty Fifth*, 211. Ironically, had Morgan continued to Lick Skillet Road, Ross's brigade would have abandoned his front because Ross was directed away from the scene at 4:00 P.M. to oppose the Stoneman-McCook raid. See *OR* 38 (3): 963.

13. Connelly, *History of the Seventieth Ohio*, 99.

14. Ibid.; *OR* 38 (3): 359; Featherston to Gale, April 26, 1865, Featherston Reports, USAHEC.

15. *OR* 38 (5): 920–21; Columbus Sykes to his wife, July 29, 1864, CS4, MS4, KMNBP; Albert Theodore Goodloe, *Confederate Echoes: A Soldier's Personal Story of Life in the Confederate Army from the Mississippi to the Carolinas* (Washington, D.C.: Zenger Publishing Co., 1907), 292; Leroy F. Banning, *Regimental History of the 35th Alabama Infantry, 1862–1865* (Bowie, Md.: Heritage Books, 1999), 55; H. Grady Howell, Jr., *Going to Meet the Yankees: A History of the "Bloody Sixth" Mississippi Infantry, C.S.A.* (Jackson, Miss.: Chickasaw Bayou Press, 1981), 229. Total casualties are estimated. Castel calculates "by conservative estimate" 120 casualties suffered from Loring's (Featherston's) division. See Castel, *Decision in the West*, 434. If the other eighteen regiments of the division averaged only a third of the casualties of the 35th Alabama, Featherston would have suffered two hundred losses at Ezra Church.

16. *OR* 38 (3): 910; "Memoirs of the Civil War: W. L. Truman," www.cedarcroft.com/about/civil-war-interests/w-l-truman-memoir/memoir-chapter-22/.

17. Excerpt of Hardee's July 30, 1864, letter to his wife quoted in Roy, "General Hardee and Military Operations," 370.

18. Scaife, *Campaign for Atlanta*, 186; *OR* 38 (5): 660–61, 904.

19. Sherman, *Memoirs*, 564; Smith diary, July 28, 1864, 422.

20. Noel Crowson and John V. Brogden, eds., *Bloody Banners and Barefoot Boys: A History of the 27th Alabama Infantry, C.S.A.: The Civil War Memoirs and Diary Entries of J. P. Cannon, M.D.*, (Shippensburg, Pa.: Burd Street Press, 1997), 87–88.

21. Maurice Report, September 9, 1864, Logan Papers, LOC; Dozier diary, July 28, 1864, in Black, "Marching with Sherman," 325; Mott to his wife, July 30, 1864; R. W. Burt to the editor, July 29, 1864, *Newark (Ohio) True American*, August 19, 1864.

22. Smith diary, July 28, 1864, 423.

Chapter 10

1. *OR* 38 (5): 917. Hood stated passively that his two corps commanders "were directed to hold" Lick Skillet Road. The only reasonable interpretation is that he was the one who directed them. No evidence exists to suggest that Lee changed Stewart's orders or commanded Stewart when Stewart arrived on the battlefield. Interestingly, Hood placed Stewart's name before Lee's, which went against the chronology of the fight but likely reinforced the hierarchy of command in Hood's mind.

2. An antithetical analysis of Hood's dispatch states the following: "This of course is nonsense and lying nonsense at that. It can only be explained, but not excused, by the well-known reluctance of all generals to admit defeat." Castel, *Decision in the West*, 434. Since the time of the dispatch is not provided, it is uncertain whether Hood understood the magnitude of his loss, or even if he thought he had lost at all. Shoup's journal entry (see *OR* 38 [3]: 688) reinforces the headquarters belief that renders Hood's summary a sensible one.

3. *OR* 38 (5): 919.

4. Stephens, *Bound for Glory*, 263–65.

5. *OR* 38 (3): 42, 105, 386. Casualty lists by division, naming all soldiers and the location of their injuries, are found in Logan Papers, LOC.

6. "Reuben" to the editor, July 31, 1864, *Toledo Blade*, August 11, 1864; Thomas Taylor to his wife, July 30, 1864, in Castel, *Tom Taylor's Civil War*, 156; John C. Arbuckle, *Civil War Experiences of a Foot-Soldier Who Marched with Sherman* (Columbus, Ohio: n.p., 1930), 78.

7. H. H. Orendorf, comp., *Reminiscences of the Civil War from Diaries of Members of the 103d Illinois Volunteer Infantry* (Chicago: J. F. Learning, 1904), 110; Humphrey to the editor, August 7, 1864, *Stark County (Ohio) Republican*, August 18, 1864; Seay diary, July 29, 1864, quoted in Gary L. Scheel, *Rain, Mud and Swamp: The Story of the 31st Missouri Volunteer Infantry* (Pacific, Mo.: Plus Communications, 1998), 73; George Hurlbut to his wife, August 2, 1864, KMNMP; Ritner to his wife, July 29, 1864, in Charles F. Larimer, ed., *Love and Valor: The Intimate Civil War Letters between Captain Jacob and Emeline Ritner* (Western Springs, Ill.: Sigourney Press, 2000), 322; Horace Park to J. S. McBeth, August 2, 1864, MS2386, Hargrett Rare Book and Manuscript Library, University of Georgia; "Condensed Letters," *National Tribune*, December 18, 1884.

8. Unidentified officer to John Cockerill, July 29, 1864, *West Union (Ohio) Democratic Union*, August 12, 1864; Bennett and Tillery, *Struggle for the Republic*, 192; Stacy Dale Allen, ed., *On the Skirmish Line behind a Friendly Tree: The Civil War Memoirs of William Royal Oake, 26th Iowa Infantry* (Helena, Mont.: Farcountry Press, 2006), 239.

9. F. H. Magdeburg, "Worden's Battalion" (n.p., 1886), 8; J. W. F. to the editor, July 29, 1864, *Warsaw Northern Indianan*, August 18, 1864; Whitsel Lewis diary, July 28, 1864, in Donald Lewis Osborn, ed., *A Union Soldier's Diary* (Independence, Mo.: Donald Lewis Osborn, 1964), 5; Gage, *From Vicksburg to Raleigh*, 228; "Report of Rebel Dead," Carton 47, Logan Papers, LOC; John Harrow to Col. R. R. Townes, July 29, 1864, Carton 46, Logan Papers, LOC; Bennett and Tillery, *Struggle for the Republic*, 192; A. B. Wetsch to David Holmes, August 3, 1864, ALPL.

10. Solomon Palmer diary, July 28, 1864.

11. L. D. McGlashon to his mother, August 6, 1864, *Crown Point (Ind.) Register*, August 18, 1864; Theodore F. Upson, *With Sherman to the Sea: The Civil War Letters, Diaries and Reminiscences of Theodore F. Upson* (Baton Rouge: Louisiana State University Press, 1943), 122; Hogan, *General Reub Williams's Memories*, 190; Ritner to his wife, July 31, 1864, in Larimer, *Love and Valor*, 325.

12. Tom Taylor to his wife, July 30, 1864, in Castel, *Tom Taylor's Civil War*, 158. This oft-told exchange was first reported in a letter two days after the battle and repeated immediately and for decades afterward.

13. *OR* 38 (3): 680.

14. Ibid., 769; *OR* 38 (5): 924–25. A curious tally by Anderson states that the division had lost "upward of 500 men and officers" at the Ezra Church fight. On July 31 General Brown submitted a casualty table of his four brigades showing the loss of 807 officers and men. *OR* 38 (3): 768. The monthly returns of the army that show Anderson's/Brown's division at 3,459 privates (i.e., men with bayonets) present for duty further muddy the waters. Ibid., 680. The discrepancies in both casualties and numbers present for duty cannot be resolved at this point.

15. David Evans, *Sherman's Horsemen: Union Cavalry Operations in the Atlanta Campaign* (Bloomington: Indiana University Press, 1996), 217–354.

16. Q. P. F., "Sherman's Army," *Cincinnati Daily Commercial,* August 5, 1864; *Chicago Tribune,* August 11, 1864.

17. *OR* 38 (3): 763.

18. Ibid., 767–68, 776–77, 799–800.

19. Ibid., 768.

20. Newton N. Davis to Bettie, September 8, 1864, Alabama Department of Archives and History, Montgomery; Douglas Jon Cater, *As It Was: Reminiscences of a Soldier of the Third Texas Cavalry and the Nineteenth Louisiana Infantry* (Austin, Tex.: State House Press, 1990), 186–87; Clayton to his wife, August 24, 1864, Henry Clayton Papers, University of Alabama, Tuscaloosa.

21. *OR* 38 (3): 699.

22. Newton N. Davis to Bettie, August 1, 1864, Alabama Department of Archives and History; William Elliott to his wife, July 29, 1864, in http://library.sc.edu/digital/collections/civilwar.html.

23. Columbus Sykes to his wife, July 29, 1864, KMNBP; Thomas P. Bailey to "My Dear Doctor," August 12, 1864, SC-2, KMNBP.

24. "Harry D." to the editor, August 1, 1864, *Painesville (Ohio) Telegraph,* August 11, 1864.

25. Gill to his wife, August 7 and 11, 1864, in Wiley, "Story of 3 Southern Officers," 33.

26. Littlejohn to his wife, August 6, 1864, KMNBP; *OR* 52 (2): 715; "General Hood Increases His Army," *Edgefield (S.C.) Advertiser,* August 17, 1864.

27. *OR* 38 (1): 115–16.

28. *Harper's Weekly Illustrated Newspaper,* August 27, 1864, 556–57; Davis, *What the Yankees Did,* 148.

29. *Harper's Weekly Illustrated Newspaper,* September 17, 1864.

30. John A. Logan, *The Volunteer Soldier of America* (Chicago: R. S. Neale and Co., 1887), 691.

31. *OR* 38 (3): 872.

32. Howard, "Atlanta Campaign: A Turning Point," *National Tribune,* March 21, 1895.

Appendix B

1. Hood to Lee, January 22, 1865, in Stephen M. Hood, ed., *The Lost Papers of Confederate General John Bell Hood* (El Dorado Hills, Calif.: Savas Beatie, 2015), 101–102.

2. *OR* 38 (3): 763.

3. Ibid., 872.

4. Richard M. McMurry, *John Bell Hood and the War for Southern Independence* (Lincoln: University of Nebraska Press, 1982), 186.

5. *OR* 38 (3): 629–30.

6. Hood, *Lost Papers,* 58–62, 115–25.

7. Hood, *Advance and Retreat,* 194–95.

8. *OR* 38 (3): 631, 688, 762, 872; *OR* 38 (5): 915–16.

Appendix C

1. James P. Snell diary, August 23, 1864. Snell's somewhat cryptic description of the church's demise ("wiped out by army operations") is open for interpretation. If the chapel was a victim of the cannonading during the siege of Atlanta, a Confederate shell is more likely responsible for the destruction since the church stood within Union lines. If it was destroyed by Union operations, it could have been destroyed for its wood.

2. Garrett, *Atlanta and Environs*, 1:750.

3. "General Loring's Ride," *Atlanta Weekly Constitution*, August 29, 1882.

4. Allen Daniel Candler and Clement Anselm Evans, eds., *Georgia: Comprising Sketches of Counties, Towns, Events, Institutions, and Persons, Arranged in Cyclopedic Form* (Atlanta: State Historical Association, 1906), 1:141; "Battle Hill Sanitarium in Most Competent Hands," *Atlanta Constitution*, May 3, 1911.

5. "Plan for National Park Has Gained New Headway," *Atlanta Constitution*, October 15, 1905.

6. "Moseley Park Retains Name," *Atlanta Constitution*, July 10, 1915.

7. "Thirtieth's Flag in Memorial Hall," *New Orleans Times-Picayune*, October 10, 1900; "Leaden Messengers of Death Preserved," *Knoxville Daily Journal and Tribune*, November 4, 1892; "War Relics Identified," *Charleston (S.C.) Evening Post*, November 25, 1908; "Backfire," *Mason City (Iowa) Globe Gazette* and *Hagerstown Daily Mail*, April 23, 1942.

8. Numerous Ezra Church items within Kurtz Collection, AHC; David O'Connell, *The Art and Life of Atlanta Artist Wilbur G. Kurtz* (Charleston, S.C.: History Press, 2013), 127–28; "Cross Is Burned by Atlanta Klan," *Columbus (Ga.) Daily Enquirer*, October 19, 1939; "Father of 4 Held in Death of 2 Children," *Augusta Chronicle*, March 22, 1981.

Bibliography

Manuscript Collections

Abraham Lincoln Presidential Library, Springfield, Ill.
    Isaiah T. Dillon letters
    Odell letters
    David Holmes letters
Alabama Department of Archives and History, Montgomery
    Newton Davis letters
Atlanta Historical Center
    Wilbur Kurtz Collection
    James P. Snell diary typescript
Auburn University, Special Collections and Archives, Auburn, Ala.
    S. H. Dent Papers
Chickamauga and Chattanooga National Military Park, Oglethorpe, Ga.
    James Binford's Recollection of the Fifteenth Regiment of Mississippi Infantry, C.S.A.
Columbia University Rare Book and Manuscript Library, New York
    Peter W. Alexander Papers
Kennesaw Mountain National Battlefield Park, Kennesaw, Ga.
    Thomas P. Bailey to "My Dear Doctor," August 12, 1864
    "The Civil War Letters of Elbridge Littlejohn," edited by Vicki Betts
    George Hurlbut letters
    Solomon Palmer diary typescript
    D. J. Spencer diary typescript
    Columbus Sykes letters
Library of Congress, Manuscripts Division, Washington, D.C.
    James Goodnow Papers
    Abraham Lincoln Papers
    John A. Logan Papers
Mississippi Department of Archives and History, Biloxi
    J. A. Biggers diary
Mississippi State University, Special Collections, Starkville
    Emmett Ross Papers
Missouri Historical Society, Saint Louis
    David Allan, Jr., letters

National Archives, Washington, D.C.
    M1064 Letters Received by the Commission Branch of the Adjutant General's Office, 1863–1870. 527 Rolls.
    RG 29 Population Schedules of the Eighth Census of the United States, Campbell County, Georgia, 1860
    RG 29 Population Schedules of the Eighth Census of the United States, Fulton County, Georgia, 1860
    RG 29 Population Schedules of the Ninth Census of the United States, Fulton County, Georgia, 1870
    RG 94 Records of the Adjutant General's Office
    RG 393 Letters Received, 1864–1865, Department of the Army of the Tennessee
Ohio Historical Center, Columbus
    Hildt Papers
    Walcutt Family Papers
U.S. Army Heritage and Education Center, Carlisle Barracks, Pa.
    Winfield S. Featherston reports
    Edward Schweitzer diary typescript
    David Thom diary
University of Alabama, W. S. Hoole Special Collections Library, Tuscaloosa
    Henry D. Clayton Papers
University of Georgia, Hargrett Rare Books and Manuscript Library, Athens
    Horace Park letter to J. S. McBeth, August 2, 1864, MS2386
University of Iowa, Libraries, Special Collections, Iowa City
    John C. Brown diary
University of North Carolina, Southern Historical Collection, Louis Round Wilson Special Collections Library, Chapel Hill
    Private William John Watson diary

Soldiers' Letters, Diaries, and Reminiscences Published in Newspapers

Burt, R. W. "To the editor, July 29, 1864." *Newark (Ohio) True American.* August 19, 1864.

"Condensed Letters." *National Tribune.* December 18, 1884.

Coombe, E. "The 28th of July before Atlanta." *National Tribune.* February 7, 1884.

"From a Private's Diary." *New York Times.* January 15, 1893.

Gage, J. S. "In the Front Line at Ezra Chapel." *National Tribune.* August 1, 1895.

"Harry D." to the editor, August 1, 1864. *Painesville (Ohio) Telegraph.* August 11, 1864.

Howard, Oliver O. "Atlanta Campaign . . . Ezra Church." *National Tribune.* March 7 and 14, 1895.

———. "Atlanta Campaign: A Turning Point." *National Tribune.* March 21, 1895.

Humphrey to the editor, August 7, 1864. *Stark County (Ohio) Republican.* August 18, 1864.

J. G. B. to the editor, August 5, 1864. *Canton (Ill.) Weekly Register.* August 22, 1864.

Jones, Wells S. "How a Great Battle Was Begun." *American Tribune.* January 30, 1891.

J. W. F. to the editor, July 29, 1864. *Warsaw Northern Indianan.* August 18, 1864.
"Liber" to the editor, August 2, 1864. *Scioto Gazette.* August 16, 1864.
Long, J. W. "Flanking Johnston: The Army of the Tennessee on the Move." *National Tribune.* September 13, 1888.
McGlashon, L. D., to his mother, August 6, 1864. *Crown Point (Ind.) Register.* August 18, 1864.
"Reuben" to the editor, July 31, 1864. *Toledo Blade.* August 11, 1864.
Ridenour, J. B. "General Logan in Line." *Elyria (Ohio) Democrat.* December 22, 1887.
Shrum, G. W. "Atlanta and Ezra Chapel." *National Tribune.* February 16, 1888.
"The Signal Corps." *National Tribune.* April 5, 1883.
Smith, Edward W. "Battle of Ezra Church: A Coffee-Cooler's Experience." *National Tribune.* July 5, 1888.
Stocker, S., to the editor, August 15, 1864. *New Philadelphia (Ohio) Tuscarawas Advocate.* September 2, 1864.
Tisdale, J. R. "Ezra Chapel." *National Tribune.* May 10, 1888.
Unidentified officer to John Cockerill, July 29, 1864. *West Union (Ohio) Democratic Union.* August 12, 1864.

Newspaper Articles

"Backfire." *Mason City (Iowa) Globe Gazette* and *Hagerstown Daily Mail.* April 23, 1942.
"Battle Hill Sanitarium in Most Competent Hands." *Atlanta Constitution.* May 3, 1911.
"The Battle of July 28, near Atlanta." *New Orleans Times-Picayune.* August 21, 1864.
"Casualties in Louisiana Regiments July 28 in the Fight before Atlanta." *New Orleans Times-Picayune.* August 21, 1864.
"Casualties in the 70th Ohio Regiment." *West Union (Ohio) Democratic Union.* August 12, 1864.
"Casualties in the 6th Iowa Infantry." *Burlington (Iowa) Weekly Hawkeye.* August 6, 1864.
"Col. Thomas Shields of the 30th Louisiana." *New Orleans Times-Picayune.* September 21, 1864.
"From Georgia." *Burlington (Iowa) Weekly Hawkeye.* July 23, 1864.
"A Gallant Ohio Private." *Sandusky (Ohio) Register.* August 17, 1864.
"General Hood Increases His Army." *Edgefield (S.C.) Advertiser.* August 17, 1864.
"General Loring's Ride." *Atlanta Weekly Constitution.* August 29, 1882.
Harper's Weekly Illustrated Newspaper. August 27, 1864.
"Leaden Messengers of Death Preserved." *Knoxville Daily Journal and Tribune.* November 4, 1892.
"List of Casualties in Gibson's Louisiana Brigade, in the Fight near Atlanta on July 28." *New Orleans Times-Picayune.* August 26, 1864.
"Memories of War." *Columbia (S.C.) State.* September 7, 1895.
"Moseley Park Retains Name." *Atlanta Constitution.* July 10, 1915.
"Plan for National Park Has Gained New Headway." *Atlanta Constitution.* October 15, 1905.

Q. P. F. "Sherman's Army: The Third Battle before Atlanta, July 28, Full Particulars." *Cincinnati Daily Commercial.* August 5, 1864.
Sherman interview with "Gath." *Cincinnati Daily Enquirer.* December 31, 1886.
"Thirtieth Louisiana." *New Orleans Times-Picayune.* May 15, 1887.
"Thirtieth Louisiana: The Veterans Come Together to Make Arrangements for the Reception of Their Old Flag." *New Orleans Times-Picayune.* May 15, 1887.
"Thirtieth's Flag in Memorial Hall." *New Orleans Times-Picayune.* October 10, 1900.
"Walthall's Charge." *Janesville (Wis.) Daily Gazette.* December 30, 1887.
"War Relics Identified." *Charleston (S.C.) Evening Post.* November 25, 1908.
Wells, Robert W. "Wisconsin in the Civil War." *Milwaukee Journal.* November 3, 1961.
"Why General Walker Remembers Macon." *Macon (Ga.) Telegram.* March 23, 1905.

Books and Articles

Allardice, Bruce S. "'It Was Perfect Murder': Stephen D. Lee at Ezra Church." In Lawrence Lee Hewitt and Arthur W. Bergeron, Jr., eds., *Confederate Generals, in the Western Theater,* vol. 3 (Knoxville: University of Tennessee Press, 2011), 221–46.
Allen, Stacy Dale, ed. *On the Skirmish Line behind a Friendly Tree: The Civil War Memoirs of William Royal Oake, 26th Iowa Infantry.* Helena, Mont.: Farcountry Press, 2006.
Anders, Leslie. "Fisticuffs at Headquarters: Sweeny vs. Dodge." *Civil War Times Illustrated* 15, no. 10 (February 1977): 8–15.
Angle, Paul A., ed. *Three Years in the Army of the Cumberland: The Letters and Diary of Major James A. Connelly.* 1959. Reprint, Bloomington: Indiana University Press, 1984.
Arbuckle, John C. *Civil War Experiences of a Foot-Soldier Who Marched with Sherman.* Columbus, Ohio: n.p., 1930.
Aten, Henry J. *History of the Eighty-fifth Regiment, Illinois Volunteer Infantry.* Hiawatha, Kans., 1901.
Bailey, Ronald H., and the editors of Time-Life Books. *Battles for Atlanta: Sherman Moves East.* Alexandria, Va.: Time-Life Books, 1985.
Banning, Leroy F. *Regimental History of the 35th Alabama Infantry, 1862–1865.* Bowie, Md.: Heritage Books, 1999.
Belknap, William W. *History of the Fifteenth Regiment, Iowa Veteran Volunteer Infantry.* Keokuk, Iowa: R. B. Ogden and Son, 1889.
Bender, Robert Patrick, ed. *Worthy of the Cause for Which They Fight: The Civil War Diary of Brigadier General Daniel Harris Reynolds, 1861–1865.* Fayetteville: University of Arkansas Press, 2011.
Bennett, Stewart, and Barbara Tillery, eds. *The Struggle for the Life of the Republic: A Civil War Narrative by Brevet Major Charles Dana Miller, 76th Ohio Volunteer Infantry.* Kent, Ohio: Kent State University Press, 2004.
Bergeron, Arthur, Jr. *Guide to Louisiana Confederate Military Units, 1861–1865.* Baton Rouge: Louisiana State University Press, 1989.

Bishop, Randy. *Civil War Generals of Tennessee.* Gretna, La.: Pelican Publishing Company, 2013.
Black, Wilfred W., ed. "Marching with Sherman through Georgia and the Carolinas: The Civil War Diary of Jesse L. Dozer." *Collections of the Georgia Historical Quarterly* 52, no. 4 (1968): 308–36.
Boedecker, Roger. *The Civil War Service of the 127th Illinois Infantry.* N.p., 2007.
Brewer, Willis. *Alabama, Her History, Resources, War Record, and Public Men: From 1540 to 1872.* Montgomery, Ala.: Barrett & Brown, Steam Printers, 1872.
Brown, J. Willard. *The Signal Corps, U.S.A., in the War of the Rebellion.* Boston: U.S. Veteran Signal Corps Association, 1896.
Brown, Norman D., ed. *One of Cleburne's Command: The Civil War Reminiscences and Diary of Capt. Samuel T. Foster, Granbury's Texas Brigade, C. S. A.* Austin: University of Texas Press, 1980.
Buck, Irving A. *Cleburne and His Command.* Jackson, Tenn.: McCowat-Mercer Press, 1959.
Candler, Allen Daniel, and Clement Anselm Evans, eds. *Georgia: Comprising Sketches of Counties, Towns, Events, Institutions, and Persons, Arranged in Cyclopedic Form.* 3 vols. Atlanta: State Historical Association, 1906.
Castel, Albert. *Decision in the West: The Atlanta Campaign of 1864.* Lawrence: University Press of Kansas, 1992.
———. *Tom Taylor's Civil War.* Lawrence: University Press of Kansas, 2000.
Cater, Douglas Jon. *As It Was: Reminiscences of a Soldier of the Third Texas Cavalry and the Nineteenth Louisiana Infantry.* Austin, Tex.: State House Press, 1990.
Committee of the Regiment. *The Story of the Fifty-fifth Regiment Illinois Volunteer Infantry in the Civil War.* Clinton, Mass.: W. J. Coulter, 1887.
Connelly, T. W. *History of the Seventieth Ohio Regiment: From Its Organization to Its Mustering Out.* Cincinnati: Peak Bros., 1902.
Crowson, Noel, and John V. Brogden, eds. *Bloody Banners and Barefoot Boys: A History of the 27th Alabama Infantry, C.S.A.: The Civil War Memoirs and Diary Entries of J. P. Cannon, M.D.* Shippensburg, Pa.: Burd Street Press, 1997.
Cryder, George R., and Stanley R. Miller, comps. *A View from the Ranks: The Civil War Diaries of Charles E. Smith, 1861–1865.* Delaware, Ohio: Delaware County Historical Society, 1999.
Davis, George B., Leslie J. Perry, and Joseph W. Kirkley, eds. *The Official Military Atlas of the Civil War.* New York: Gramercy Books, 1983.
Davis, Stephen. *What the Yankees Did to Us: Sherman's Bombardment and Wrecking of Atlanta.* Macon, Ga.: Mercer University Press, 2012.
Deupree, J. G. "The Noxubee Squadron of the First Mississippi Cavalry, C. S. A., 1861–1865." In *Publications of the Mississippi Historical Society*, ed. Dunbar Rowland, 2:132–43. Jackson, Miss., 1918.
Dodge, Grenville M. *Personal Recollections of General William T. Sherman*, delivered at the 28th annual encampment, Department of Iowa, Grand Army of the Republic, May 21, 1902. Des Moines, Iowa, 1902.
Ecelbarger, Gary. "An Ambitious Goal Indeed: An Evaluation of General John B. Hood's Plan and Generalship during the Battle of Atlanta, July 22, 1864." *North & South Magazine* 13, no. 2 (July 2011): 22–31.
———. *The Day Dixie Died: The Battle of Atlanta.* New York: Thomas Dunne Books, 2010.

Eddy, Thomas M. *The Patriotism of Illinois*. Vol. 2. Chicago: Robert Clarke Company, 1865.
Editors of Time-Life Books. *Atlanta*. Voices of the Civil War. Richmond, Va.: Time-Life Books, 1996.
———. *Shenandoah 1862*. Voices of the Civil War. Alexandria, Va.: Time-Life Books, 1997.
Evans, Clement A., ed. *Confederate Military History: A Library of Confederate States History*, vol. 8. Atlanta: Confederate Publishing Co., 1899.
Evans, David. *Sherman's Horsemen: Union Cavalry Operations in the Atlanta Campaign*. Bloomington: Indiana University Press, 1996.
Fletcher, Samuel. *History of Company A, Second Illinois Cavalry*. Chicago: n.p., 1912.
Fordyce, Samuel W., IV, ed. *An American General: The Memoirs of David Sloan Stanley*. Santa Barbara: Narrative Press, 2003.
Gage, M. D. *From Vicksburg to Raleigh; or, A Complete History of the Twelfth Regiment Indiana Volunteer Infantry*. Chicago: Clarke and Company, 1865.
Garrett, Franklin M. *Atlanta and Environs: A Chronicle of Its People and Events*. 3 vols. Athens: University of Georgia Press, 1969.
Goodloe, Albert Theodore. *Confederate Echoes: A Soldier's Personal Story of Life in the Confederate Army from the Mississippi to the Carolinas* Washington, D.C.: Zenger Publishing Co., 1907.
Hattaway, Herman. *General Stephen D. Lee*. Jackson: University Press of Mississippi, 1976.
Hess, Earl J. *The Battle of Ezra Church and the Struggle for Atlanta*. Chapel Hill: University of North Carolina Press, 2015.
Hewitt, Janet B., Noah Andre Trudeau, and Bryce A. Suderow, eds. *Supplement to the Official Records of the Union and Confederate Armies*. 100 vols. Wilmington, N.C.: Broadfoot Publishing Company, 1994–98.
Hogan, Sally Coplen, ed. *General Reub Williams's Memories of Civil War Times: Personal Reminiscences of Happenings That Took Place from 1861 to the Grand Review*. Westminster, Md.: Heritage Books, 2004.
Hood, John B. *Advance and Retreat: Personal Experiences in the United States and Confederate States Armies*. New Orleans: G. T. Beauregard, 1880.
Hood, Stephen M., ed. *The Lost Papers of Confederate General John Bell Hood*. El Dorado Hills, Calif.: Savas Beatie, 2015.
Hope, Henry M. *The Poor Houses*. Camarillo, Calif.: Xulon Press, 2008.
Howell, H. Grady, Jr. *Going to Meet the Yankees: A History of the "Bloody Sixth" Mississippi Infantry, C.S.A*. Jackson, Miss.: Chickasaw Bayou Press, 1981.
Hughes, Nathaniel C., ed. *The Civil War Memoirs of Philip Daingerfield Stephenson*. Conway, Ariz.: UCA Press, 1995.
Hughes, Nathaniel C., Jr., and Gordon D. Whitney. *Jefferson Davis in Blue: The Life of Sherman's Relentless Warrior*. Baton Rouge: Louisiana State University Press, 2002.
Jenkins, Robert D. *The Battle of Peach Tree Creek: Hood's First Sortie, 20 July 1864*. Macon, Ga: Mercer University Press, 2013.
Johnson, Robert Underwood, and Clarence Clough Buel, eds. *Battles and Leaders of the Civil War*. 4 vols. New York: Century Co., 1887.
Jones, Charles Edgeworth. *Georgia in the War, 1861–1865*. Augusta, Ga.: n.p., 1909.

Kellogg, Mark E., comp. *Army Life of an Illinois Soldier, Including a Day-to-Day Record of Sherman's March to the Sea: Letters and Diary of Charles W. Wills.* Carbondale: Southern Illinois University Press, 1996.

King, Stephen Lynn, comp. *History and Biographical Sketches of the 46th Tennessee Infantry, C.S.A., Henry County, Tennessee.* Bowling Green, Ky.: Stephen Lynn King, 1992.

Larimer, Charles F., ed. *Love and Valor: The Intimate Civil War Letters between Captain Jacob and Emeline Ritner.* Western Springs, Ill.: Sigourney Press, 2000.

Logan, John A. *The Volunteer Soldier of America.* Chicago: R. S. Neale and Co., 1887.

Lucas, D. R. *New History of the 99th Indiana Infantry.* Rockford, Ill.: Horner Printing, 1900.

Magdeburg, F. H. "Worden's Battalion." Paper presented at the first annual reunion of the 14th Wisconsin Veteran Vol. Infantry, Fond du Lac, Wis., June 16–17, 1886.

McMorries, Edward. *History of the First Regiment Alabama Volunteer Infantry, C.S.A.* Montgomery, Ala.: Brown Printer Company, 1904.

McMurry, Richard M. "A Policy So Disastrous: Joseph E. Johnston's Atlanta Campaign." In Savas and Woodbury, *Campaign for Atlanta*, 2:223–50.

———. *John Bell Hood and the War for Southern Independence.* Lincoln: University of Nebraska Press, 1982.

Montgomery, Frank C. *Reminiscences of a Mississippian in Peace and War.* Cincinnati: Robert Clark Company Press, 1901.

O'Connell, David. *The Art and Life of Atlanta Artist Wilbur G. Kurtz.* Charleston, S.C.: History Press, 2013.

Orendorf, H. H., comp. *Reminiscences of the Civil War from Diaries of Members of the 103d Illinois Volunteer Infantry.* Chicago: J. F. Learning, 1904.

Osborn, Donald Lewis, ed. *A Union Soldier's Diary.* Independence, Mo.: Donald Lewis Osborn, 1964.

Rennolds, Edwin H. *A History of the Henry County Commands.* Kennesaw, Ga.: Continental Book Co., 1961.

Report of the Proceedings of the Society of the Army of the Tennessee, at the Twentieth Meeting. Cincinnati: Published by the Society, 1893.

Reunion of the 37th Regiment O. V. V. I. Toledo, Ohio: Montgomery and Vrooman Printers, 1890.

Rood, Hosea Whitford. *Story of the Service of Company E, and of the Twelfth Wisconsin Regiment, Veteran Volunteer Infantry in the War of the Rebellion.* Milwaukee, Wis.: Swain and Tate Co., 1893.

Roy, T. B. "General Hardee and the Military Operations around Atlanta." *Southern Historical Society Papers* 8 (September 1880): 337–87.

Salling, Stuart. *Louisianans in the Western Confederacy.* Jefferson, N.C.: McFarland & Company, 2010.

Savas, Theodore P., and David A. Woodbury, eds. *The Campaign for Atlanta and Sherman's March to the Sea.* 2 vols. Campbell, Calif.: Savas Woodbury Publishers, 1992, 1994.

Scaife, William R. *The Campaign for Atlanta.* 4th ed. Cartersville, Ga.: Civil War Publications, 1993.

Scheel, Gary L. *Rain, Mud and Swamp: The Story of the 31st Missouri Volunteer Infantry.* Pacific, Mo.: Plus Communications, 1998.

Sherman, William Tecumseh. *Memoirs of General W. T. Sherman*. New York: Literary Classics of the United States, 1990.
Simpson, Brooks D., and Jean V. Berlin, eds. *Sherman's Civil War: Selected Correspondence of William T. Sherman, 1860–1865*. Chapel Hill: University of North Carolina Press, 1999.
Smith, Daniel P. *Company K, First Alabama Regiment*. Prattville, Ala.: privately published, 1885.
Stephens, Larry D. *Bound for Glory: A History of the 30th Alabama Infantry Regiment, Confederate States of America*. Ann Arbor, Mich.: Sheridan Books, 2005.
Stuart, A. A. *Iowa Colonel and Regiments*. Des Moines, Iowa: Mills & Company, 1865.
Swan, James B. *Chicago's Irish Legion: The 90th Illinois Volunteers in the Civil War*. Carbondale: Southern Illinois University Press, 2009.
Thompson, Illene D., and Wilbur E. Thompson. *The Seventeenth Alabama Infantry: A Regimental History and Roster*. Bowie, Md.: Heritage Books, 2001.
Tower, R. Lockwood, ed. *A Carolinian Goes to War: The Civil War Narrative of Arthur Middleton Manigault, Brigadier General, C. S. A.* Columbia: University of South Carolina Press, 1983.
U.S. War Department. *War of the Rebellion: A Compilation of the Official Records of the Union and Confederate Armies*. 128 vols. Washington, D.C.: 1880–1901.
Upson, Theodore F. *With Sherman to the Sea: The Civil War Letters, Diaries and Reminiscences of Theodore F. Upson*. Baton Rouge: Louisiana State University Press, 1943.
Warner, Ezra. *Generals in Blue: Lives of Union Commanders*. Baton Rouge: Louisiana State University Press, 1959.
———. *Generals in Gray: Lives of Confederate Commanders*. Baton Rouge: Louisiana State University Press, 1959.
Welsh, Jack D. *Medical Histories of Confederate Generals*. Kent, Ohio: Kent State University Press, 1995.
Wiley, Bell I. "A Story of 3 Southern Officers." *Civil War Times Illustrated* 3, no. 1 (April 1964): 26–34.
Willett, Elbert D., Joseph J. Willett, and John H. Curry. *History of Company B (Originally Pickens Planters), 40th Alabama Regiment, Confederate States Army, 1862–1865*. Anniston, Ala.: Norwood Printers, 1902.
Wooster, Ralph, ed. "Four Years in the Confederate Infantry: The Civil War Letters of Private R. F. Eddins, 19th Louisiana." *Texas Gulf Historical and Biographical Record* 7 (1971): 11–37.
Wright, Henry H. *A History of the Sixth Iowa Infantry*. Iowa City: State Historical Society of Iowa, 1923.
Wynne, Lewis N., and Robert A. Taylor, eds. *This War So Horrible: The Civil War Diary of Hiram Smith Williams*. Tuscaloosa: University of Alabama Press, 1993.

Websites

American Civil War Research Database. Historical Data Systems. www.civilwardata.com.

Branch, Paul. "Johnston, George Doherty." NCpedia. http://ncpedia.org/biography/johnston-george-doherty.

Diggins, Milt. "Cecil County's Civil War General." Historical Society of Cecil County. www.cecilhistory.org/mackall.html.

Elliott, William. Letter to his wife, July 29, 1864. The New University Library Web Site. http://library.sc.edu/digital/collections/civilwar.html.

46th Tennessee Volunteer Infantry, Company K. "The History of the 46th Tennessee." http://46thtn.homestead.com/history46.html.

Greer, Darroch. "Counting Civil War Casualties, Week-by-Week, for the Abraham Lincoln Presidential Library and Museum." BRC Imagination Arts. www.brcweb.com/alplm/BRC_Counting_Casualties.pdf.

Jackson, Billy. "Reverend James Hugh McNeilly, Chaplain, 49th Tennessee Infantry Regiment, C.S.A." Sons of Confederate Veterans, Camp 260. www.scvcamp260.org/mcneilly.html.

"Memoirs of the Civil War: W. L. Truman." Cottage on the Knoll at Cedarcroft Farm. www.cedarcroft.com/about/civil-war-interests/w-l-truman-memoir/memoir-chapter-22/.

Smith, Ron, ed. "The Civil War Diaries of Mifflin Jennings, 11th Iowa Infantry." RootsWeb, an Ancestry.com community. www.rootsweb.ancestry.com/~ialcgs/mifflinj.htm.

Ullrich, Dieter C., ed. "Civil War Diaries of Van Buren Oldham." Civil War Virtual Archives. www.utm.edu/departments/special_collections/E579.5%20Oldham/text/vboldham_indx.php.

Index

Adams, Edward (Major), 211
Adams, John (Brigadier General), 214
Adams, Robert N. (Lieutenant Colonel), 154, 211
Adams's brigade, 154, 169, 171, 178–79, 214
Alabama infantry regiments: 1st, 165, 215; 1st (sharpshooters), 215; 17th, 150–51, 156, 212; 17th (battalion sharpshooters), 215; 18th, 214; 19th, 80, 104–106, 187, 212; 22nd, 79–80, 104–105, 193, 212; 24th, 102, 213; 25th, 73, 104, 212; 26th, 150, 215; 27th/35th/49th, 179, 215; 28th, 102, 213; 29th, 150, 215; 30th, 184; 32nd/58th, 214; 34th, 102, 107, 213; 36th, 214; 37th, 142, 150, 214; 38th, 214; 39th, 104, 212; 40th, 142, 145, 214; 42nd, 142, 145, 214; 50th, 74, 80, 104–106, 212; 54th, 142, 145, 214; 55th, 215; 57th, 215
Alcorn, Milton S. (Major), 214
Alexander, Isaac N. (Lieutenant Colonel), 211
Anderson, J. Patton (Major General), 44, 189–90
Andrews, A. R. (Lieutenant), 212

Arkansas cavalry regiments: 1st Mounted Rifles, 215; 2nd Mounted Rifles, 215
Arkansas infantry regiments: 4th, 157–58, 215; 9th, 215; 25th, 216
Armstrong, Frank C. (Brigadier General), 60, 216
Armstrong's brigade, 216
Army of the Cumberland, 11, 46, 76
Army of the Ohio, 12, 59
Army of the Tennessee, 12, 24, 26, 29–30, 46–48, 58–59, 63, 66, 112, 185, 200–201, 209
Arnold, George W. (Captain), 80, 105, 212
Atlanta and West Point Railroad, 11
Augusta Railroad. *See* Georgia Railroad
Austin, John E. (Major), 213
Avirett, John A. (Captain), 214

Baker, Alpheus (Brigadier General), 116, 141–42, 145, 184, 214
Baker's (Higley's) brigade, 116, 122, 141–42, 144–46, 197, 206, 214
Bassett, W. L. (Captain), 214
Batchelor, S. S. (Major), 213
Beckham, Robert F. (Colonel), 44
Belknap, William W. (Colonel), 27, 152–53, 212

Bell, Charles J. (Major), 125, 127, 213
Benton, Samuel (Colonel), 75
Berkey, John M. (Lieutenant Colonel), 211
Binford, James (Major), 169–70
Bishop, William H. (Colonel), 212
Bisland, Thomas A. (Captain), 213
Blair, Francis P. (Major General), 211
Boggess, Jiles S. (Lieutenant Colonel), 176, 216
Boughter, Sam (Captain), 163
Bragg, Braxton (Major General), 32–33, 35, 41, 173–74
Brannon, Thomas J. (Captain), 212
Brantly, William F. (Brigadier General), 75, 90, 92, 98, 140, 193, 213
Brantly's brigade, 75, 90, 92, 94, 96, 101, 118, 153, 193, 201, 205, 213
Brown, John C. (Brigadier General), 39, 44–48, 71–73, 75, 76, 78, 102, 104, 108, 139–40, 189, 193–94, 204, 212, 218
Brown, William B. (Major), 124–25, 128, 211
Brown, William N. (Colonel), 214
Brown's division, 73, 76, 77, 89, 101, 108, 120, 132–33, 158, 167–68, 179, 193
Bryan, David F. (Major), 215
Buie, Duncan (Major), 130, 213
Bunn, Henry G. (Colonel), 158, 215
Burnett, Thomas J. (Major), 156, 215
Butler, William L. (Lieutenant Colonel), 213

Campbell, Francis L. (Lieutenant Colonel), 213
Cantey, James (Brigadier General), 150
Cantey's brigade. *See* O'Neal's (Cantey's) brigade
Carskaddon, David (Colonel), 144, 209
Cavins, Aiden G. (Lieutenant Colonel), 211
Chapel Road, 51, 59–60, 62, 70
Chattahoochee River, 9, 10, 12, 51, 176
Cheatham, Benjamin Franklin (Major General), 39–40, 43, 174, 189
Cladek, John J. (Colonel), 211
Clayton, Henry D. (Major General), 39, 76, 89, 120, 122, 131, 138, 141–42, 145–46, 184, 194, 207, 212, 218
Clayton's division, 76, 89, 120, 132, 138, 140–41, 168, 179, 193, 204, 213
Clune, William H. (Captain), 211
Collins, Robert A. (Captain), 214
Coltart, John G. (Colonel), 74, 80, 212
Corse, John M. (Brigadier General), 26, 100
Coursey, James, 65
Coursey, William, 65, 92
Crumbecker, Abraham M. (Major), 152
Cunningham, Edward H. (Lieutenant Colonel), 122–23
Curtis, John (Orderly Sergeant), 82
Curtiss, Francis S. (Lieutenant Colonel), 210

Dalton, William, 127
Darden's battery, 160
Davis, Harry, 127, 197
Davis, Jefferson (President), 31, 33, 35, 41–43, 45, 102, 113, 173
Davis, Jefferson C. (Major General), 148–49
Davis, Theodore R., 116–17, 143, 197
Deas, Zachariah (Brigadier General), 80
Deas's brigade. *See* Johnston's (Deas's, Coltart's, Toulmin's) brigade

De Gress, Francis (Captain), 66, 75, 210
Dodge, Grenville M. (Major General), 26, 46–47, 57–58, 211
Doss, Washington L. (Lieutenant Colonel), 214
Downing, J. B. (Lieutenant), 212
Dozier, Jesse, 181
Duncan, Austin N. (Captain), 215
Dyer, Samuel M. (Lieutenant Colonel), 214

East Point, 48, 50, 70, 176
Ector, Matthew D. (Brigadier General), 49, 183
Ennis, Thomas J. (Major), 96, 211
Ezra Church, 60, 62–63, 65, 68, 71–73, 77–80, 87, 89, 100, 113–15, 117, 119–20, 130–34, 137, 141, 143, 148, 151–52, 159, 172, 175, 182, 197, 220, 222; destruction of, 229

Farrell, Michael (Colonel), 214
Featherston, Winfield S. (Brigadier General), 170, 178, 187, 214
Featherston's brigade, 178–79, 214
Ferreby, Thomas G. (Lieutenant Colonel), 209
Ferrell, James O. (Adjutant), 213
XV Army Corps, 14–15, 27–29, 58–59, 62, 66, 73, 75, 77, 83, 86, 92, 99–101, 111, 115, 132–33, 138, 143, 146–47, 151–55, 166, 175, 177, 185, 188, 190, 197, 200–201, 205, 209
Foster, John A. (Captain), 215
French, Samuel D. (Major General), 49, 173, 179–80
French's division, 173–74, 179
Froehlich, George (Captain), 210
Fulton, Robert A. (Lieutenant Colonel), 59

Fulton County Alms House (Poor House), 69, 71, 76, 90, 102, 119–20, 138, 150, 174, 179, 219, 229
Funk, John, 83

Galloway, Morton G. (Lieutenant Colonel), 215
Galvin, Michael (Captain), 98, 211
Georgia Railroad, 10, 12, 59
Getzen, Thomas W. (Captain), 213
Gholson, Samuel J. (Brigadier General), 151
Gholson's brigade, 151, 216
Gibson, Randall L. (Brigadier General), 120–23, 128, 131–32, 141–42, 213, 218
Gibson's brigade, 121–23, 126, 128, 131–32, 137–39, 142, 146, 193, 213
Gill, Robert (Lieutenant), 195–96
Gillmore, Robert A. (Colonel), 105, 161, 164, 210
Godwin, Aaron S. (Lieutenant Colonel), 215
Goodnow, James (Lieutenant Colonel), 211
Granger, George (Major), 209
Grant, Ulysses S. (Lieutenant General), 9, 28, 198
Griffin, Thomas J. (Captain), 214
Guibor's Missouri battery, 179
Gulley, Ezekiah S. (Major), 145, 214

Hall, Hiram W. (Major), 96–98, 211
Hall, William (Colonel), 27
Halleck, Henry W. (Major General), 12, 17, 20, 30
Hamilton, Andrew J. (Sergeant), 96
Hardee, William (Lieutenant General), 40, 41, 71, 119, 136, 172–74, 184, 194, 203, 222, 227–28
Harper's Weekly Illustrated Newspaper, 15, 116–17, 143, 197

Harris, Aaron W. (Lieutenant), 179
Harrison, Richard (Colonel), 215
Harrow, William (Brigadier General), 29, 63, 124, 187, 210
Harrow's division, 63, 78, 81, 101, 108, 128, 132–33, 146, 151, 158–59, 178, 199
Hart, Benjamin R. (Colonel), 79–80, 193, 212
Hawkins, Edward R. (Colonel), 216
Heath, Albert (Lieutenant Colonel), 211
Hemphill, James A. (Lieutenant), 162
Herndon, Thomas H. (Lieutenant Colonel), 214
Hibbetts, Jefferson J. (Lieutenant Colonel), 212
Hildt, George (Lieutenant Colonel), 85
Higley, John H. (Colonel), 145, 184, 214
Higley's brigade. *See* Baker's (Higley's) brigade
Hindman, Thomas C. (Major General), 76
Hipp, Charles (Major), 93–94, 210
Holtzclaw's brigade. *See* Jones's (Holtzclaw's) brigade
Hood, John B. (General), 31–45, 50–57, 62, 65, 69–73, 113–14, 118–19, 134–39, 168, 171–74, 178, 182–85, 189, 192–96, 201–203, 207, 212, 217–28
Hood's corps. *See* Lee's (Hood's) corps
Hooker, Joseph (Major General), 24–25, 47
Horne, Elijah W. (Captain), 213
Hoskins, James A. (Captain), 30, 180, 216
Hoskins's Mississippi battery, 130, 180, 216

Hotaling, John R. (Major), 86, 94, 96, 106
Howard, Oliver O. (Major General), 20–23, 25, 30, 46–48, 59, 64, 72, 86–88, 93, 109, 112, 140, 175, 200, 202, 206–209
Hubbard, T. S. (Captain), 94, 96, 213
Hufstedler, Eli (Lieutenant Colonel), 216
Huger, Charles L. (Lieutenant), 213
Hulme, Isaac N. (Colonel), 215
Hunley, Peter F. (Lieutenant Colonel), 214
Hunter, Samuel E. (Colonel), 213
Hutchinson, Frederick S. (Lieutenant Colonel), 211

Illinois artillery unit, 1st (Battery A), 66, 210
Illinois infantry regiments: 12th, 153–54, 211; 26th, 64, 105, 152, 158, 161, 163–64, 210; 31st, 97, 153, 211; 40th, 95–98, 100, 211; 48th, 104–105, 151, 160, 211; 55th, 81–84, 86–87, 104–105, 107–108, 187, 210; 64th, 153, 211; 66th, 154; 90th, 64, 152, 160–61, 211; 103rd, 124, 128, 185–86, 211; 111th, 81, 83, 153, 156, 210; 116th, 81–83, 86, 107, 210; 127th, 81, 93, 96, 210
Indiana infantry regiments: 12th, 64, 79, 105, 152, 161, 163, 211; 83rd, 81, 83–84, 86–87, 92, 210; 97th, 151, 211; 99th, 64, 124, 126, 151–52, 187, 211; 100th, 64, 188, 211
Iowa infantry regiments: 3rd, 212; 4th, 185, 209; 6th, 95–98, 211; 9th, 144, 209; 13th, 151, 160, 212; 15th, 27, 152–54, 212; 25th, 145, 187, 210; 26th, 186, 209; 30th, 209; 31st, 143, 210

INDEX 271

Iverson, Alfred (Brigadier General), 192
Ives, Samuel S. (Colonel), 215

Jackson, Moses (Captain), 214
Jackson, William H. (Brigadier General), 60, 70, 118, 138, 176, 183, 216
Jackson's division, 70–71
Jaensch, Frederick (Major), 210
Johns, Benjamin F. (Lieutenant Colonel), 212
Johnson, Abda (Colonel), 89, 141
Johnson, Ashton (Lieutenant), 166
Johnson, James M. (Lieutenant Colonel), 90, 213
Johnson, Oscar (Corporal), 82
Johnson, Polk G., 166
Johnson, William E. (Captain), 215
Johnston, George D. (Brigadier General), 73, 79, 170, 212, 225
Johnston, Joseph E. (General), 31–33, 41, 126, 191, 221, 225
Johnston's (Deas's, Coltart's, Toulmin's) brigade, 73–74, 78–80, 85, 90, 95, 101, 104, 106, 118, 140, 157, 169, 193
Joliff, Reuben W. (Captain), 210
Jones, Bushrod (Colonel), 146, 214
Jones, Dudley W. (Colonel), 216
Jones, John W. (Captain), 213
Jones, Theodore (Colonel), 85, 210
Jones, Wells S. (Colonel), 27, 59, 94, 100–101, 140
Jones's (Holtzclaw's) brigade, 122–23, 141–42, 146, 168

Kaercher, Jacob (Lieutenant Colonel), 210
Keen, Robert L. (Captain), 213
Kelsey, Robert G. (Lieutenant Colonel), 82, 213
Kendrick, William B. (Captain), 145, 214

Kennedy, Hyder A. (Lieutenant Colonel), 213
Kile, Augustus (Captain), 215
Knox, Samuel L. (Major), 165, 215
Krepp, John W. (Lieutenant), 178
Kurtz, Wilbur G., 232–33

Landgraeber, Clemens (Major), 140, 210
Lavender, John W. (Captain), 157
Ledergerber, Frederick T. (Major), 210
Lee, Robert E. (General), 9, 35, 43
Lee, Stephen D. (Lieutenant General), 42–44, 50–53, 56–57, 62, 69, 70–73, 76, 89, 102, 108–109, 115, 118–20, 122–23, 134–41, 146–47, 168, 174, 179, 183, 193–94, 202–203, 205, 212, 219–25
Lee's (Hood's) corps, 71, 101, 174, 184, 194
Levings, Edwin, 97
Lewis, Joseph C. (Colonel), 213
Lick Skillet Road, 51–53, 55–56, 60–62, 69–76, 79, 89, 90–92, 119–20, 134–35, 138, 142, 146–47, 150–51, 169, 175, 177, 182, 190–91, 202, 204, 219–20, 222, 226–27, 229
Lightburn, Joseph A. J. (Brigadier General), 27, 59, 90–91, 100–101, 200, 210
Lightburn's brigade, 67, 93, 100, 104, 153, 155, 157
Lincoln, Abraham, 28, 198
Linnell, Lewis T. (Lieutenant), 212
Logan, John A. (Major General), 13–20, 25, 29, 46–47, 59, 64–65, 82, 86–88, 94–96, 106, 111, 124, 132, 140, 185, 199–200, 209
Loring, William W. (Major General), 169–70, 173, 178, 182, 206, 214, 217, 230

Loring's division, 168, 179, 184, 214, 221
Louisiana infantry regiments: 1st (regulars), 213; 4th, 121, 129, 213; 4th (battalion), 129, 213; 12th, 215; 13th, 121, 124, 128, 213; 14th (battalion sharpshooters), 213; 16th/25th, 121, 129, 131, 213; 19th, 120, 129, 130–31, 213; 20th, 121–22, 124, 128; 30th (battalion), 121–22, 124–29, 186, 197, 213
Lowell, Mansfield (Major General), 39, 41
Lowry, Robert (Colonel), 171, 214
Lyles, William W. (Lieutenant Colonel), 97, 213

Mackall, William W. (Brigadier General), 32–33
Macon & Western Railroad, 11, 17, 29, 49, 191
Magdeburg, F. H. (Captain), 187
Maney, George E. (Brigadier General), 39, 43
Manigault, Arthur M. (Brigadier General), 75–76, 101–104, 106, 108, 139–40, 193–94, 213
Manigault's brigade, 75, 101, 103–104, 107–108, 118, 139–40, 155, 193, 213
Manning, Michael W. (Lieutenant Colonel), 211
Martin, James S. (Colonel), 81, 93, 210
Martin's brigade, 63, 81, 83, 85–86, 90, 103–104, 153, 155, 164
Maurice, Thomas D. (Major), 66, 180–81
Maxwell, William W. (Lieutenant Colonel), 216
McBee, Joshua T. (Major), 216
McCane, Thomas A. (Captain), 215
McCook, Edward (Brigadier General), 191

McGuirk, John (Colonel), 151, 157, 160, 216
McKelvaine, Robert P. (Colonel), 90, 97, 213
McPherson, James B. (Major General), 13–14, 17, 22, 24, 35
Medal of Honor, 94, 96, 127
Mercer, Hugh (Brigadier General), 38–39
Meumann, Theodore (Colonel), 210
Michigan infantry regiment, 15th, 169, 214
Military Division of the Mississippi, 9, 36, 70, 196, 209
Milligan, Augustus L. (Captain), 215
Minter, John A. (Colonel), 214
Mississippi cavalry regiments: 1st, 60, 216; 2nd, 61, 216; 28th, 216
Mississippi infantry regiments: 1st (battalion sharpshooters), 214; 3rd, 214; 6th, 179, 214; 7th, 74, 84–85, 95, 212; 9th, 74, 84–85, 95, 98, 212; 9th (battalion sharpshooters), 74, 212; 10th, 74, 82–83, 212; 14th, 214; 15th, 169, 214; 20th, 214; 22nd, 214; 23rd, 214; 24th/27th, 75, 90, 97, 213; 29th/30th, 75, 90, 98, 213; 31st, 214; 33rd, 214; 34th, 75, 90, 96, 213; 37th, 156, 215; 40th, 214; 41st, 74–75, 84–85, 95, 98, 195, 212; 43rd, 215; 44th, 74, 82–83, 95, 107, 187, 213
Missouri artillery unit, 2nd Light (Battery F), 210
Missouri infantry regiments: 3rd, 210; 6th, 81, 83, 85, 87, 92, 153, 210; 12th, 130, 210; 17th, 120, 210; 27th, 209; 29th, 129–30; 31st, 210; 32nd, 186, 210
Montgomery, Frank C. (Lieutenant Colonel), 60
Moore, Israel T. (Major), 210
Morgan, James (Brigadier General), 149, 176–77

Morgan's division, 177
Moritz, Carl (Captain), 210
Mott, Samuel R. (Lieutenant Colonel), 81, 210
Murphy, Philip H. (Major), 130–31
Murphy, Robinson, 96
Myers, George B. (Lieutenant Colonel), 212

Nabers, James F. (Captain), 212
Nelson, Noel L. (Colonel), 215
New Jersey infantry regiment, 35th, 153, 156, 211
Nichols, Samuel D. (Major), 209
North, Benjamin (Captain), 210

O'Connor, Dennis (Major), 209
Ohio artillery unit, 4th Battery (Light), 66, 210
Ohio infantry regiments: 30th, 58, 81, 84–85, 153, 210; 32nd, 152–53, 212; 37th, 93–94, 100, 210; 46th, 100, 124, 126, 128, 197, 211; 47th, 91–92, 100–101, 155, 210; 53rd, 65, 71, 73, 90–91, 210; 54th, 92, 100, 155, 210; 57th, 81, 210; 70th, 124–26, 128, 132, 177–78, 186, 211; 76th, 58, 186, 209; 81st, 154–55, 211
Oliver, John M. (Colonel), 78, 123, 178, 211
Oliver, Starke H. (Captain), 213
Oliver's brigade, 63, 78, 85, 106, 123, 132, 158, 160–61, 171
O'Neal, Edward A. (Colonel), 150, 156, 215
O'Neal's (Cantey's) brigade, 150, 154–55, 157, 159–60, 215
Osterhaus, Peter (Brigadier General), 28–29
Owens, Robert A. (Colonel), 215

Palmer, John (Major General), 29, 47, 148–49
Palmer, Solomon (Major), 80, 212

Pearson, Robert N. (Lieutenant Colonel), 211
Perry, John J. (Major), 216
Perry, John S. (Captain), 215
Phillips, Henry L. (Captain), 177–78
Picolet, Arthur (Captain), 213
Pinson, R. A. (Colonel), 60, 216
Polk, Leonidas (Major General), 38, 44
Poor House. *See* Fulton County Alms House (Poor House)
Posey, Benjamin L. (Captain), 214
Post, Franklin C. (Captain), 211
Proctor's Creek, 47, 57, 81, 117
Proudfit, James K. (Lieutenant Colonel), 211
Presstman, Stephen W. (Colonel), 45

Quarles, William A. (Brigadier General), 151, 160–61, 164–66, 171, 215
Quarles's brigade, 151, 160–61, 165, 215

Ray, Archibald D. (Captain), 212
Reynolds, Daniel H. (Brigadier General), 34, 150, 157, 159–60, 165, 215
Reynolds's brigade, 154, 157–58, 160, 215
Richardson, William C. (Major), 215
Ritner, Jacob (Captain), 188
Rittenbury, J. J. (Captain), 215
Roberts, Aurelius (Lieutenant Colonel), 209
Rogers, Jefferson W. (Lieutenant Colonel), 215
Romer, Francis (Lieutenant Colonel), 210
Ross, Lawrence "Sul" (Brigadier General), 176–77, 216
Ross, Peter F. (Lieutenant Colonel), 216
Ross's brigade, 176–77, 216
Rouse, Napoleon B. (Captain), 212

Roy, Thomas B. (Adjutant General), 173

Schofield, John (Major General), 12, 57, 137, 172
Scott, Thomas M. (Brigadier General), 215
Scott's brigade, 179, 215
Seay, Abraham J. (Major), 210
XVII Army Corps, 97, 99, 101, 133, 151–52, 155, 175, 185, 190, 201
Shane, John (Colonel), 211
Sharp, Jacob H. (Brigadier General), 74–75, 79, 82–83, 95, 102, 140
Sharp's brigade, 74–75, 82–83, 85–86, 90, 95, 98, 101–103, 118, 155, 164, 212
Shaw, Francis H. (Captain), 210
Sherman, William T. (Major General), 9–13, 17–20, 22–25, 28–30, 33, 46–48, 50, 65–66, 69, 87–88, 100, 110, 130, 137, 148–49, 175–77, 192, 196, 209
Shields, Thomas (Lieutenant Colonel), 125, 127, 213
Shoup, Francis A. (Brigadier General), 44–45, 50–51, 182–83, 219, 227
Simpson, Samuel P. (Lieutenant Colonel), 210
XVI Army Corps, 26, 59, 62, 66, 151, 155, 175, 185, 201, 211
Slaughter, John N. (Major), 107, 213
Slocumb, Cuthbert (Captain), 214
Smith, Giles (Brigadier General), 27–28, 151–52
Smith, James T. (Lieutenant Colonel), 215
Smith, Milo (Colonel), 144, 209
Smith, Morgan L. (Brigadier General), 27–28, 59, 64–65, 68, 91, 152, 154, 200, 210
Smith, Thomas H. (Captain), 166

Smith's (Morgan) division, 63, 78, 81, 84, 101, 103, 108, 124, 128, 132–33, 151–52, 154, 199
Smith's brigade, 143–45
Smyth, William (Colonel), 210
Snodgrass, John (Colonel), 215
South Carolina infantry regiments: 10th, 102–103, 107, 213; 19th, 102–103, 107, 213
Stevenson, Carter (Brigadier General), 38–39, 141
Stewart, Alexander P. (Lieutenant General), 38, 44, 50–57, 69, 72, 89, 114, 118, 134–35, 137–38, 147, 151, 168–69, 173, 178, 182, 205–206, 214, 217–18, 220–22, 224–26
Stewart's corps, 134–35, 184, 214
Stigler, James M. (Major), 214
Stone, George A. (Colonel), 210
Stoneman, George (Major General), 49, 191–92
Stuart, Owen (Colonel), 211
Sullivan, Paul A., 162
Sweeny, Thomas W. (Brigadier General), 25–26

Taylor, Thomas T. (Major), 91, 101, 210
Tennessee infantry regiments: 42nd, 160, 215; 46th/55th, 161, 163–64, 215; 48th, 215; 49th, 160, 166, 215; 53rd, 164, 215
Terral, Samuel H. (Major), 215
Texas cavalry regiments: 1st, 216; 3rd, 176, 216; 6th, 216; 9th, 176, 216
Thomas, George H. (Major General), 11, 18, 29–30, 47, 137, 172
Thrasher house (Hood's headquarters), 31–32, 50, 69, 135, 138, 172
Tisdale, John R., 130
Torgler, Ernst, 94

Touchstone, Benjamin, homestead, 65, 91, 150
Toulmin, Harry T. (Lieutenant Colonel), 80, 95, 104, 106, 193, 212
Turner, Richard W. (Colonel), 130, 213
Turner's Ferry, 65, 148–49, 176
Turner's Ferry Road, 49, 59, 65, 69, 148–49, 176–77

Utoy Creek, 70, 177, 190, 197

Van Deusen, Delos (Lieutenant Colonel), 210
Van Sellar, Henry (Lieutenant Colonel), 211
Voelkner, Louis (Captain), 210
von Zinken, Leon (Colonel), 122–24, 213

Walcutt, Charles C. (Colonel), 29, 99–100, 124, 133, 211
Walcutt's brigade, 63
Walker, C. Irvine (Lieutenant Colonel), 103, 107, 213
Walker, William H. T. (Major General), 37–38
Walthall, Edward C. (Major General), 150–51, 157, 164, 166, 167, 171, 174, 178, 189, 192–93, 214–15, 217
Walthall's division, 168–69, 171, 179, 199, 201, 205, 215, 221
Wangelin, Hugo (Colonel), 62, 129, 210
Wangelin's brigade, 129
Watson, Samuel H. (Captain), 92
Weirick, John H. (Lieutenant), 62
Wells, Joseph M. (Colonel), 214
Wells, Robert K. (Captain), 145
Wheeler, Joseph (Major General), 49, 60

White, Charles C. (Captain), 213
White, James L. (Major), 107
White, John R. (Colonel), 215
Whitney, Isaac M. (Captain), 105, 212
Williams, J. Byrd (Colonel), 85, 87, 212
Williams, Reuben (Colonel), 78, 104–106, 159, 161, 210
Williams, Richard (Captain), 165, 215
Williamson, James A. (Colonel), 143–45, 209
Williamson's brigade, 143, 145
Williams's brigade, 78, 81, 85, 105–106, 158, 160, 162
Wilson, Joseph D. (Lieutenant Colonel), 161, 163, 215
Wilson, William D., 162–64
Windsor, John S. (Captain), 210
Wisconsin infantry regiment, 12th, 97–98, 101, 153, 211
Woods, Charles R. (Brigadier General), 28, 116, 143, 209
Woods, William B. (Colonel), 209
Woodson, Edward C. (Captain), 216
Woods's division, 58, 63, 116, 133, 143, 146, 197
Worden, Asa (Major), 211
Worden's battalion, 187, 211

Yates, James H. (Captain), 216
Yates's Mississippi battery, 166, 216
Young, William F. (Colonel), 166, 216
Young, William H. (Colonel), 49, 174
Youngblood, E. H. (Major), 151, 216
Youngblood's battalion, 151, 157–58, 216
Young's brigade, 179, 183

www.ingramcontent.com/pod-product-compliance
Lightning Source LLC
Chambersburg PA
CBHW020833160426
43192CB00007B/630